HOSTAGES
to
FORTUNE

*The United Empire Loyalists and
the Making of Canada*

PETER C. NEWMAN

PUBLISHED BY SIMON & SCHUSTER

New York London Toronto Sydney New Delhi

SIMON &
SCHUSTER
CANADA

Simon & Schuster Canada
A Division of Simon & Schuster, Inc.
166 King Street East, Suite 300
Toronto, Ontario M5A 1J3

"When I Went Up to Rosedale." From *The Gods* by Dennis Lee
(McClelland & Stewart, 1979). Copyright ©1979 Dennis Lee.
With permission of the author.

This Simon & Schuster Canada edition November 2016

For information about special discounts for bulk purchases,
please contact Simon & Schuster Special Sales at 1-800-268-3216 or
CustomerService@simonandschuster.ca.

Library and Archives Canada Cataloguing in Publication
Newman, Peter C., author
Hostages to fortune: the United Empire Loyalists and the making of
Canada / Peter C. Newman.
Issued in print and electronic formats.
ISBN 978-1-4516-8609-8 (hardback).—ISBN 978-1-4516-8615-9 (html)
1. United Empire loyalists—History. 2. Canada—History—
1763–1867. I. Title.
FC426.N48 2016   971.02'8   C2016-901488-6
                        C2016-901489-4

Manufactured in the United States of America

1 3 5 7 9 10 8 6 4 2

ISBN 978-1-4516-8609-8
ISBN 978-1-4516-8615-9 (ebook)

The one contributor to this book who trumped all others was my precious wife, Alvy. We met twenty years ago and our lives spilled into each other as we revelled in the mix. For fairy tales to work, one must believe in them. This one took us by storm. Instead of remaining the eternal pest with a notebook, I joined life and tried to become a mensch—all for the love of Alvy. It was the American author and poet Willa Cather who so memorably described the process of never-ending love: "One cannot divine or forecast the conditions that will make for happiness—one only stumbles into them by chance, in a lucky hour at world's end." As I did.

CONTENTS

NORTH AMERICA 1776

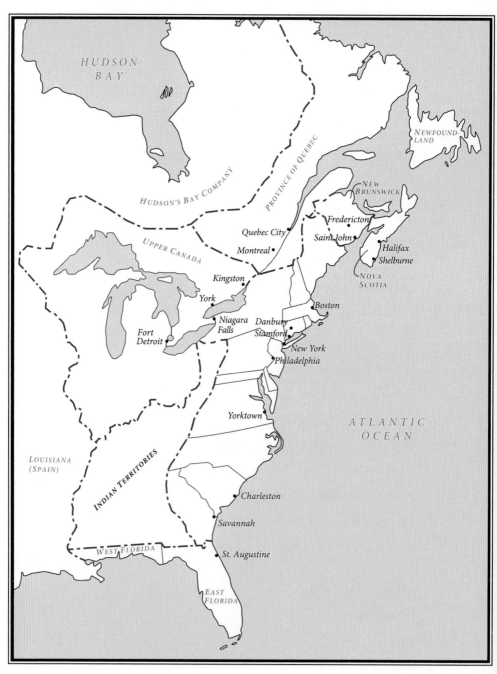

HUDSON
BAY

NEWFOUND-
LAND

HUDSON'S BAY COMPANY

PROVINCE OF QUEBEC

NEW
BRUNSWICK

Fredericton

Quebec City
Saint John

Montreal

UPPER CANADA

Halifax
Shelburne

Kingston

NOVA
SCOTIA

York

Boston

Niagara Danbury
Falls Stamford

Fort
Detroit

New York
Philadelphia

Yorktown

ATLANTIC
OCEAN

LOUISIANA
(SPAIN)

INDIAN TERRITORIES

Charleston

Savannah

WEST FLORIDA

St. Augustine

EAST
FLORIDA

WAR OF 1812

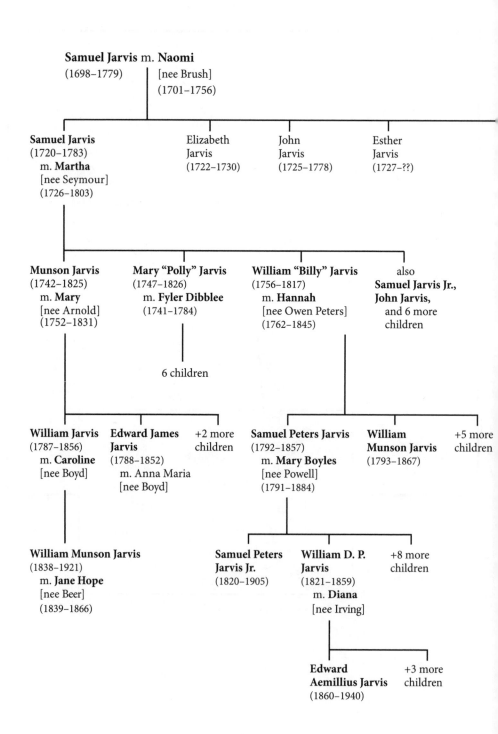

Samuel Jarvis m. **Naomi**
(1698–1779)   [nee Brush]
           (1701–1756)

Samuel Jarvis
(1720–1783)
m. **Martha**
[nee Seymour]
(1726–1803)

Elizabeth
Jarvis
(1722–1730)

John
Jarvis
(1725–1778)

Esther
Jarvis
(1727–??)

Munson Jarvis
(1742–1825)
m. **Mary**
[nee Arnold]
(1752–1831)

Mary "Polly" Jarvis
(1747–1826)
m. **Fyler Dibblee**
(1741–1784)

William "Billy" Jarvis
(1756–1817)
m. **Hannah**
[nee Owen Peters]
(1762–1845)

also
**Samuel Jarvis Jr.,
John Jarvis,**
and 6 more
children

6 children

William Jarvis
(1787–1856)
m. **Caroline**
[nee Boyd]

**Edward James
Jarvis**
(1788–1852)
m. Anna Maria
[nee Boyd]

+2 more
children

Samuel Peters Jarvis
(1792–1857)
m. **Mary Boyles**
[nee Powell]
(1791–1884)

**William
Munson Jarvis**
(1793–1867)

+5 more
children

William Munson Jarvis
(1838–1921)
m. **Jane Hope**
[nee Beer]
(1839–1866)

**Samuel Peters
Jarvis Jr.**
(1820–1905)

**William D. P.
Jarvis**
(1821–1859)
m. **Diana**
[nee Irving]

+8 more
children

**Edward
Aemillius Jarvis**
(1860–1940)

+3 more
children

The Descendants of Samuel and Naomi Jarvis

Names in **bold** appear in *Hostages to Fortune*

Stephen Jarvis Sr.
(1729–1820)
  m. **Rachel**
[nee Starr]
(1733–1824)

Isaac
Jarvis
(1733–??)

Naomi
Jarvis
(1736–??)

Nathan
Jarvis
(1737–1820)

Abraham
Jarvis
(1739–1813)

Polly
Jarvis
(1742–1746)

Hezekiah
Jarvis
(1746–1838)

Stephen Jarvis Jr.
(1756–1840)
  m. **Amelia**
[nee Glover]
(1756–1819)

Eli Jarvis
(1768–1854)

+6 more
children

Elizabeth
"Betsey" Jarvis
(1784–1874)
  m. **Rev. Dr.
Thomas
Phillips**
(1781–1849)

Frederick
Starr Jarvis
(1786–1852)
  m. **Susan**
[nee Merigold]
(1786–1863)

Frances
"Fanny"
Jarvis
(1787–1867)
  m. **Major
John Maule**

Rachel
Isabella
Jarvis
(1794–1887)

George
Stephen
Benjamin
Jarvis
(1797–1878)

William
Botsford
Jarvis
(1799–1864)

12 children

14 children

INVOCATION

T HEY CAME because there was nowhere else to go. They came
because they were being offered virgin soil, hungering for
crops. They came to reclaim the marrow of their lives. They came to
exercise their rage for life. They came to adopt a new home country
so untried and unsung it didn't even have a name—but sight unseen,
it had agreed to adopt them. They were offered heaven's most precious gift: a second chance. Their exodus had created the backbone
of a new northern nation, bigger and bolder than their dreams, that
became their sanctuary. They called it Canada.

PROLOGUE

No smear of their sweat or echo of their prayers reaches out to us, yet in their time the Loyalists gave substance to the unformed notion of Canada and the even less likely ideal that British North America could spawn a distinct and lasting new nationality in the free-range wilderness on the frigid side of the 49th parallel.

A LAND FULL OF WONDERS, Canada's future domicile was the globe's second largest landmass, colonized first by fishermen from the west of England landing in forbidding coves of Newfoundland, and then by New France colonists clustered in primitive huts along the riverbanks of the mighty St. Lawrence. That led to the frowning ridges of the Canadian Shield, marching northward into the silent eternities of Arctic solitude.

In mid-continent, the brooding forests stood as tall as the sailing ships' masts they would become, leaving behind rotting stumps that strained the pioneers' backs as they turned foraged meadows into farms. At the same time, the western plains beckoned to explorers, pulled across the continent by the assurance that beyond the next valley they would gain access to the spices of the Orient, and if not, then the valley after that. Instead, they encountered beavers whose waterproof fur could profitably be turned into hats. By habit, the furry rodents were not nomadic, so when a stream or lake was fished out, the fur traders had to keep moving ever westward for more pelts. And that was how so much of Canada was first explored and later settled.

By exercising their Darwinian adaptability to its limits, the Loyalists established a frontier society that operated according to British Canada's founding catechisms. Neither elitist nor servile, their motivating intent was to claim residency, but more as free agents than bonded citizens. The Loyalists moved from their original hovels into log cabins that coalesced into huddles of villages and aspiring counties. It was not a conquest in any manner except one: the feeling of empowerment triggered by the newcomers' revived sense of possession—minor as it was. Still, the land under their blistered feet belonged to them now, and that felt like a daily miracle.

They gradually prospered enough to lead decent lives. But it was never easy. Regardless of their formal religions, the first generation of Loyalists shared the inner loneliness of being stranded in unfamiliar landscapes, never certain whether they still enjoyed God's good graces. Salvation was always in doubt, something to be earned by the courage of each early morning.

They joined a loose collection of hard-bitten settlers in a sophomoric land, largely occupied by unwilling exiles—feeling as though they were the last to fill a lifeboat that might or might not float. They occasionally cursed their fate, but accepted it. "If the Loyalist exile was the end of one saga, it was also the beginning of another," wrote Will Ferguson, the prize-winning author who defined Canadians as "Americans with manners." According to Ferguson, "The Loyalists' discovery of Canada proved that it was not simply a wilderness; it was the Land of Second Chances." No longer squatters, the newcomers were still outcasts, but eventually they became wardens of the new nation's barely mapped potential. The pioneer families learned to treasure small, private epiphanies, getting in touch with the freshly tilled earth, the tangles of this new land's conflicting moods, and the vicissitudes of its weathers—all sensations that provided a rough-hewn, welcoming domicile.

Loyal by nature and by circumstance, the Loyalists gradually created a rough wilderness culture that flowed from the principles of adherence rather than social contract. Their sense of tradition tended to trump the adjoining Yanks' trigger-happy assertions of will, so that even in their early stirrings one could detect the longings for tidiness, the avoidance of risk, and the parsimony of emotions. That was their birthright. "The United Empire Loyalists represented a declaration of independence against the United States—a determination to live apart from that country," decreed Professor J. M. S. Careless, the great University of Toronto historian.

Political, intellectual, personal, emotional, spiritual, and, in some cases, opportunistic—"Loyalism" was complex and multifaceted. Having publicly taken sides in the American Revolution, Loyalists, who might have chosen to remain in the U.S. once the war ended, were banished and had no choice except moving to Canada or migrating to other lands under British control. Later, if they could, some did return to America. Others were not motivated by ideological principles at all or by a love for the British way of life, but opted to leave the U.S. in search of economic gain. Nonetheless, in the larger perspective, Professor Careless's assertion remained valid: the Loyalists, he rightly argued, "helped create not only a new province but a new nation."

It was the Loyalists who introduced Liberalism to Canada in the mid-1780s. They combined their opposition to American-style republicanism with support for individual liberty to forge a new approach that was much closer to Liberal values than Tory beliefs.

That was what separated levelheaded "Canadians" from the flag-happy, impulsive assertions of "life, liberty and the pursuit of happiness" by America's Patriots. The rebels of yesterday had turned into bodacious adventurers who opted for swashbuckling independence under the proud banner of the United States of America. (Canadians of later generations could only agree with former Mexican president Porfirio Díaz's lament: "So far from God; so near to the United States.")

The subservient system of colonialism had more than served its time. The American Revolution cut the apron strings to Mother England—with about as much regret as discarding a frayed Walmart apron. The blood spilled in the passionately held and contradictory causes of both sides turned this quixotic rebellion of colonial Brits into an abattoir-style slaughter. It was the most vicious bloodbath ever fought on American soil, only excepting the great Civil War of the 1860s. The cost in human suffering was incalculable. Even more disturbing, it was a case of former compatriots slaughtering one another and families splitting up as their members chose sides. It was, primarily, a civil war over how to settle grievances with the Mother Country that had unceremoniously moved on to more pressing concerns—such as His Majesty's declining sanity.

History was impatient and the American colonies' resentment had long been a-simmering. It took an eight-year struggle for the Yanks finally to realize their lode-star destiny as pledged by their noble Declaration of Independence. In the process they forced most Loyalist Americans into exile—first by intimidation, then by confiscation, and finally by threatening their very existence.

According to Phoenix historian Ted Rushton, the Thirteen Colonies would have become "the Arizonas of the 19th Century British Empire—contributing little, complaining much, forever restless, rejecting any and all fresh ideas. The revolutionary freedom movement that swept Latin America might never have been ignited without the heady example of the Declaration of Independence," he wrote. "Likewise, France's revolution was inspired in part by the same document—with very different results." Without that revolution to set the stage, Napoleon Bonaparte would not have acted like such a testosterone-driven contenda'—the master of everything that moved, including the sensual Josephine. The alternate exodus might have consisted of Loyalists fleeing to the reggae beaches of the French islands in the Caribbean or joining the funeral marching bands of New Orleans.

Without the War of Independence, Canada would likely not have existed. It was the massive Loyalist influx from south of the border that saved the northern territory from being annexed by the Yanks. The newcomers, having formed a hard core of settlers loyal to their adopted grubstakes, became the mothers and fathers—nurturers and role models—of the new nation.

EVENTS RECORDED IN THIS BOOK assay the steep price demanded by loyalty, a trait described by New York psychologist Eric Felten as "the vexing virtue." In the contemporary age when alliances shifted as rapidly as the hues in a pigeon's neck feathers, loyalty seemed as obsolete a virtue as chivalry.

Both of these emotions are outdated, but without true believers in these qualities at precisely the most appropriate time and place, Canada would not have come into being. The Loyalists' dogma was the forerunner of the Canadian experience, which was based on self-discipline of the spirit in place of the armed assertions of temper and tantrum—wild Yankee style.

The displaced Loyalists were true hostages to fortune, steadfastly faithful to the vague causes that characterized their quest, yet never certain they would, should, or could, abandon their consciences. This was an issue governed by emotional moods instead of moral absolutes. And yet it was the moral absolutes that really mattered. The source for that bit of wisdom was the chiselled inscription on the cairn mounted at Tusket, in Nova Scotia's Yarmouth County. As the commemorative inscription so accurately and concisely put it: "They sacrificed everything save Honour." That diagnosis was echoed by contemporaries who encountered the original Loyalists, or like Lady Emily Tennyson, the British poet laureate's talented widow, who had studied Canadian history, and gushed: "You Canadians should be proud of the founders of your country. The Loyalists were a grand type of law-abiding, God-fearing men. No country ever had such founders, no country in the world—not since the days of Abraham."

It was Sir Guy Carleton (later promoted to Lord Dorchester, governor in chief of British North America) who directed that "as a Mark of Honour the families of those immigrants who had left the Thirteen Colonies between 1776 and 1783, ought to be distinguished by the letters U.E. affixed to their names." That was an abbreviation for Unity of the Empire, later expanded to United Empire Loyalists. It remains a significant honour and Canada's only hereditary title.*

Canada was the ideal colony to sponsor such a distinction, as a people united in reconciliation, and yet reflecting the wilderness in the process of morphing into an emancipated and prosperous society. "Carrying forward the principles of parliamentary democracy transferred in triumphant vindication from an ancient capital to a new one," so proclaimed the British scribe James Morris in *Pax Britannica*. It seemed as if there never would be such a construct as average Canadians—as there still isn't. That didn't matter, so long as we weren't considered to be failed Yanks.

THE ENTHUSIASTIC BACKING of the Loyalists for such causes as their support for the Canadian side during the War of 1812 convinced the population at large that their country was well worth preserving. "It represented a varied way of life they didn't want to see submerged—a collective pride in themselves and a sense not only of their powers but also of their rights," according to the West Coast intellectual George Woodcock. "Here again the importance of settlement emerged. When men owned land and created a way of life, they were ready to risk their lives in its defence."

The Loyalists also provided strong support for municipal and provincial self-government. It was their flowering that forced Britain to introduce representative assemblies in Upper and Lower Canada,

---

* During my research, I met a leading Belleville physician who had been awarded that distinction and swore that it was much more difficult to qualify for than his original medical degrees.

areas of jurisdiction that were, in terms of their existence, just as much the children of the American Revolution as the United States. In virtue of their very presence and, by extension, their mind-set, the Loyalists survived and settled along the northern shores of Lake Ontario and Lake Erie as well as many more in the Maritimes—a new country was in the process of being born.

THE SAGA OF THE LOYALISTS who came up against the Americans' never-ending quest to sanctify their sacred exceptionalism provides the narrative arc of the pages that follow. The Loyalists who moved north were far too down-to-earth (literally) for such boastful vanities as feeling exceptional themselves. But by the end of the eighteenth century, the handful of inhabitants of that largely barren land that would become Canada could feel vindicated for sharing their properties with the waves of refugees driven out by Yankee excesses. What emerged from their banishment and resettlement was an allegiance to the wild geography they had been invited to share. It was a country with one big "VACANT" sign across it—that had yet to flex its muscles and assume the mantle of nationhood. But by God, it was on the way!

The Loyalists achieved something truly magnificent: castaways in a tight-fisted land and caught in dire circumstances, they endured. Then, they became dance partners in Canada's slow waltz to nationhood.

1

A GLORIOUS DAY
FOR AMERICA

From an American start, a British interregnum, and ultimately a Canadian base, the Jarvis family's evolution and remarkable involvement in national and international affairs—coloured their days and inspired their nights—became the hallmark of passionate lives.

J UST BEFORE DAWN ON April 19, 1775, at the common green in the puppy bush settlement of Lexington, Massachusetts, in the shadow of its white steeple church and cozier meeting house, there occurred an unexpected confrontation between seven hundred British regulars, resplendent in their colonials' distinctive bright scarlet uniforms, and sixty local militiamen trying to shake themselves awake. The exchange of musket fire that followed triggered the real beginning of the American Revolution. It was an uncharacteristically minor-note overture to a brutish war that lasted eight interminable years without respite, drastically altering the trajectories of its contestants. A new pecking order was being born that foreshadowed evolving mainline history. More than a century later in 1886, in an ironic twist, the Montreal-born artist Henry Sandham immortalized the Battle of Lexington in his painting *The Dawn of Liberty*, which portrayed the New England militiamen as defiant, polished, and as brave as the British. The ultimate promise of what transpired on Lexington Green that April morning was indeed momentous: it was an early warning signal that being Canadian would be less a nationality and more of a condition.

The townsfolk, some descendants of the Puritans who had settled the area in the late 1630s, had been alerted the evening earlier by silversmith and Patriot Paul Revere (who was on a clandestine mission and never did shout, as was alleged, "The British Are Coming!"—since by then the British had been there as colonizers for 150 years). Still, British troops were on the march towards nearby Concord via Lexington and it was Revere and his famous ride that was immortalized in American history. At forty years of age in 1775, Paul Revere was a skilled artisan and "a New England Yankee to the very bottom of his Boston riding boots," as one of his many biographers depicts him. He spoke in a "harsh, nasal New England twang," was energetic, ambitious, and devoutly devoted to the Patriot cause. That night, the British were in search of a cache of arms and the rebel leaders Samuel Adams and John Hancock, who were attending the Massachusetts Provincial Congress in Concord. Both men were staying with Reverend Jonas Clark in Lexington at the home previously owned by Hancock's grandfather, also named John Hancock, a respected minister in the town for more than five decades.

But on the evening of April 18, a sympathetic source close to General Thomas Gage—"circumstantial evidence" suggested it was his American-born wife, Margaret, who was profoundly distressed by the British-colonial rift—had alerted Dr. Joseph Warren, a young Patriot leader and a "gentleman revolutionary," about the action. Warren was not prone to rush to judgment, yet in this case he trusted his source. He immediately dispatched his couriers, Revere and William Dawes, to warn the citizens of Lexington and Concord.

The Lexington militia was no ragtag band of hick farmers. As tensions had escalated, the militiamen regarded with utmost seriousness their duty to protect their families and property. Under the command of Captain John Parker, a forty-five-year-old veteran of the French and Indian War (1754–1763), the North American part of the Seven Years' War that began in Europe in 1756, the men had drilled as intensely as any Napoleonic army.

It was four-thirty in the morning by the time the British regulars, led by Major John Pitcairn, reached the outskirts of Lexington, and another twenty minutes until the militiamen assembled on the town common and he saw them. A crowd, among them the wives and children, had gathered at a safe distance to watch the unfolding spectacle.

Parker did not want any trouble, nor did he want any of his men hurt or killed. Yet his military and patriotic instincts were acute and he was prepared to stand his ground. "Let the troops pass by," he firmly emphasized to his men. "Don't molest them, without they [*sic*] being first." Seeing the mass of red coats advancing towards them, one of the assembled colonists exclaimed, "There are so few of us here, it is folly to stand here!" Parker, however, would not countenance such talk in the ranks and threatened to shoot any man who ran. "Stand your ground! Don't fire unless fired upon!" he ordered. "But if they want to have a war let it begin here."

The British soldiers on foot, and the officers on horseback, moved closer. Pitcairn yelled towards Parker, "Lay down your arms, you damned rebels!" Parker was bold, but not stupid. His militia was completely outnumbered. So he instructed them to disperse and not to fire. Some began to move away, but there was confusion: most of the militiamen stayed put with their muskets at the ready.

Suddenly a shot rang out. No one knew who had fired, British or American. It made no difference. The British regulars let loose a volley of musket balls in reaction and a few of the American militiamen shot back. Two colonists were killed instantly and another six in the tussle which followed. One of the men, Jonathan Harrington, was severely wounded. He stumbled and crawled back to his house and died as his wife and son tried desperately to save him. Another ten colonists were wounded and the rest ran for cover in the nearby woods and buildings. Only one British soldier died.

Regrouping, the British troops continued on toward Concord. But many more colonial militiamen awaited them at the North Bridge in a scene later described by Ralph Waldo Emerson in the first stanza of his stirring poem "Concord Hymn":

By the rude bridge that arched the flood,
Their flag to April's breeze unfurled,
Here once the embattled farmers stood,
And fired the shot heard round the world.

By the end of the day, ninety-three Americans had been killed and forty-one wounded. However, the Brits were stunned: they had lost 273 soldiers and hundreds more were wounded. The Revolutionary War had begun to move into the history books.

Earlier that morning, while they fled from Lexington just as the British regulars arrived, Sam Adams and John Hancock, having heard the gunfire on the Common, stopped to talk.

"It is a fine day," said Adams.

"Very pleasant," commented Hancock, figuring Adams was referring to the weather.

"I mean," Adams replied, "this is a glorious day for America."

And so it was. Slightly more than a year later, Adams and Hancock both would be among the esteemed signatories of the American Declaration of Independence.

Meanwhile, in the town of Danbury, Connecticut, a different type of skirmish was under way. This was between a father and son, both with the same name: Stephen Jarvis. Their family feud was initially about Amelia Glover, the splendid young woman Stephen wanted to marry. Yet in the turmoil of those dangerous times that engulfed them, their quarrel soon became about choosing sides in the civil war that was about to tear the colonies asunder.

In this life-and-death struggle, young Stephen Jarvis (1756–1840)—later immortalized in family folklore as "the Colonel," one of the patriarchs of the Jarvis family branch whose members were to rise to prominence in Upper Canada—would emerge as a fierce defender of the British Empire and a man who took great pride in his designation as a Loyalist. He was most aptly described by his Boswell and great-great-granddaughter, the sympathetic chronicler Ann Jarvis Boa, in her definitive biography titled *My Eventful Life*. His "story is really about one brave and reckless man who, always anxious to please, throws himself headlong into situations from which, once committed, there is no turning back," she concluded. "As a Loyalist, who has declared himself on the British side, he had no choice but to be in the fight until he dies, or it is over."

As a young man of nineteen in 1775, all Stephen Jarvis desired was to marry his love, the tempting, tempestuous Amelia. The only portraits of Stephen and Amelia were painted when they were much older. Wearing a distinguished morning coat with a high collar and a white cravat, Stephen was the model of an upper-class gentleman and a trooper who had experienced a full life. Though he was balding and appeared somewhat weary, the painting still attests to his strength and sense of purpose. Amelia, her head covered by a white frilly bonnet, or mob cap as it was called, was then a handsome woman with a kind demeanour. Yet even in her advanced age, her spirit, her dark eyes and slender nose suggested that she truly was the walking miracle who had caught Stephen's eye.

Stephen Jarvis Sr. (1729–1820) was a proud man of substantive standing in Danbury, like many of the extended members of his family who populated the town. His father, known as "Captain" Samuel, had lived nearby in Norwalk, thirty-six kilometres south on the shores of the Long Island, where he was involved in the shipping trade. As a young man, Stephen Sr. had moved inland to Danbury, become a farmer, and married Rachel Starr in 1756. Later that year their first child, Stephen Jr., was born. Rachel's roots were in Danbury, a typical settlement in the mid-eighteenth century with a population of 1,527. Within two decades, on the eve of the revolution, that number had increased to 2,526—though that did not include the African American slaves and servants, who were then common in

Connecticut towns. (In the 1770s, Connecticut had a slave population of 6,464, the most among the New England colonies.)

There was no documentation on whether Stephen and Rachel owned slaves or had servants, yet Danbury's ministers, lawyers, and town officials certainly did. There were colony-wide laws against any black servant or slave travelling beyond where they lived. And by 1730, any black, Indian, or mulatto slave guilty of uttering or publishing any words that a white person found objectionable received forty lashes as punishment.

Daily life as elsewhere revolved around religion, a bevy of chores, and family responsibilities. The Jarvises were devoted Episcopalians, an Anglican offshoot, which reinforced their British ties. In any confrontation with the Mother Country, few Anglicans, and certainly no Anglican ministers, disavowed King George III, the Supreme Governor of the Church of England. Mostly everyone else in Danbury, however, was Congregationalist, an autonomous Protestant sect that soon fostered the spirit of the revolution. The seeds of independence had been planted decades earlier by outspoken preachers such as Jonathan Mayhew, a twenty-nine-year-old pastor of the West (Congregational) Church in Boston. In 1750, Mayhew, in a widely circulated sermon assessing King Charles I's legacy as a martyr, stated that in the face of tyranny, it was "warrantable and glorious" for people "to disobey the civil powers in certain circumstances . . . in order to redress their grievances; to vindicate their natural and legal rights . . . and free themselves and posterity from inglorious servitude and ruin." A year before his death in 1766, he publicly decried the British attempts to extort the colonists through unfair taxation.

At the handful of Danbury churches, simple and unelaborate structures, Sunday was a serious occasion, as it was throughout the Thirteen Colonies. The Jarvises and their neighbours might not have been subjected to the God-fearing fire-and-brimstone of the early Puritans, but it was damn close. The Lord's Day remained a time of piety, prayer, and reflection, a consequence of the First Great Awakening, the evangelical religious revival that engulfed (and divided)

Connecticut in the 1730s and 1740s. At the same time, a visit by the English Methodist George Whitefield, one of the movement's chief proponents, literally brought entire towns like Danbury to a complete standstill. For Nathan Cole, a farmer from Middleton, a town eighty kilometres east, south of Hartford, hearing Whitefield speak made him feel as if he was one of the Apostles. Or so he claimed. "When I saw Mr. Whitefield come upon the Scaffold he looked almost angelical, a young, slim slender youth before some thousands of people with a bold undaunted countenance," Cole recorded in his journal.

> And my hearing how God was with him everywhere as he came along it solemnized my mind, and put me into a trembling fear before he began to preach; for he looked as if he was [clothed] with authority from the Great God, and a sweet solemn solemnity sat upon his brow. And my hearing him preach gave me a heart wound; by God's blessing my old foundation was broken up, and I saw that my righteousness would not save me; then I was convinced of the doctrine of Election and went right to quarrelling with God about it, because all that I could do would not save me; and he had decreed from Eternity who should be saved and who not.

Right.

SUCH POWERFUL MEMORIES resonated for decades after, making religion an institution to be revered. There was no doubt that Stephen and Rachel inculcated their sons and daughters to heed the Almighty and their parents—not necessarily in that order. At the dinner table, meals were usually eaten in silence. According to the customs of the day, children "were ordered never to seat themselves at the table until after the blessing had been asked, and their parents told them to be seated. They were never to ask for anything on the table; never to speak unless spoken to; always to break the bread, not to bite into a whole slice; never to take salt except with a clean knife; not to throw bones under the table."

After Stephen Jr. was born, Rachel gave birth to another eight children, about the norm in colonial America. Her youngest, a son, Eli, was born in 1768, which meant that during the first twelve years of her marriage, she was pregnant more often than she was not. The Jarvis clan knew how to procreate, ranking that activity as their favourite indoor sport. Stephen Sr.'s older brother, Samuel Jarvis (1720–1783), was Stamford's town clerk and Anglican Church warden. He and his wife, Martha (1726–1803), had eleven children, six of whom were boys. Those six boys—the two most prominent were William (Billy) (1756–1817) and Munson Jarvis (1742–1825)—had more than forty children, many of whom later lived in New Brunswick and Toronto. One of their five daughters was Mary (Polly) (1747–1826), who married lawyer Fyler Dibblee (1741–1784), and also left a record of her tragic experience as a Loyalist.

Until he was twelve years old, Stephen Jr. and his siblings were educated at the church-run public school or tutored at home. Rachel's great-great-grandfather, Comfort Starr, a physician, left £800 in his will for the establishment of a school fund in Danbury. However, parents and children were occupied six days a week with field work, wood chopping, manning the fireplaces, weeding the gardens, tending to the farm animals, preparing food, and sewing clothes. In a diary entry from 1775, young Abigail Foote from Colchester, Connecticut, described her packed workday like this:

> Fix'd gown for Prude,—Mend Mother's Riding-hood,—Spun short thread,—Fix'd two gowns for Welsh's girls,—Carded tow,— Spun linen,—Worked on Cheese-basket,—Hatchel'd flax with Hannah, we did 51 lbs. apiece,—Pleated and ironed,—Read a Sermon of Doddridge's,—Spooled a piece,—Milked the cows,— Spun linen, did 50 knots,—Made a Broom of Guinea wheat straw,—Spun thread to whiten,—Set a Red dye,—Had two

Scholars from Mrs. Taylor's,—I carded two pounds of whole wool and felt Nationly,—Spun harness twine,—Scoured the pewter.

Even with such a rigorous list of household duties, the Jarvis family prospered and found comfort and support in each other. Their wooden-frame farmhouse on Wooster Street was not large, but suited their needs. The houses were heated by fireplaces, though in the winter it was often still necessary to warm the inner sheets with pans of hot coals. Much of the daily focus involved the kitchen, wrote Alice Morse Earle in her 1898 account, *Home Life in Colonial Days*. "The walls were often bare, the rafters dingy; the windows were small, the furniture meagre; but the kitchen had a warm, glowing heart that spread light and welcome, and made the poor room a home." Sunday supper was a favourite event and would have featured goose, chicken, pheasant, or quail served with pumpkin bread, which was popular in Connecticut. The children sipped on milk, which became a routine part of a New England diet in the late 1720s.

Slightly more grandiose, but still middle-class, was Sunday dinner at the home of John Adams. A guest later noted that "the first course was a pudding of Indian meal, molasses, and butter; then came a course of veal and bacon, neck of mutton, and vegetables." Adams was by no means wealthy, and later, when he was in Philadelphia in 1774 as a congressional representative, was overwhelmed by the hospitality and the "sinful feasts," as he referred in his diary to the sumptuous culinary experiences he frequently attended. "Dined with Mr. [Benjamin] Chew, Chief Justice of the [Province of Pennsylvania]," Adams recorded about one such dinner. "Turtle and every other thing. Flummery, jellies, sweet meats of twenty sorts. Trifles, whipped syllabubs, floating islands . . . and then a dessert of fruits, raisins, almonds, pears, peaches—wine most excellent and admirable. I drank Madeira at a great rate and found no inconvenience in it." Clearly, the American colonists enjoyed the finer aspects of life, and Adams noted that "even plain Quakers . . . served ducks, hams, chickens, beef, creams and custards."

———————

THE REVOLUTION INTERCEDED in the idyllic lives of Stephen Sr.,
Rachel, and their children in a profound way. From a Patriot perspective, the darkest day in Danbury's history was April 26, 1777,
the day the town was occupied and then partially destroyed by British forces under the command of General William Tryon, who was
also the governor of New York from 1771 to 1780. Danbury had
been specifically targeted by the British. Stephen Jarvis was later suspected of having guided Tryon to Danbury, though at the time he
claimed he was fifty-eight kilometres away in Greenwich—an alibi
that proved to be true because the Americans were using the town to
store arms and supplies.

Munson and William Jarvis participated in the destruction as
members of the Prince of Wales Loyal American Volunteers. Most
of Danbury's residents had fled before the British troops arrived.
According to the town's history the "enemy" soldiers captured and
killed several Patriot supporters.

Throughout the Revolutionary War, almost all Loyalists were
derisively denigrated as "Tories," allegedly upper-class Brits who
were traitors and had to be driven from the colonies with the same
resolve as a dreaded plague that had to be expunged. The Tory
label, as will be seen, hardly fit all Loyalists—in truth, it did not fit
most of them. There was no off-the-rack Loyalist, despite later mythology that portrayed them as diehard monarchists. The Loyalists
meshed British traditions with American republicanism and were
forced to live with this unholy contradiction between authority and
liberty wherever they settled. But in the case of the Jarvises, "Tories" was an accurate depiction. The family's roots stretched back to
fifteenth-century England, the time of the Tudors and Robert Ger-
vayes of Chatkyll, County Staffordshire, northeast of London. By
the early 1600s the family's name had changed to Jervice when one
of Robert's grandsons, John, who was born in the 1580s, emigrated
to the colony of Virginia, establishing the Jarvis presence in the New

World. John's three sons settled in Boston, a town still under control of the Puritans.

Even after two generations, the Jarvis family retained its strong connection to England. Even more so when the call for revolution was heard in the colonies. From the start, Stephen Sr. made it clear to his son, friends, and associates that the Jarvises were on the side of the King. Or as Stephen Jr. put in his memoirs, "my father was one of those persons called Torries [*sic*]."

When the citizens of Danbury heard about Lexington and Concord, a wave of patriotism swept through the town—except at the home of the Jarvises and the other hundred or so Loyalists. The bell at the First Congregational Church rang nonstop, cannon was fired, and bonfires were lit, as James Montgomery Bailey related in his history of Danbury. "A public meeting was held, and the village orators who were not friends of King George made fervid speeches, urging the able-bodied to enroll themselves in defence of the country," Bailey added. That presumably did not include Stephen Jarvis Sr.

Stephen Jr. (hereafter Stephen Jarvis) was not about to allow his father's stubborn disapproval of Amelia to stop him from making her his bride, no matter how precarious the political situation might be. "Some time in the month of April, 1775, when the first blood was shed at Lexington," he later recorded, "I became acquainted with a Lady to whom I paid my address, and who I afterwards married; this attachment was disapproved of by my father, who carried his displeasure to great lengths and I was under the necessity of visiting the Lady only by stealth." Stephen Sr.'s anger only increased; father and son barely spoke.

Two months after Lexington and Concord, hostilities continued unabated with the far bloodier conflict between the rebels of Massachusetts and the British forces at Boston's Battle of Bunker Hill (more accurately Breeds Hill nearby), the unsuccessful British attempt to occupy Boston. The fighting was intense and the colonial troops under the command of William Prescott put up a fierce resistance. One of the Patriot casualties was Joseph Warren. The thirty-four-year-old physician had been shot in the face before British soldiers repeatedly stabbed him with their bayonets. It was that kind of war.

Boston did not fall that day; indeed, more than a year later the siege ended in a stalemate as the British evacuated the city. Though technically victorious at Bunker Hill, they sustained heavy casualties, proving that an army of colonials would not crumble before the mighty British regulars. "We have . . . learned one melancholy truth," a British officer conceded after the battle, "which is, that the Americans, if they were equally well commanded, are full as good soldiers as ours."

The courageous stand of the colonials at Bunker Hill, who had heeded the orders of their magical commander, General George Washington, provided a psychological boost. In New England and the other northern colonies, young men were drafted into local militias mainly to protect New York, thought to be the Royal Navy's next target.

Regardless of his family's loyalties, Stephen Jarvis was drafted. He might have avoided it, or he could have found a substitute. But because of the bitterness over his relationship with Amelia and in a fit of high pique, Stephen insisted on angering his father even more by picking the least forgivable gesture: he joined the rebel militia and went to New York against his family's enduring faith and then current wishes.

"I was obstinate and declared my intentions of going as a soldier," he remembered.

> For this declaration [my father] took me by the arm and thrust me out of the door; during the evening, however, I went to my room and went to bed. The next day was Sunday and I kept out of sight, the next morning we were to march, a Brother of my Mother was the officer commanding. On leaving the house I passed my father and wished him "good-bye," he made me no reply, and I passed on to the house of my uncle, the place

of rendezvous, but before the Troops marched my father so far relented as to come to me and after giving me a severe reproof, ordered me a horse to ride, gave me some money, and I set off. We arrived in New York the next day, and my uncle took up his quarters at Peck Slip [southwest of Manhattan] and took me into his house. He had a son with him, a little younger than myself, with whom I spent my time very agreeable.

After two weeks, the unit Jarvis had joined was inexplicably dismissed, possibly due to the disorganized state of the American revolutionary military in the early days of the conflict. When Stephen returned home, he theatrically swore to his enquiring father that he would break off his "suit with Miss Glover" thereby unintentionally spreading an essential bit of evidence about his long-term intentions. The father took him at his word. And Stephen changed out of whatever he wore as a rebel militiaman, donned his courting clothes, and dutifully trotted off to pass on the bad news to his beloved. But there was many a slip twixt the cup and the lip—or in this case between the Jarvis farm and the Glover homestead. Seeing Amelia face-to-face melted whatever resolve Stephen may have accumulated. "Before we parted, we renewed our vows of love and constancy."

That night of ardent promises had to face the cold light of day when Stephen confronted his father and reported on his mission. "My reception the next morning was everything but pleasant. I continued, however, to visit her as often as I could." Stephen's layover would last less than a year, during which time the Continental Congress meeting in Philadelphia issued the Declaration of Independence and the British, led by General William Howe, occupied New York City. By early 1777, local Patriots were hell bent on capturing Stephen for his part in helping Loyalist prisoners escape Connecticut. The teenager sought refuge in the home of Loyalist William Hawley, who was married to one of Amelia's sisters. This couple kindly arranged to have Amelia visit them, since they sensed that the mounting hostilities would soon be separating the young lovers until the revolution could be resolved. Stephen appreciated the rendez-vous and later wrote, "the pleasure I spent in her society surely can be better imagined than described," which proved not only that he was mature beyond his years as a lover, but that he had a way with words. Finally, a rebel relative arrived at the Hawley house to take Amelia home. Loath to leave any earlier than she had to, Miss Glover pretended that she had more packing to do and asked the relative to wait. In Jarvis's words, she "left him and visited me in my apartment. In this manner we kept him until a late hour, when we at last took leave of each other."

Stephen then fled Connecticut and joined the British garrison in New York as a sergeant with the early promise of a commission that would accord him a respectable wage and status as an officer. He would not see Amelia again until the spring of 1783.

Stephen Jarvis's story and that of his cousins in Stamford pro-vide a personal and intimate account of the trials and tribulations of Loyalism. Stephen's cousin Polly Dibblee later reflected on their "Burdens of Loyalty" and, as the Jarvis family saga demonstrated, that turned out to be a gross understatement.

There was no such thing as a "typical" Loyalist refugee experi-ence. Yet the Jarvis family's collective saga is historically significant because it touched on so many varieties of experience. Most Loyal-ists were middle- or working-class, while the Jarvises were decidedly middle-class. The Jarvis men and women were literate and the men, like Stephen Sr., had professions or readily moved into them follow-ing the revolution. Many adherents came from New York—where half of the population were Loyalists compared to only a tenth's of New England's and about a third in the South—whereas the Jarvis clan, based in Connecticut, had New England roots. Unlike Stephen Jr. and his cousins, however, a majority of Loyalists did not take up arms against the rebels. (Some years ago, American historian Paul H. Smith calculated that 15 percent of adult white male Loyalists—or about 21,000—were active in provincial corps or in the British army.) It was thus accurate to state, as New Brunswick Loyalist historian

Stephen Davidson put it, "that many Loyalists shared some of the Jarvis family's experiences, but not all Loyalists experienced all of the elements of the Jarvis saga. The Jarvises illustrate the Loyalist refugee experience the way old book plates illustrated the key points of a novel but didn't give away the whole story."

2

FOUNDING THE REPUBLIC
OF IMPUDENT DREAMS

A kaleidoscope of fugitive longings which seized the glories of political independence: this was the fever in the blood that triggered the American Revolution.

JOHN ADAMS, who within less than a year would rank among the revolution's chief machers—and eventually become the second American president—was at his farm in Braintree, south of Boston. It was there that word reached him about the events at Lexington and Concord. Immediately grasping the significance of the hostilities, he rode by horseback the fifty kilometres, "past burned-out houses and scenes of extreme distress," to inspect the battle area for himself, as his biographer David McCullough related. Two months later, his wife, Abigail, did the same thing when the Battle of Bunker Hill, the first all-out conflict of the revolution, broke out. The terrifying crescendo from that confrontation could be heard as far away as Braintree. She took their seven-year-old son, Johnny (the future U.S. president John Quincy Adams), and climbed up Penn's Hill close to the family farm. From that high vantage point, a steady cloud of smoke was visible. "How many have fallen we know not," she wrote to her husband that evening. "The constant roar of the cannon is so distressing that we cannot eat, drink, or sleep."

Decades later, John Adams suggested that before the first shot was fired at Lexington, the American Revolution had already commenced. "The Revolution," he wrote in 1818 a few months after his eighty-second birthday, "was in the minds and hearts of the people." If so, at the crux of this bitter separation was the universal eighteenth-century truth which decreed that a mother country had the God-given right to rule her colonies in any way she deemed.

Certainly that was the way His Majesty King George III, the thirty-seven-year-old English monarch, saw it. "I have no doubt but the nation at large sees the conduct in America in its true light," he wrote to Prime Minister Lord North several weeks after the Battle of Bunker Hill, "and I am certain any other conduct by compelling obedience would be ruinous and . . . therefore no consideration could bring me to swerve from the present path which I think myself in duty-bound to follow."

One way or the other, America would be made to submit to the dictates of the King and Parliament, as a child who refused to obey his parents' will. So firm was this view held by the King and his key political advisors that the royal forces forged ahead no matter what the human cost. In 1775 and for the next six years at least, backing down, compromising, reconciliation, or a negotiated settlement— such as proposed in the 1775 Olive Branch Petition to ease tax and trade regulations—were not considered serious options.

King George III was a slow learner, unable to read until he was eleven, and didn't make friends easily. George actually met his wife, the German-born Princess Charlotte of Mecklenburg, for the first time on the afternoon of their wedding day. They immediately had fifteen children and she didn't learn much English—never enough to divert regal intentions. His Majesty was remembered mainly for his deranged bouts of insanity, as diagnosed by his doctors because his urine had turned dark blue (he may, in fact, have suffered from porphyria, a hereditary disease, though scientific efforts to prove it conclusively have fallen short). During his lapses, he talked incessantly, until he was foaming at the mouth. His eyes were bloodshot, the shade of squashed red currants. His keepers had to sit on him so that he wouldn't harm himself.

During the years of the American Revolution, however, he was a more vibrant and polarizing figure. His stewardship was profoundly flawed by his inflexibility and narrow-mindedness. "In all that related to his kingly office," concluded Jeremy Black, his able modern biographer, "he was the slave of deep rooted selfishness and no feeling of a kindly nature ever was allowed to access to his bosom, whenever his power was concerned, either in its maintenance, or in the manner of exercising it." This style of misanthropy even applied to the most marginal of concerns. When his lord chancellor asked the royal presence for permission not to wear a wig while not engaged in official functions, the King harrumphed: "I will have no innovations in my time!" It could have been his epitaph.

The King imagined himself the moral guardian of his subjects, many of whom in his opinion were weak and depraved and required rescuing from themselves and the corruption around them. At the end of October 1775, when he rode in a grand procession from St. James's Palace to the Palace of Westminster to officiate at the opening of Parliament, more than sixty thousand enthusiastic Londoners turned out to gaze at him riding by in his extravagant "fairy-tale" royal coach, as it was described by officials of the Royal Mews, where the coach and other royal transportation were kept. Built in 1762, the coach was "gilded with 22 carat gold leaf and sumptuously decorated with sculptures of cherubs, tritons and dolphins. The panels on the carriage were painted by the Italian artist Giovanni Cipriani. The coach, seven meters long, weigh[ed] four tonnes and [was] drawn by a span of eight horses." Few who watched the spectacle that October in 1775 would have doubted that the rebellion in the American colonies was doomed to fail.

The monarch, who would occasionally refer to himself as "the last King of America," had considerable patronage at his disposal and restored some of the throne's waning powers. While his views carried weight in Parliament, his interventions into the affairs of state were not entirely appreciated by all politicians in the vehement debate about America's future and its obligations to contribute to the defence of the colonies. On this subject, he ardently sided with his key ministers and opposed MPs such as Edmund Burke, the brilliant political theoretician, who argued that America would be best controlled "through a wise and salutary neglect."

The father of modern conservatism and a member of the British Parliament, Burke argued in a series of luminous lectures that while there were limits to freedom, at some point forbearance ceased to be a virtue. In his Commons "Speech on the Conciliation with American Taxation" on April 19, 1774, he tore apart the moral foundations of the British Empire: "Reflect how you are to govern a people who think they ought to be free, and think they are not," he noted. "Your scheme yields no revenue; it yields nothing but discontent, disorder, disobedience; and such is the state of America, that after wading up to your eyes in blood, you could only end just where you began; that is, to tax where no revenue is to be found. A great empire and little minds go ill together."

IF THE BIG ISSUE in the revolution was the power of a mother country to rule its colonies as it wished, the more specific cause was money—or, rather, the lack thereof. Defeating the French in the Seven Years' War (1756–1763) had greatly enhanced Britain's empire around the globe, extending its power in the West Indies, West Africa, and India. In North America, the victory was a complete humiliation of the French that gave the British all of its former New France territory, with the exception of the tiny islands of Saint-Pierre and Miquelon off the coast of Newfoundland. But it was enormously costly. By the time the Treaty of Paris—agreed to by the British, French, and Spanish—that ended the conflict was signed in 1763, the British national debt had nearly doubled to approximately £130 million, or the equivalent today of about US$16.5 billion. With the decision to maintain troops in the colonies, a succession of prime ministers—starting with the Earl of Bute, then followed by George Grenville, Marquess of Rockingham, and Lord North, among others—determined that the only viable policy was enforcing the Navigation Acts, increasing custom duties, as well as imposing direct and indirect taxes.

Grenville's Stamp Act of 1765, which instituted the detested fee on all paper products and legal documents, typified the seemingly arbitrary and arrogant British treatment of the colonies. It fostered protest organizations like the Sons of Liberty, a clandestine underground group formed at Boston in 1765 with a mission to defend the colonists' rights in any way necessary including violence in the streets. The official stamp distributors responsible for collecting the tax became prime targets for irate colonial mobs—fearing for their lives, most quickly resigned. Even when the stamp tax was repealed in 1766, Parliament concurrently passed the Declaratory Act, which reasserted its absolute authority to tax the Americans "in all cases whatsoever."

The tax fees were only part of the problem. Far more significant from the Americans' point of view was that the Brits were ignoring, even mocking, their legitimate political and natural rights, no different from the British philosopher John Locke's theories about the British in his 1689 essay *Two Treatises of Government*. "Be it remembered," John Adams wrote in 1765, "that liberty must at all hazards be supported. We have a right to it, derived from our Maker. . . . Our fathers have earned and bought it for us at the expense of their ease, their estates, their pleasure, and their blood."

The problem for Britain's North American colonies was their lack of representation in Westminster's elected lower house. The colonies were governed by the Executive Branch (King George in full froth) with no checks or balances. While the people of England—in fact, property qualifications meant that the vast majority of Englishmen could not vote until the twentieth century—took advantage of their democratic privileges that had evolved over centuries, the colonials enjoyed no such rights. The "free" Englishmen who moved across the Atlantic were no longer free, but subject to the unchecked authority of an uncaring, distant monarchy. However, the main point the colonists argued consistently was that they could not be taxed without their consent. Hence the cry of the revolution, "No Taxation Without Representation!" though even if they had had representatives in the British House of Commons, it would hardly have mattered.

In the spring of 1764, following the passage of the Sugar Act that increased custom duties on items imported into colonies, Samuel Adams had framed the quintessential American position in an interesting light.

> For if our Trade may be taxed why not our Lands? Why not the Produce of our Lands & everything we possess or make use of? This we apprehend annihilates our Charter Right to govern & tax ourselves–It strikes at our Brittish [*sic*] Privileges, which as we have never forfeited them, we hold in common with our Fellow Subjects who are Natives of Brittain [*sic*]: If Taxes are laid upon us in any shape without our having a legal Representation where they are laid, are we not reduced from the Character of free Subjects to the miserable State of tributary Slaves?

Well, yeah.

British authorities would hear none of this then or later. Instead, they held firm in their resolve, angering the colonists and exacerbating the tension with other detested measures like the Currency Act, which restricted the colonies' right to print money, and the Quartering Act, which mandated that the colonists had to provide shelter and supplies for British troops. To the colonists these taxes and acts amounted to nothing less than slavery. "[Britain] will make Negroes of us all," bitterly declared New York lawyer Robert R. Livingston, a Founding Father.

Discontented American politicians and merchants did not really want to rebel or go to war. The eruption of violence in 1775 was the culmination of a decade of being rebuffed and punished by the British for their ongoing defiance. American petitions led to boycotts of British goods, which in turn led to angry protests, effigy burnings, vicious attacks on real or suspected Loyalists, property destruction, and finally to the deadly musket battle on Lexington Green. From 1765 to 1775, the British, who were determined to suppress any and all resistance, sent more soldiers to police the colonies and passed more repressive acts. The celebrated Boston Tea Party on December 16, 1773—in which a group of Patriots masquerading as Indians dumped East India tea into the harbour as a protest against the trifling, but highly symbolic, tea tax—was a turning point. Had the British government not penalized all of Boston and Massachusetts by shutting down the colony's harbours, the revolution might never have begun.

Parliament responded to the tea protest in 1774 with the Coercive Acts, or Intolerable Acts, which, among other provisions, ended local self-government in Massachusetts and stifled Boston's commercial endeavours. Colonists up and down the Thirteen Colonies in turn reacted to these Coercive Acts with additional acts of protest and by convening the First Continental Congress, which petitioned the British monarch for repeal of the acts and coordinated colonial resistance to them. By 1775, the crisis had escalated, and the American Revolutionary War began in earnest with the opening shots being fired in a suburb of Boston.

IN 1776, the American colonies were in a very different place from Mother England, which had nurtured them. The island nation was on the cusp of the Industrial Revolution that would change everything. British society for generations had been plagued by landless, itinerant lower classes, composed primarily of underemployed farm workers who coalesced into grim industrial slums, as would be chillingly portrayed by Charles Dickens and Karl Marx. (It was a classic Malthusian dilemma, which doesn't mean much except that it sounded impressive.) Eldest sons inherited the family farms and were married off to their neighbours' eldest daughters. Then what? Then the wedding guests went home and had to fend for themselves.

That was not quite the situation in America. The Thirteen Colonies were not without class distinctions, especially in the southern sphere, yet the easy availability of open, fertile ground also provided welcome opportunity to acquire property and create individual security, leading to the possibility of wealth. Fledgling industries provided employment but no troublesome surplus labour was created in the process; those who could not get work in towns easily found vacant farmlands to till.

This was the realization of Thomas Jefferson's rural ideal, a nation of independent, self-sufficient farmers with room to grow. And it worked. Open acreage created a distinct entrepreneurial society. As a result, Jefferson and commercial advocates such as Alexander Hamilton felt constrained by the rule of British authority that was busy dealing with radically different domestic social conditions. Until 1763, an armed English presence was needed in the colonies as protection against French conquest. After that there was no such pressing requirement, though it materialized once the American uprising turned into full-scale war.

At this time of a spirited move to independence, expectations of public service were far different from modern conventions. In a society where 90 percent of the people were farmers, serving in government was based on having the time and means to live without pay. Benjamin Franklin, for example, was able to manage this due to the success of his printing business; likewise for some lawyers. But the bulk of government service was provided by slave owners who relied on the work of others to provide their privileged lifestyles.

Franklin had been negotiating with Prime Minister North and Secretary of State for the Colonies Lord Dartmouth to reach a compromise over the Americans' complaints about British rule and perceived repression in the colonies, but Franklin insisted that the British government must first agree the colonies had the right to govern and tax themselves. Meanwhile, word reached North that the King was impatient and the cabinet was ready to remove him as prime minister. At a cabinet meeting on January 12, 1775, North abandoned conciliation efforts, agreeing to pursue policies to eliminate all trade with the Thirteen Colonies and declare that persons within the colonies not actively loyal to the Crown be recognized as rebels. Intransigence on both sides set the stage for the fatal confrontation at Lexington.

Not being the tea-swilling laggards that the Yanks imagined them to be, the British responded with a vengeance, even though the grim reality at the start was that in most situations the American militia were bumbling amateurs compared to the British regulars and their paid Hessian allies—mercenaries brought in to ensure the job got done quickly and efficiently. The backwoods Yankee militia initially regarded bayonets as handy implements for cutting up the meat of animals they shot, and their troops fled in panic when faced by British bayonet assaults. But both sides fully realized that there was no turning back.

The stage was now set for a showdown between executive authority and the will of the people. Westminster was forced to pay strict attention to George Washington's guns. Britain's American colonies were founded upon profoundly idealistic principles which guided the victors and the losers—the Loyalists—to very different conclusions. Rejection of the structured law and order of a monarchical society meant a lawless interval when nothing would be sacred. The image of a distracted King was as discomforting to monarchists as was the shadow of a troubled Pope to Roman Catholics. The most compelling, if awkwardly tempting, summons was dealing with that vexing virtue, loyalty. It came at a high price and yielded few dividends but it was good for the soul and became a bargaining chip.

Taking up arms against England meant flat-out war, prompting resident genius Benjamin Franklin to confide that the instigators of the revolution would "all hang separately" if their initiative failed. By the same token, for the Americans involved, those identical manoeuvres constituted the grand potential of being recognized as the highest acts of patriotism—or they might, if they succeeded. Although Franklin and his friends feared being hanged, the reaction of the empire was actually one of leniency. As early as November 28, 1776, a Loyalist officer had granted pardons to all Nova Scotia's Cumberland County soldiers who had attempted (without success) to promote the revolution, profoundly frustrating the Loyalists who wanted the authorities to crack down on the Patriots and their misguided Nova Scotia allies. American history books would later try to disguise the fact that the revolution was actually a civil war. Patriots preferred to imagine the war as a conflict between mistreated colonies and a tyrannical empire. This mythology was such an intricate part of American self-perception that when *Star Wars* innovator George Lucas created Luke Skywalker for his blockbuster space opera, his young hero had to be a republican rebel who fought against an evil empire. Who among Patriot historians wanted to describe the founding of their nation as being drenched in the blood of brothers fighting against one another? The conflict set off a flash of violent crescendos, as sudden and deadly as an unexpected earthquake. Without being willing and certainly without being ready, America was thrust into the Gulliverish burden of leading the New World.

Individual states jumped in as if they were engaged in a giant toffee pull and they didn't want to miss out. North Carolina, once the calmest of backwaters and usually bypassed as a hotbed of tranquility, came out angrily for independence and foreign alliances. The state of Georgia, which at the time had a highly favourable fiscal subsidy arrangement with London, went against its self-interest and voted to fight. South Carolina was next, when its last royal governor, William Campbell, was forced to escape aboard a British man-of-war; as was Lord Dunmore, the royal governor of Virginia. Rhode Island was more careful but began to omit the King's name in public documents.

Massachusetts went all the way. Delegates to Boston town hall meetings endorsed a keynote declaration that accused the English King of every misdeed this side of spreading the Black Plague, endorsing this declaration: "For prayers of peace, the King has instead tendered the sword; for liberty, he has chains; for safety, there is death; loyalty to him is now treason to our country." That all-purpose run-down shifted the onus from protest to retribution. A congressional resolution of May 15, 1776, rejected the continuation of Americans taking routine oaths supporting the British government. Only New York hesitated. On July 2, 1776, the United States Congress supported and disseminated their sacred Declaration of Independence. John Adams, who "more than anyone . . . had made it happen," wrote McCullough, believed that it would be that date which "will be celebrated by succeeding generations as the great anniversary festival." Yet it turned out to be July 4 when the final vote was taken in far less pomp and circumstance than has been mythologized. (In fact, the Declaration was not actually ready to be signed until early August, although decades later both Adams and Jefferson insisted the significant signing took place on July 4.)

The Founding Fathers were happy to brand George III as a tyrant, though South Carolina, Georgia, and several northern delegates drew a line at Thomas Jefferson's suggestion that the King was guilty of perpetuating the slave trade. That went too far. Black slavery was so institutionalized in the colonies that any hint of a rebuke was considered excessive. In 1776, the American population was approximately 2.5 million people and 20 percent (or 500,000) of them were slaves. Of that number, 40 percent (or 200,000) were in servitude in Virginia, Jefferson's home colony. According to David McCullough, an estimated one third of the members of the Second Continental Congress owned slaves.

In what is a well-known case of historical hypocrisy, Jefferson, the voice and chief author of the independence declaration that, more than any document in the history of statesmanship, gave a new nation its *raison d'être*, and who penned its most eloquent and enduring

phrase proclaiming the "self-evident" truth that "all men are created equal," owned with his wife, Martha, about two hundred slaves.
This included his mistress, Sally Hemings, a mulatto who was thirty
years his junior and not more than fourteen when their affair began.
Hemings, the mother of Jefferson's children, was not officially freed
until after his death in 1826. (He purposely left her name out of his
will specifying which of his slaves would be freed, though she had
born and nurtured two of his sons.) But such was the way of the
times: Jefferson never stopped believing in white racial superiority,
and as a plantation owner, keeping slaves was economically sound.
George Washington also had two hundred slaves and, though he
was much more intellectually opposed to it than Jefferson, he still
owned slaves when he became the first U.S. president. John Dickinson, the Pennsylvania delegate who opposed a violent rebellion
against the Brits, kept eleven, and at one point Benjamin Franklin,
an early abolitionist, owned two slaves. There was no real distinction
between Patriots and Loyalists on the subject of slavery; Loyalists
were committed slave owners as well and many brought their slaves
with them to Canada. The fact that the British Parliament abolished
slavery throughout the empire in 1833 later reaffirmed the Loyalists'
sense of moral authority, but that did not alter the fact of their earlier
support of that shameful institution

Apart from the issue of slavery, every informed individual who
read the 1776 Declaration of Independence was aware that the
Americans were not challenging lawful authority; instead, they were
protesting the *absence* of lawful authority and as such had the right
to rebel in order to reinstitute it on fairer terms. John McCain, the
American naval hero who dared speak out of turn on vital issues,
echoed the same contemporary interpretation, saying, "This was
what the War of Independence was all about: more of a civil war
among like-minded people than a conquest to seize territory or
booty."

———

HISTORY MOVED INTO a new unexplored quadrant. Soon after it was passed by the Congress, the independence resolution was adopted by the Patriot assembly of New York with no recorded objections. New York had the largest percentage of loyal colonists, so it was not the colony itself that accepted the Declaration of Independence, but the assembly of its Patriot politicians. This group would relocate their "capital city" a number of times during the revolution, finally locating it in New York City after the British scrambled home in November of 1783. That changed everything.

The Loyalists were no longer the "Loyal Opposition." Now they were foxes inside the chicken coop, suspected traitors, targets of abuse, rogues galore, and yet, still heroes to themselves. As usual, such bleats were accompanied by humour, with some cynical observers pointing out that America had advanced rapidly toward independence—by becoming independent of principle; independent of credit, independent of good manners, and independent of gratitude to the Mother Country.

It was a time for fundamental shifts and of resistance to arbitrary British misgovernment. The possibility of breaking the colonies' bonds with England had been a separate issue, but suddenly it was on the table. All but one of Boston's political opinion leaders urged revolution. And yet, as one of the negotiators conceded, "the golden leaf of independence was too thin to conceal the wicked winks of treason." Samuel Adams, the upright rabble-rouser with the loudest voice, was the monarchy's chief messenger. A slip of the tongue at the time provided much amusement. A proclamation of faith by provincial invocations, which customarily ended with the rote salutation "God Save the King!" now pointedly declared, "God Save the People!"

Next on the agenda was finding a way of creating the appearance of legality in prosecuting the Loyalists. The 1775 Provincial Congress resolved part of the issue by passing a law that all persons who were "disaffected to the cause of America" must immediately be disarmed. The guns, it should be added, usually had less to do with war than with bagging tomorrow's dinner. This was not just a new law but a new kind of law setting up barriers to ordinary lifestyles.

When American colonists adopted the Declaration of Independence in 1776, one third of the subcontinent's inhabitants were opposed to gaining independence from England. This raised significant issues about understanding the mentality of the Loyalists, many, though certainly not all, of whom never wavered in their faith to the British constitutional monarchy, no matter how scatterbrained George III might become. Boston, which was the commercial and intellectual hub of the colonial regimes, was generally in favour of independence. New York, more cosmopolitan, remained Loyalist. The balance of the population was against everybody. They held their noses, but surreptitiously supported whoever was winning.

At the time, the Loyalists were still untried and unorganized, isolated aboard a perishable platform. British monarchy had for uncounted millennia been effective and flexible. It had evolved away from the concepts of "divine right" and autocratic rule to a more democratic, constitutional monarchy, decades—and in some cases, centuries—before the other royal houses of Europe followed suit. Loyal Americans were convinced that the problems could be resolved by compromise. Their differences with the Patriots reflected two opposing European philosophies: the first claimed that governmental powers were based on the natural rights of citizens and thus should be directly controlled by voters. To others this sounded like raising the spectre of assured anarchy in which law and order could never coexist. They were both right. But history, as usual, was in a hurry and moved at its own pace to force a premature denouement. The voters won.

The Yanks were not prepared for a war that was to last eight desperate years, endangering almost daily the lives and limbs of civilian-soldiers who were not sophisticated enough to know if and when to quit. There was in fact, no turning back on either side.

Still, there certainly was hope. Though threatened and reviled, the Loyalists were alive and kicking—glad to be so—since that was no longer a guaranteed option in their former homelands in the Thirteen Colonies. There was a definite split growing wider between the Patriots and Loyalists that was almost physical, like the earth opening into two separate gullies after an earthquake.

3

MAYHEM UNCONFINED

The firestorm of change ignited by the Revolutionary War was profound and unnatural. There was no middle ground. Either you were a daring revolutionary thug or a gutless bottle-washer for the foppish King of England. Both caricatures were accurate.

W HEN IT WAS FINALLY OVER, all that remained for Polly Jarvis Dibblee were the bitter memories of her terrible ordeal. The revolution had driven her and her children from their home in Stamford, Connecticut; forced her into exile in, as she recalled, the "frozen climate and barren wilderness" of New Brunswick; and caused the tragic suicide of her husband, Fyler.

"O gracious God, that I should live to see such times under the Protection of a British Government for whose sake we have Done and suffered everything but that of Dying," she wrote from New Brunswick to her brother William in mid-November 1787. "May you never Experience such heart piercing troubles as I have and still labour under. . . . You may Depend on it that the Sufferings of the poor Loyalists are beyond all possible Description. The old Egyptians who required Brick without giving straw were more Merciful than to turn the Israelites into a thick Wood to gain Subsistence from an uncultivated Wilderness."

Until the 1770s, life had been good for Polly, the daughter of Samuel and Martha Jarvis of Stamford, and a sister to Munson and William, two of her nine siblings. She was born in 1747 and grew up as her siblings did, heeding their parents' credo to "fear God and honour the King." By the time she was sixteen, Polly had married her sweetheart, Fyler Dibblee, a twenty-two-year-old lawyer and the son of Reverend Ebenezer Dibblee, the pastor of St. John's Anglican Church in Stamford, and his wife, Joanna. A graduate of Yale University, Fyler must have studied or "read law" with a local lawyer or judge for two years before he was admitted to the bar. He was ambitious and a community leader. He headed Stamford's militia company with the rank of captain and served as the town's representative to the Connecticut General Assembly. When the revolution began, Polly and Fyler had five children—Walter, William, Margaret (Peggy), Ralph, and Sally—and owned a fine house with its own library, a sure sign that they valued reading, an interest they would have imparted to their children. Benjamin Franklin, who conceived the public library, wrote in his *Autobiography*, published a decade after the Revolutionary War ended, that his lifelong passion for learning and literature started for him as young man with his father's small collection of books.

Stamford had first been settled by Puritans in 1641 and was then known by its Indian name, Rippowam. By the mid-1770s, the town's population had grown to approximately three thousand. As in Danbury, some of the more prominent residents had black servants or slaves, and that may have included the Jarvis and Dibblee families. Stamford hugs the Long Island Sound, which was a boon for its merchants, who took advantage of its maritime location and conducted a prosperous trade shipping the area's diverse agricultural produce to New York City and points beyond.

But they did not always conform to British trade laws. In November 1700, the Earl of Bellomont, writing from New York, reported to the English Lords of Trade, the royal advisors responsible for enforcing mercantilist regulations, about a Stamford merchant named Major Selleck. "There is a town called Stamford in Connecticut colony, on the border of this province, where one Major Selleck lives," the earl noted. "He has a warehouse close to the sea, that runs between the Mainland (Long Island). That man does great mischief with his warehouse, for he receives abundance of goods from our vessels, and the merchants afterwards take their opportunity of running them into this town. Major Selleck receives at least ten thousand pounds worth of treasure and East India goods, brought by one Clarke of this town from Kidd's sloop and lodged with Selleck." Not all that surprisingly, seven decades later, several of Selleck's grandsons were among Stamford's estimated one hundred Loyalists.

Stamford had a reputation as a "well-to-do" town, a lively place with a range of businesses, shops, schools, and Protestant churches. The most important establishment was the village grist mill, where farmers in the area delivered their grain so it could be processed into flour. During the French and Indian War, several of Stamford's young men fought and died defending British interests. So loyal was the town then that at meeting in 1757, the citizens voted to bear the cost of room and board for visiting British regulars. The following year, a committee led by Abraham Davenport, arguably Stamford's most prominent citizen, agreed to supply British soldiers with firewood for their guard room and hospital. Less than twenty years later, that devotion to the King would be dramatically transformed; in a sermon of November 16, 1775, Dr. Noah Welles referred to the same British regulars as the "enemy" and called for the town to resist oppression at all costs.

THERE ARE NO known portraits of either Polly or Fyler, but it is easy to imagine Fyler, a gentleman lawyer in breeches and stockings, black pumps fastened with silver buckles, a tailored doublet, a white frilly shirt with a cravat, a frock coat, and a three-corned and cocked broad-brimmed hat. He probably also sported a wig tied with a colourful ribbon, popular in the colonies despite being expensive, heavy, and hot to wear. Polly's daily attire, no doubt homemade, would have been a tasteful patterned coloured gown and petticoat, along with a mob cap covering her long hair tied in a bun or a wide brimmed hat to shelter her from the sun during the hot summer days.

While Fyler conducted legal business—since crime was not a huge issue in Stamford, his law practice dealt primarily with contracts and commercial matters: drafting deeds, writs, and bills of sale; debt collection; and land transactions—Polly (or her servants) supervised their children and the household. As with her relatives in Danbury, that meant a day filled with washing, cooking, polishing silver and pewter, preparing food, knitting, garden weeding, milking a cow, and likely dealing with wrangy geese. In those days, according to Alice Morse Earle, "geese were raised for their feathers more than as food . . . and in some towns every family had a flock, and their clanking was heard all day and sometimes all night." Polly performed the arduous task of plucking the feathers (a stocking was pulled over the bird's head to prevent biting) so Fyler might have a ready stock of quill pens for his office and library.

Polly was educated, though as per the custom of the times she would have deferred to Fyler on most issues, especially the subject of Stamford's role in Connecticut politics and the colonies' relationship with Britain. Her focus was her family. "The home of pre-revolutionary days was far more than a place where the family ate and slept," writes Carl Holliday in his 1922 study, *Women's Life in Colonial Days*.

> Its simplicity, its confidence, its air of security and permanence, and its atmosphere of refuge or haven of rest are characteristics to be grasped in their true significance only through a thorough reading of the writings of those early days. The colonial woman had never received a diploma in domestic science or home economics; she had never heard of balanced diets; she had never been taught the arrangement of color schemes; but she knew the secret

of making from four bare walls the sacred institution with all its subtle meanings comprehended under the one word, home.

Connecticut was somewhat more somber than the other colonies, but for amusement Polly and Fyler attended local balls and dances. There was fishing and hunting for Fyler and his male companions; and for the more adventurous a glass of ale and wagering on cockfights. And for Polly and the children there was skating and sleigh riding during the winters.

THE TRANQUIL FAMILY and happy life Polly and Fyler had built for themselves and their children began to unravel in 1776. As was the case with their respective families, Polly and Fyler were "loyal servants of the Crown," as they might have described themselves, and therefore targets for Patriot mobs.

In the black-and-white world of the American Revolution, you were either unblushingly for the Patriots or violently against them. There was no middle ground, especially after the publication of philosopher and radical Thomas Paine's popular political pamphlet, *Common Sense*, in January 1776, which passionately and convincingly made the case for American independence and that was followed three months later by Lexington and the Declaration of Independence. George Washington seemed to have approved of mob persecution of the Tories. In 1776, Israel Putnam, one of Washington's generals, met a procession of the Sons of Liberty parading a number of Tories on rails up and down the streets of New York and attempted to halt this inhuman proceeding. On hearing this, Washington reprimanded the general, stating that "to discourage such proceedings was to injure the cause of liberty in which they were engaged," and that "nobody would attempt it but an enemy of his country." Likewise, Samuel Adams, the onetime calming figure, grew notorious for his extremism, going so far in speeches before Congress in 1778, to call the Loyalists "traitors," "wretches," and "dastardly criminals."

On November 3, 1778, he praised the Banishment Act of Massachusetts but deplored the fact that its General Court had allowed a few
exceptions to the death penalty. Though a tolerant and just man,
Adams wrote in 1780 that he would have hanged his own brother
had he taken the British side. Patriots still repeated with glee the
definition of a Loyalist as "a thing whose head is stretched in England
and its body in America, and its neck ought to be stretched too."

Following the publication of the Declaration of Independence,
the tens of thousands of Loyalists in the colonies were deprived of
their right to vote. The glorious new home of freedom, liberty, and
democracy turned out, for the moment, to be a tightly controlled
one-party state. Even the legal right to dispose of one's fortune as
one wished was limited to republican voters. Sworn fidelity to the
state was a required qualification to serve on juries or to hold any
semi-public office. Those involved in commercial activity were forced
to abandon any chance of success, unless they belonged to the Patriot
"Mafia"—and that included abandoning any criticism, however mild
or constructive. "There is more liberty in Turkey than in the Domin-
ions of Congress" was the studied conclusion of one of the republic's
best minds—careful to remain anonymous, of course. The system did
not allow free comment.

And always there were the fines that doubled at the drop of an un-
kind adjective. Levied at will by floating prosecutors, such fines and
the penalty system drove the economy. The birth pangs of this magnificent democratic achievement included a wee rider. By federal
edict, half of all imposed fines—which went as high as $20,000 for
significant transgressions—were pocketed by the prosecutors themselves. It was the most profitable game in town. The new America
at first was financed largely by these fines levied against Loyalists.
Patriots also sold any land, furniture, or slaves that they seized from
their Loyalist neighbours, using the profits to fund their civil war.
The insurgent Tories accused their enemies of disarming them to
the point of having to hunt with clubs. That was rapidly turning into
a valid complaint.

Not having Patriot land to seize and use to finance their side of the war, all that Loyalists could do was sit back and watch their Patriot counterparts' difficulties in launching a new paper currency. They did their best to prevent the circulation of Continental dollars while at the same time spreading distrust in their inherent value. This seriously hindered the Americans' efforts to finance their military requirements. *Rivington's Royal Gazette*, New York City's Loyalist newspaper, gleefully pointed out that the rebels' zeal in printing too many Continental dollars "would have depreciated the Gold of Ophir," causing the currency to depreciate in value.*

It wasn't long before most of the dispensable authority was being dedicated to ensuring that the Loyalists would cease to be a factor in the new republic's political pecking order. No. That was putting it too mildly: the motivating purpose was to *eliminate* the Loyalists, either by involuntary exile, or worse. "Eliminate" was a gangland version of "rub out" but in this context it signaled their exclusion, persecution, and eventual expulsion. At first the language was mellow: "We would humbly wish that this Act [the Massachusetts Government Act that closed Boston Harbor] had been couched with less vigour and that the execution of it had been delayed to a more distant time . . ." and so on. Then the rhetoric hardened: "In the presence of God and in good faith we have agreed with each other to suspend all commercial intercourse with Great Britain until these hateful Acts be repealed." Although the Loyalists had commanded the votes of a third of the pre-revolutionary electorate, the equations of power kept changing. The raw truth was that, even among the

---

* Ophir was a mystical port in the Red Sea referred to in the Hebrew Bible, where King Solomon went to resupply his hoards of gold and precious stones. According to legend, the area's mountains consisted of pure gold. Several of Edgar Rice Burroughs's novels in the Tarzan series were located in and around the lost city of Opar, which was another name for Ophir that was also the destination of the adventurers in the 1957 film *Legend of the Lost*. The final adoption of the enduringly alluring location—that has never been authenticated—was Ophur, the name of a Chicago rock band that expired noisily in 2003.

Patriots' rioting adherents, no one dared admit to themselves that mob rule was taking over. Yet that is precisely what happens in revolutions: the rule of law becomes a joke, then a target, and finally a discarded absurdity. The unrest was everywhere. When court convened at Great Barrington, the judges were ordered to leave town; and they meekly complied. In the counties, farmers would not grind their corn. The forty-three blacksmiths of Worcester County ceased their essential labours. Those careful folk who were still obeying the colonies' now defunct regulations were considered "infamous betrayers of their country."

The revolution thus meant that a difficult and dangerous choice had to be made—to support the Mother Country or abandon her for what must have seemed like a republican pipe dream. As nearly every Loyalist, such as Polly and Fyler, was to quickly understand, siding with the Crown came with a high price. Angry mobs rarely asked questions; instead they acted as judge and jury and meted out their distorted version of frontier justice. In retrospect, by their brutish actions, the Patriots were hardly helping promote their cause or persuading Loyalists to switch their allegiances. In fact, the mob violence had the opposite effect. The outrageous assaults were a major reason for the Loyalists' unwillingness to join the Patriot cause. The terrorist activities of mobs, fanned into flames by the rhetoric of their leaders, tainted whatever merit the Patriot complaints against Britain might have had. While Loyalists might not have appreciated further taxation any more than the Patriots did, they certainly did not approve of the plundering, vandalism, and tortures of the mob.

THROUGHOUT THE PRECEDING DECADE, Patriot anger had been mainly directed against customs officers, tax collectors, and merchants who were intent on enforcing unpopular British trade regulations and taxes. In Boston in January 1774, an unruly mob turned on John Malcolm, a sea captain and customs official with a nasty temper. One day, Malcolm became embroiled on the streets in a one-sided verbal assault on a young boy, who was rescued from possible harm by one George Hewes. Malcolm did not appreciate Hewes's interference in his business and the two men exchanged insults. Before it was over Malcolm struck Hewes on the side of his head, and Hewes required medical care from Dr. Joseph Warren, the Patriot physician.

Hewes swore out a complaint against Malcolm to a local magistrate. However, that evening, the impatient members of the Sons of Liberty—who hated Malcolm for his bullying, but more so for his zealous obedience to his British masters—took matters into their own hands. A large mob invaded Malcolm's home and dragged him into the street. They tore his clothes off and subjected him to the popular Patriot punishment of tarring and feathering. Malcolm was smeared in a mixture of moderately warm pine tar and pitch and then humiliated by being doused with goose feathers. After that treatment, he was carted through the street to the gallows. A rope was placed around his neck and the Sons threatened to hang him. Eventually, after further abuse, they let him go.

Tarring and feathering was not, as was commonly thought, an American invention. It dated back at least to the late twelfth century (and likely earlier), when King Richard I, or "Richard the Lionheart" as he was dubbed, was in France en route to retake the Holy Land from the so-called Muslim infidels. To maintain discipline and order, he issued a decree that any of his soldiers or sailors who were convicted of theft were to have their heads shaved and be covered in hot pitch and feathers. At some point in the 1760s, tarring and feathering started being the standard practice for gangs of American sailors intent on retribution against anyone they felt had wronged them.

Unlike the tar or asphalt currently utilized in road construction, which when heated likely would be deadly if applied to a person's skin, the pitch or pine tar used during the American Revolution had a lower melting point. The tar must have stung badly, but it was not usually fatal to the victim. Still, the Patriot mobs were particularly adept at the practice and anyone unfortunate enough to have it done to them did not easily forget it.

The main object was to humiliate the sufferer and instill the fear of God in him. Being partially stripped, then having distilled jack pine oil poured on your bare skin, including your private parts, and finally being dumped screaming into a vat of duck or chicken feathers usually did the trick. As in the case of John Malcolm, victims were subsequently propped up in a cart and paraded around their own neighbourhoods as a mark of contempt before their friends and families. That must have been the worst punishment, since the cruel treatment cast them into the comical appearance of giant, unplucked roosters, wobbling from the pain between their legs and elsewhere. An alternative was having the offender ride a rail around the neighbourhood, carried on the tall shoulders of his torturers. Since there was nothing between his body and the steel rail that he had to perch on, the damage to his reproductive organs was simple to imagine, if impossible to endure. The brutality of such situations was difficult to accept, or even imagine. "Oil did gradually take off the tar and feathers from the skin of victims," Loyalist John Melchoir File of New York's Hudson Valley later recalled, "but the psychological effect of this cruel treatment lasted a lifetime."

In File's opinion, Loyalists "were the most persecuted group" of the American Revolution. "You must try to walk in our shoes in order to understand the effect persecution had on our lives," he added in his reminiscences written soon after the conclusion of the War of 1812. Certainly by the summer of 1776, that assessment was all too true. (In December 1776, the Provincial Congress of New York went so far as to order the Committee of Public Safety to purchase all the available pitch and tar necessary for its dark uses.) The maltreatment of Loyalists quickly turned into a monstrous manhunt. It was always open season on the Tories. They were tracked down as if they were the last of their breed, haunted by the clear, if so far unrealized, threat of extinction.

———————

THE EXTENT OF the torment the Loyalists were subjected to was hard to imagine and harder to believe. It crossed all boundaries of paying the penalty for being on the revolution's losing side. Threatened with expropriation of property, violence, and torture, the Loyalists ran for their lives. Asked to plead, they would proudly confess to remaining loyal to the Crown and being profoundly committed to fundamental British values. Their loyalty was more cultural than ideological, but they could get decidedly emotional when describing their persecutors, who they characterized as "an army of Banditti whose sole objective was cowardly plunder."

The terrible tribulations endured by Jessie Dunbar, Jacob Bowman, Thomas Brown, and Ebenezer Slocum, among scores of others, were telling and all too representative of Loyalist misery.

In the days leading up to Lexington, a farmer named Jessie Dunbar, who lived in Bridgewater, Massachusetts, thirty-two kilometres west of Plymouth, had unknowingly disobeyed a revolutionary edict forbidding Patriots to purchase livestock from Loyalists—in this case, an equally innocent farmer named Nathaniel Thomas who lived nearby and who had an ox to sell. Dunbar drove his newly acquired animal home, where he skinned the ox and hoisted the carcass up on a rack for sale of its desirable parts. When local Patriots aware of the sale came by, they forced Dunbar into the dead animal's bleeding, gut-filled belly, then took him on a four-mile cart ride until they dragged the stunned Dunbar out of the belly of the beast and whipped him about his face and body with its entrails—all because he had bought the animal from a Loyalist.

Several months later and about five hundred kilometres to the southwest, Jacob Bowman, a farmer who lived with his wife and children on the Susquehanna River (in present-day Pennsylvania), was abruptly attacked by a gang of Patriots. Bowman, of German heritage, had served in the British army during the war against the French and was awarded 1,500 acres of land for his service. He and his eldest son, Adam, who was sixteen years of age, were taken prisoners. "The house [was] pillaged of every article except the bed on which his sick wife lay, and that they stripped off all but one blanket," later recounted Elizabeth Bowman, Jacob's granddaughter (the daughter of Bowman's second son, Peter.) "Half an hour after my grandfather was marched out, his youngest child was born. This was in November [1775].There my grandmother was, with an infant babe and six children, at the commencement of winter, without any provisions, and only one blanket in the house. Their cattle and grain were all taken away." The family survived the winter with the assistance of friendly Aboriginals in the vicinity who provided them with food and supplies. Together with other fleeing Loyalists, the family eventually made it north into British-controlled territory.

Jacob and Adam were taken to Philadelphia and locked up for the next eighteen months. They were released when an exchange of prisoners was agreed to, but they had no knowledge that the family had relocated. On their journey, they encountered Patriot scouts who shot at them, severely wounding Adam. Taken to a Patriot outpost, Jacob tended to his son, saving his life. The Patriots demanded that Jacob denounce his loyalty to the British, but he refused. He was incarcerated again in a jail at Lancaster, Pennsylvania, with another Loyalist by the name of Hoover. "They were there fastened together by a band of iron around their arms, and a chain with three links around their ankles, the weight of which was ninety-six pounds; and then fastened by a ring stapled to the door," Elizabeth Bowman recalled. "In that condition they remained four years and a half, until the flesh was worn away and the bones laid bare four inches." (He might have taken comfort with the fact that his son Peter, Elizabeth's father, as soon as he turned thirteen joined Butler's Rangers, a fierce Loyalist regiment.)

THOMAS BROWN WAS a son of privilege. He was only twenty-five in the summer of 1775 when he arrived in the British colony of Georgia from his father's estate in Whitby, North Yorkshire, to establish a plantation near Augusta. His retinue numbered seventy-four indentured servants who cleared the land, subdivided its 5,600 acres into farms, and erected the magnificent wilderness mansion that became his home. His stables filled with productive animals, his workers occupied the three dozen farmhouses he had built for them. He felt exalted, reborn on a new continent with an unlimited future. He seemed blessed by the mandate of heaven.

As a recent arrival from an ancient and infinitely more orderly society, Brown was unprepared for the formidable challenges of the infinite contingencies which no doctrine could encompass and no grand design could subjugate. Revolutionaries are not called revolting for nothing. Brown recognized that the essential issues of settling in an unfamiliar hunk of distant geography would not be simple. But with the advantages of youth, wealth, and an adventurous spirit he figured that calling on the necessary Stations of the Cross ought to be manageable. He saw himself as a creative improviser possessed by the capacity to move ahead with as little unpleasantness to himself as possible. After all, there was nothing very wrong, and much that was very right, about the dependable British tradition of muddling through.

Then, on the hot day of August 17, 1775, breaking the lazy mood of Georgia on his mind, Brown's reverie was interrupted by the tattoo of 130 armed men, a contingent from the local Sons of Liberty chapter, marching in step formation to the mansion he had recently finished building. Their mission was to enlist him in support of the revolution. Feeling the supportive weight of the British Empire on his shoulders, Brown calmly replied that he could never enter into an engagement to take up arms against the country which gave him his being. In the temper of the times, that was enough excuse for half a dozen of the ruffians to lunge at Brown, one of them smashing him on the top of his head with a rifle butt in such fury that it fractured his skull. Dazed into a semiconscious state, he later recalled having the top half of his body stripped and bound to a tree while

his legs and feet, splayed on the ground in front of him, were tied
to stakes. His limbs were set on fire by being dipped in flaming tar,
with kindling kept burning under his legs at the same time to increase the heat and intensify the searing pain. Two of his toes were
reduced to stubs.

There he was, tethered to a tree so he couldn't move, his lower
limbs inflamed, and his head caved in. Only one indignity remained: to scalp the poor man. That would have meant certain
death. Brown actually was half scalped, with the skin on the left
side of his head hanging down and blood spurting up in tiny foun-
tains on his head, gushing down his neck, and pooling behind his
ears. At this point, whatever tiny flicker of mercy remained among
his torturers kicked in. Miraculously, they stopped torturing him.
Even more miraculously, he lived. All this, one must remember, because he had admitted that in the vote to follow, he would support
the British monarchy under which he had grown up—and this was
meant to be America's first free election. Instead of running, he decided to fight back. That would require an army of his own, so he set
about recruiting one and arranging to be named its commanding
lieutenant-colonel.

Once Brown had more or less recovered, hobbling from village to
village, acting and looking like a mutilated scarecrow, he recruited
his own fighting unit—the King's Carolina Rangers—including a
mounted troop of cavalry. They were divided into seven companies,
played a key role in the defence of Savannah and Charleston, and
fought hard and bravely until the war ended in 1783. Later that year,
the regiment was disbanded at Halifax where most of its members
took up residence.

It was difficult to calculate the impact of the physical outrages
that had been inflicted on Thomas Brown's body. Or to speculate
why he deserved such Spanish Inquisition treatment simply because
he admitted that he planned to vote for his home team in what was
supposed to be a free and fair election. These acts of random and
unjustified cruelty were perpetrated by the self-styled sponsors of the

world's proudest democracy, conceived by America's political aristocrats who were supposed to represent enlightenment, compassion, and the freedom of choice.

Some enlightenment, some compassion; some freedom of choice.

Loyalty to the King had equally devastating consequences for the Slocum family. On April 5, 1777, a rebel mob arrived at Charles Slocum's door and demanded to see his son, Ebenezer. The Patriots were angry over the discovery that Ebenezer had been taking provisions and intelligence to Lord Hugh Percy's British forces stationed on the Rhode Island coast. Anxious to be rid of a spy in their midst, the mob tracked the young man to his father's home. When Charles Slocum went to answer the door, he was shot dead by a North Kingston man named George Babcock.

Ebenezer Slocum was twenty-seven at the time of his father's death. The Patriots of North Kingston seized the Slocum family's goods and property, while the Rhode Island Assembly ordered them to move ten miles inland. Being a widow with ten children was only the beginning of Sarah Slocum's problems. She was charged with having paid rent using forged currency—money that was in their home when her husband died. Found guilty, she was punished by having her cheeks burned and her earlobes cut off (the actual account used the word "cropped"). To add to this indignity, she was forced to stand for half an hour with her head and arms in the town pillory. The arrest had more to do with her loyalty to the King than her use of questionable currency, and the treatment of their mother only strengthened the Slocums' resolve to fight the rebels. At the end of the war, Esther and Ebenezer Slocum left Long Island Sound in the company of their children, but Ebenezer's mother, Sarah, was forced to travel on her own on a different ship. She had nine other children besides her Loyalist son, but many of them were already married and happily established in Rhode Island. Their wives and husbands did not want to give shelter to a British sympathizer such as Sarah, especially one whose loyalty was evident in her lobe-less ears and branded cheeks.

Such incidents were not at all rare in what turned out to be a savage and profoundly personal feud. For all its cruelties, this was a quarrel among neighbours—the 2.5 million Americans who had settled in the Thirteen Colonies facing down the increasingly voiceless minority of the Loyalists, who had every right to vote in the first American election. How often such treatment was inflicted was impossible to record, but certainly frequently enough for the Patriots to win the war and become the first—and formative—governors of the newly United States.

THE VINDICTIVE STRUGGLE between Loyalists and Patriots left no fighting ground unturned, including religion. One of Deerfield, Massachusetts's, most vocal Loyalists was the Reverend Jonathan Ashley, who had been the pastor of the town's Congregational Church since 1732. Having prayed for the health of the King for more than two thousand Sundays, the clergyman was not about to join a rebellion that involved crates of tea being dumped in Boston's harbour. In fact, Ashley's Patriot neighbours no longer drank tea as an act of political defiance.

On July 22, 1774, the Congregational minister made his own political statement—he announced that he was having a tea party at his home. To underscore the point, he then had one of his sons purchase a pound of tea at a local Loyalist's store and deliver it to another clergyman in nearby Greenfield.

Another of the most trusted leaders among local Loyalists was the Reverend John Beach, rector of Christ Anglican Church, in the small community of Redding Ridge, deep in the wilds of Connecticut. "Obedience to my King is to me as obligatory as obedience to my God," he trumpeted, and neither threats nor persecution could move him from that thorny path. After July of 1775, Anglican services were suspended in most of the state because clergymen felt that they would draw inevitable destruction upon themselves. The exceptions were in the tiny communities of Newtown and Redding

Ridge, where Beach resided and presided. He was remembered as declaring that "he would pray for the King till the rebels cut out his tongue."

The seventy-five-year-old Beach was not what the Patriots considered an "active Loyalist," having signed an agreement not to discourage enlistments in the American army among his parishioners. However, in the use of the liturgy in his worship services, Beach flatly refused to leave out the prayers for His Majesty, a position that soon enough triggered the active persecution of local Patriots. One Sunday a squad of soldiers marched into his church and threatened to shoot him if he prayed for George III. Their muskets were pointed at the vicar's head, but he ignored them and went on with his supplications without so much as a tremor in his voice. Unlikely as it sounds, the soldiers were so struck with admiration that they stacked arms and remained to hear the preacher's sermon.

Beach did not always fare so well. Once a band of out-of-towners took him to where an axe and block were prepared for his execution. One soldier said, "Now you old sinner, say your last prayer." Beach knelt down and prayed, "God bless King George, and forgive his enemies and mine for Christ's sake." His stunned captors once again let him go. At another Sunday worship service, seven soldiers were hired specifically to assassinate Beach. In the midst of a service, they burst through the church door and opened fire while he was delivering his sermon from a pulpit that was directly down the aisle from the church's main door. A bullet lodged in the sounding board only a foot above Beach's head. The congregation sprang to its feet to flee the church. But Beach quickly quoted Scripture to calm the worshippers: "Fear not them which kill the body, but are not able to kill the soul; but rather fear Him which is able to destroy both soul and body in hell." Beach then continued with his sermon as if nothing had happened. He died in his sleep, passing away a year before the war officially ended. His last words were: "I have fought a good fight." And he had.

———

IN STAMFORD, the Jarvises faced a similar host of problems and perils. Life for Polly and Fyler and their families became dangerous indeed. British retaliation was quick after the Continental Congress issued its Declaration of Independence. The King's troops took control of New York City in August 1776, and by the end of September they occupied all of Long Island. Suddenly, Stamford was on the frontier that separated Patriot and British forces. It was no longer a safe place for a Loyalist lawyer and his wife and children to live. In fact, the entire Jarvis tribe was at risk.

Polly's father, Samuel, who was fifty-six in 1776, and mother, Martha, who turned fifty that same year, were elderly for the times. They were permitted to remain in their home in Stamford for four years, though they lived under a constant threat because of their well-known Loyalist sympathies. One night in 1780, without any warning, Samuel and Martha were ordered by the Patriot commander in the area to vacate their home and leave almost all of their belongings behind. (Patriots later claimed that Samuel and Martha were also stripped naked before they were forced to depart.) They were put in a boat, taken across Long Island Sound, and made to wade ashore where they sought shelter among the trees. The British rescued them the next day, but the shock of the experience aged Samuel. He died a short time later.

Earlier, in July 1776, Polly's brother Munson, a silversmith in Stamford who had been under intense suspicion for months by the town's revolutionary committee of safety, was, as he later described it, "condemned and advertised as inimical to the Liberty of America and an Obstinate Adherent to the Ministerial Cause." Soon after, he fled to Long Island where his brother William accompanied him. For a brief time, Munson recruited fellow Loyalists for the Prince of Wales Loyal American Regiment, before setting up a business in New York City.

In a painting done many years later when he was a top-ranking official in Upper Canada, William Jarvis was the model of an English aristocrat—certainly in his own mind at any rate, since his income never met his expectations—wearing a fine white wig with curls and regal British uniform with golden epaulettes. An accompanying painting is of William's wife, Hannah Owen Peters (1762–1845). She was the daughter of the Reverend Dr. Samuel Peters of Hebron, Connecticut. Peters was a devoted Loyalist, landowner, and Anglican missionary. He enjoyed the finer things in life and was an early target of Patriot mobs out for vengeance even before the revolution officially began. In 1773, when Hannah was only eleven years old, she watched in horror as her house was ransacked and her father was assaulted by the Sons of Liberty and driven out. With assistance from the Royal Navy, he escaped to London, where Hannah joined him in 1776.

A year after that, William joined the Loyalist brigade the Queen's Rangers, which was then being reorganized under the command of John Graves Simcoe, later the first lieutenant-governor of Upper Canada. In late 1776, both Munson and William, and their brother Samuel were captured by the Americans, who "chained up each with a Negro on their right." They were imprisoned at Fishkill, New York, north of New York City, but were able to escape disguised as women. They took refuge in the nearby forest for several days, evading the Americans searching for them, and eventually reached New York without being apprehended.

Samuel then signed on with the British forces across the sound on Long Island. He was assured the rank of brigadier-general if he raised thirty men for a Loyalist regiment. He did recruit the men, but the promotion never happened. Almost as bad, the promised refund for the expenses he incurred in conscripting new troops was never paid. Angry, Samuel Jarvis resigned, but he did not waver in his loyalty. He took a job in the fall of 1776 in the British commissary department which supplied the King's troops with provisions.

In the spring of 1778, Patriot soldiers again captured Samuel and dragged him off to Poughkeepsie, New York, where he was imprisoned in a ten-foot-square cell with fourteen other Loyalists for six months. For three weeks of this term, he was chained by hands and feet to a dungeon floor. To make matters worse, Jarvis had to pay for his own food or starve to death. As his trial date for high treason approached, he and his fellow prisoners were able to break through the prison wall. The escaping Loyalists were fired upon and several were wounded, but Samuel and one other managed to elude their captors, hiding in the woods and neighbouring barns for six weeks. Later, in his petition to the Crown for restitution, Samuel described how he "suffered beyond description with hunger, wet and cold . . . not once enjoying the comfort of a bed."

By the winter of 1778, Samuel Jarvis had rejoined the staff of the commissariat in New York City. He noted that he received nothing more than "his small pay and allowance for fuel and provisions which was not adequate to the necessary expenses in a garrison town." A year later the men in the commissariat were split into a corps. Jarvis became a lieutenant, had to buy his own uniform, and found himself doing a great deal of garrison duty in addition to his earlier responsibilities.

Polly and Fyler's wartime ordeal took a turn for the worse in December of 1776, when Fyler had to flee to Long Island to escape a violent Patriot mob. Polly and her children were evicted from their home and took refuge with Fyler's parents and his sister, Mary, who lived with them. Mary's experiences during the revolution drove her mad. During the next seven years, she watched in horror as people she knew and trusted turned on her family in a vicious civil war. What Reverend Ebenezer Dibblee, his wife, Joanna, and Mary endured throughout the revolution can only be imagined from the smallest of details left behind in family correspondence and Anglican Church records. Mention is made of "stark poverty," "personal dangers," "family troubles," and the Dibblees being "haunted by the spectre of want." All this took its toll on Mary's sensitive nature.

Although they were committed Loyalists, Ebenezer, Joanna, and Mary Dibblee remained in Stamford throughout the revolution. Ebenezer had a lasting commitment to the welfare of his congregation, but he may also have stayed in his republican parish out of concern for his single daughter. A move would have only added further stress to Mary's worsening mental state. The conflict had been too much for Mary Dibblee. Repeated attacks on her parents' home, the violence toward her Loyalist brothers, and the poverty of the war years led to a nervous breakdown. A 1788 letter from Stamford to Loyalists in New Brunswick recounted how Mary had "gone mad from fear" and "raves about the house." Eventually she was chained to the floor of the vicarage so that she would not wander off. The times were desperate, but it was the cruelest of treatments.

In 1789, thirty-nine-year-old Mary was described in a letter to former members of Dibblee's congregation in these vivid terms: "No Bedlamite was ever more raving than [Mary] has been for four weeks past and no appearance of her being better. They have been obliged to chain her some part of the time." (It is important to remember that the Bedlam Asylum for the Criminally Insane was the most infamous mental hospital in Great Britain, a place known for the terrifying screams and wails of its patients. Such was Mary Dibblee's condition.) Mary's father was seventy-four in 1789; her mother was sixty-seven. It was hard to imagine how they found the strength to care for their daughter.

Polly and her children had joined Fyler on Long Island in the spring of 1777. But they were easy targets for a roving band of rebels who attacked the family and stole almost everything they owned. The rebels even took the children's hats. Fyler and Polly and the children were sent to New York City under a flag of truce. However, it was less expensive to live on Long Island, which was also not too far from their family home in Stamford, Connecticut. No doubt figuring the British military would protect them from future attacks, Polly, Fyler, and their family eventually returned to Long Island, settling among other Loyalists at Oyster Bay. Polly must have felt that their five children, ranging from three to thirteen years of age, were now finally at a safe distance from any further Patriot attacks.

But her logic was flawed. Oyster Bay was close to Fort Franklin, the largest of all of Long Island's British garrisons. That only made it an irresistible target for the Americans.

Polly's worst nightmare came true in April of 1778 when Connecticut Patriots, whale boat raiders, invaded their home and took Fyler away. Six months later, following a negotiated prisoner exchange, Fyler was finally set free, but not until undergoing the hellish experience of incarceration in an American prison—possibly locked up in New Gate Prison, where "the light of the Sun and the light of the Gospel are alike shut out from the martyrs."

The common prisons that housed Loyalists who had blundered into disrepute were often nightmarish to behold. By far, the worst was this New Gate Prison, a former copper mine in Simsbury (now East Granby) in northern Connecticut—ironically named after Newgate Prison in London. It was called the "Catacomb of Connecticut" for a good reason: the approach was through a trapdoor, which led to another, larger trapdoor that was covered with bars and bolts of iron. The heavy gates were lifted by muscular guards, opening into a vertical shaft three feet in diameter, sunk through solid rock, and leading into a larger shaft that the guards maintained was a bottomless pit. Then, thirty-eight feet down, the prisoners reached one final platform that opened into their dimly lit quarters with pots of charcoal used to dispel the foul air. It was said, somewhat incomprehensibly, about this worst of the bad prisons, that it "fed the dead and starved the living."

Most rebel jails (or "gaols") were so poorly constructed that Loyalists could readily escape if they hadn't been chained down. Often rebel guards were more than open to bribes and looked the other way. Alexander Fairchild, a Connecticut Loyalist fighter who later found refuge in New Brunswick, even escaped from New Gate Prison after two months of incarceration with, as he later recalled, "the greatest risk of life, attended with hunger and fatigue." In May

1781, two Loyalist privateers, Ebenezer Hathaway, captain of the His Majesty's imperial privateer *The Adventure*, and his shipmate, Thomas Smith, helped free several prisoners. They had been locked up in New Gate for twenty days when they and some of their men were ordered to cook the prisoners some food in a kitchen that was on the surface. They subdued their guards and freed as many prisoners as they could. "This adventure," relates David B. J. Snyder, a Loyalist descendant, "was recorded in the summer edition of *Rivington's Royal Gazette*, a New York Loyalist newspaper, the accuracy of which Connecticut rebels found so unpalatable that they confiscated papers and denied that such an event had happened."

Besides local jails and the copper mines of East Granby and Simsbury, Patriots also incarcerated Loyalists in ships anchored off key rebel strongholds. The Boston prison ships began lodging loyal Americans as early as 1776, and the rebel prison ships in New London, Connecticut, operated until at least 1782. In 1777, the rebel Provincial Congress of New York started imprisoning its Loyalist inmates aboard a "fleet prison" that was anchored in the Roundout River near the rebel capital of Esopus (New York). These fleet lockups were not set up as torture chambers, but they were in no way comfortable, heated, or ventilated. The stench must have been deadly. Rations included three quarters of a pound of meat plus one pound of bread daily, with salt and vinegar included three times a week. Fortunately, there were no second helpings. The fleet prison in Kingston only lasted five months; British soldiers liberated its prisoners and set the ships afire in October of 1777.

Some Loyalists who were considered unreliable were put on special "guard-ships" that eventually dropped them off in Europe or the West Indies. The passengers had to pay their own fares but could take with them the proceeds from the forced sale of whatever American assets they still possessed. There was no chance of their returning. Anyone caught trying to do so would automatically be sentenced to "death without benefit of clergy." (That was shorthand for "no appeal.")

Fyler Dibblee was set free in a prisoner exchange in October 1778. He and Polly and their children then relocated from Oyster Bay to West Hills, New York, a seemingly safer location a short distance to the south-east. Again, raiders found them and attacked, even threatening to "put to the bayonet" the children if they made a fuss. Somehow the Dibblees made it to South Hempstead, east of Brooklyn. There, in November 1779, Polly gave birth to a son, Ebenezer, her sixth child. Soon, the joy over welcoming a new child was tainted by the news that the Dibblee property in Stamford had been confiscated. All of Fyler and Polly's possessions—their house, barn, furniture, books, clothing, cows—had been divvied up by their one-time neighbours, all in the name of the Patriot cause. Loyalists like Fyler and Polly Dibblee had paid an enormous price for their steadfast devotion to Britain and they had to search deep within themselves to find the necessary resolve to carry on. Such determination enabled the vast majority of them to face subsequent challenges in new lands with integrity, dignity, and pride. Heroism wears many faces.

4

WAR OF NO ROSES

*From the opening crack of musket fire at Lexington in 1776
to the downing of British colours at Yorktown in 1783, the
American Revolution did not merely give birth to a nation.
It forged an original republic with balls.*

THE CHANGE IN the America that Patriot sympathizers envied
was suddenly devoid of familiar signposts and customary
echoes. The Revolutionary War (1775–1783) obliterated everything
except death in the afternoon. It was fought by the American colonists against then resident British occupiers and hired Hessian (German) mercenaries. It was this clash of arms and men that created the
United States of America—and exported the idea of freedom and
equality around the world. This was also a chronicle of the original,
pastoral American Dream falling apart, to be replaced overnight by
the dedication to armed independence. The mood was now in tune
with the evolving brash subcontinent on the march to overthrow its
colonial status.

It was the ultimate, high-stakes royal poker game, with the earth's
richest subcontinent being the prize. It took eight years of uninter-
rupted terror in the course of eighty-four momentous clashes of
arms on land and sea for the revolutionaries to declare victory. The

price in deaths and destruction was so steep that the war could not be counted as a triumph for either side—only as less of a massacre for American Patriots than for American Loyalists.

It was the continent's first civil war between Europeans. As such, the slaughter was on such an unprecedented scale that only one of its historic consequences was beyond doubt: that its most obvious loser was the incumbent King of Great Britain, George III. It was his last waltz. He lost America, the Thirteen Colonies—arguably Britain's most significant overseas territory and the pride of his empire. There was no single cause. But it came down to his monumental lack of respect for his courageous citizens who he considered to be uncouth and not worthy of his concerns.

Although General George Washington, a slave owner, reigned as the revolution's leader—successfully impersonating an austere saint and later becoming his country's first president—his belief system was attached to creative pragmatism. If that creed had ever elected its leader in sacred conclave, he would have been chosen Pope by acclamation. In the bitterly polarizing circumstances of the eight-year war, he was precisely the right choice, not being worth a damn as a military strategist and losing many more battles than he won. Yet he was, writes Ron Chernow, his most recent biographer, "a sensitive, complex figure, full of pent-up passion, whose judgement and great self-command always made him appear a man of a different cast in the eyes of the world." Great leaders exude such qualities. And George Washington led through his inspired acts of conscience and commanded through his ability to inspire. It was perfect casting.

In June 1776, while Washington was in New York, attempting to fend off an inevitable British assault on the city, the Patriot Conspiracy Committee led by Founding Father John Jay discovered (from interrogating an arrested Loyalist named Isaac Ketchum) a plot to kidnap or kill the American military leader and bribe Patriots to join the British side. The conspirators included one of Washington's bodyguards, Thomas Hickey, and possibly both David Mathews,

New York's mayor, as well as William Tryon, the governor of the Province of New York.

Hickey was arrested, court-martialed, and then publicly hanged before a crowd of two thousand New Yorkers on a field in the Bowery. Mathews was temporarily held in custody before escaping and then resumed his mayoralty duties once the British took charge of New York in September; while Tryon, who probably financed the entire affair, avoided capture.

Washington's futile attempt to defend New York City against the British attack was a long shot at best. Essayist James Morris best caught the grand purpose and the imperial might of the Royal Navy. "It was the Navy which made Britain great, guaranteeing the island's immunity and giving its people the freedom of imperial action," he wrote. In return, the navy received a loyalty given no other department of state. Its crews and flag officers assumed a mythic character: hard drinking but always alert, eccentric but superbly professional, breezy, posh, kindly, tough like Admiral Nelson, ready to disobey an order for any good cause, or blow any number of deserving foreigners out of the water.

And it was during the most nakedly sun-washed of the long days at the end of June 1776 that an armada of 136 British ships sailed into the waters surrounding New York City, marking the start of the nearly eight years of British occupation that spanned the American Revolution. By mid-August, General Washington faced a British naval force of 1,200 cannon, 400 transports, 32,000 troops, and 13,000 sailors. Washington's original ragtag army initially lacked shoes as well as adequate gunpowder. A month earlier, when two British warships had started the fighting, Washington was shocked at the ineptitude of his men. "His artillery did more harm to themselves than to the enemy," relate historians Edwin G. Burrows and Mike Wallace in their mammoth history of New York City. "[The] only casualties of the day occurred when an ill-trained gun crew on the Battery blew themselves up—while many of [Washington's] men and officers abandoned their positions to gawk at the spectacle. 'Such unsoldierly conduct,' he explained to the Provincial Congress, would 'give the enemy a mean opinion of the army.' "

That was precisely what happened at one of the war's biggest battles, on August 27, 1776, near the Red Lion Inn where Gowanus Road, the main artery to the village of Brooklyn near Manhattan, intersected with Martense Lane and Narrows Road (in present-day Brooklyn this would be in the vicinity of 39th Street and Fourth Avenue). Vastly outnumbered when the first attack began, the Americans, who had been told to fight "at all hazards," ran. They were reorganized and joined by a few thousand other Continental soldiers under the command of Major General William Alexander—who fancied himself the Earl of Stirling—but in the end were vastly outnumbered by about twenty-five to one. The British commander, General James Grant, who detested the Patriots, urged his men to be as fierce as possible. For a while, both sides fired cannon shells and musket balls at one another. But then thousands of British regulars, Scottish Highlanders, and Hessians, who had circled behind the unsuspecting Americans, arrived—and all hell broke loose.

"The Hessians and our brave Highlanders gave no quarter," a British officer later reported. "It was a fine sight to see with what alacrity they dispatched the rebels with their bayonets after we had surrounded them so they could not resist. Multitudes were drowned and suffocated in morasses—a proper punishment for all Rebels."

Stirling was able to escape with hundreds of his men to Brooklyn Heights, though in a subsequent attack on the British line, many were killed. By the end of the day, hundreds of Patriots had been killed or captured; and many of those, including officers, were treated roughly. "I shall never forget the [robberies], blows and Insults I met as well as the hunger," Lieutenant Jonathan Gillett, a farmer from West Hartford, Connecticut, later recalled. The Hessians were especially brutal with the Patriots they apprehended or who surrendered to them, subjecting them to revolutionary-era waterboarding. Some of the men were stripped, beaten, and hung with a rope around their necks from a tree. When they were nearly strangled to death, the mercenaries cut them down, revived them with rum—and then tortured them again. Anywhere from three hundred to five hundred Patriots died that day and as many as two thousand were taken prisoner—and that included three generals, Stirling, Nathaniel Woodhull, and John Sullivan—in a battle that cost Washington about a third of his force. "The fields and woods [of Brooklyn] are covered with dead bodies," one New Yorker later reported. The British left the corpses to rot, and the stench of death lingered in the area for at least a year.

The battle for New York City lasted a few more months. In the fight for Brooklyn in August, the Americans lost, but after the clash on Harlem Heights in October, Washington believed he had won, though British historians regarded this skirmish as having been inconclusive. The Patriots had a few other victorious moments, but those, as well as the illusory success on Harlem Heights, proved hollow and the battle statistics were not reassuring: 3,600 Patriots under Washington's command had died or were wounded and another 4,300 had been taken prisoner. From the American commander's point of view, the one positive was that the revolution had not been crushed.

AGAINST ALL ODDS, the lacklustre American army eventually turned itself into a stormy river of determined men—proving that fighting for a cause, rather than defending the rights of an aristocracy, will always win the day. Most of the Thirteen Colonies fielded dedicated commandos bent on fulfilling their mission of gaining freedom and their own space in which to grow. This involved not only the two main armies locked in eighty-four decisive confrontations that tested the endurance of both sides, but also the accompanying clashes of arms in dozens of smaller, yet equally murderous, venues.

Apart from well-trained, if burnt-out, British regulars and German mercenaries who opposed them, the Americans also faced a highly effective "fifth column" behind the major lines of combat, aimed against the Patriots with often devastating results. By the authoritative count of two dedicated researchers—Thomas B. Allen and Todd W. Braisted—there was a shadowy army of Loyalist Provincial Corps in existence that consisted of 150 disciplined and hyper-active military units of armed Loyalists fighting to back up their cause inside American territory. These Loyalist fighters battled American forces throughout the Thirteen Colonies, from Connecticut to South Carolina.

They were part of guerilla units who fought alongside pro-British Indian allies in deadly raids and acted as spies for British military commanders in the New York area. The criteria for enrolment included being willing, able-bodied, between sixteen and sixty, and brave enough to accept the consequences of being captured by Patriots. Loyalist soldiers went into battle knowing that if taken prisoner, they would be treated as criminals. Every state passed laws enumerating captive penalties. They ranged from exile to execution, with not much in between, but giving preference to the latter.

More than 1,500 American Loyalists were commissioned as officers of these freelance regiments, equipped by the British, including half a dozen generals, but there was no dependable count of the non-commissioned volunteers. Regiments were formed not only on the basis of military experience but also on the ability of recruiters to persuade men to sign up. Some units, such as Butler's Rangers, King's Royal Regiment of New York, the British Legion, the Royal Highland Emigrants (with a fighting strength of 1,800), and the Queen's Rangers (named in honour of Queen Charlotte, the wife of George III), were full-scale regiments with infantry cavalry and even their own marching bands; others were more modest in size (but not in spirit), such as the Virginia Volunteers, disbanded when their two members were taken prisoner, or Stewart's Troop of Light Dragoons, garrisoned on Staten Island with a complement limited to two dozen. These armies were American in the King's service on enemy territory, and that could be a tricky wicket.

Among these marginal fighting outfits was the New York Volunteers, a witches' brew of splendid petulance but lousy discipline, better known as "Coffin's Cavalry," named after its dazzling commanding officer, Major John Coffin, who was a direct descendant of the legendary Tristram Coffin of the original *Mayflower* expedition. Major Coffin's brave exploits on behalf of the Loyalists were abruptly halted when he was blacklisted for being too forthright by publicly exposing the cowardice in battle of King George III's eldest son during a cavalry charge. Coffin vanished from sight after the incident and the rebel army placed a price on his head.

His reappearance near Charleston in North Carolina was not accidental, since he had been wooing Ann Mathews, a gutsy young woman on St. John's Island, near the city then held by the Rebels. The major crept through enemy lines, then sprinted for his intended bride's house. Within minutes, a rebel officer burst through its front door, and, catching sight of Miss Mathews rearranging her hooped crinoline skirt on the living room divan, asked her permission to search the premises. "A Redcoat has been seen near these grounds," he warned. "He's believed to be Major Coffin, a Tory scoundrel, a real bad one." He brushed past Miss Mathews, ran upstairs, searched every nook and cranny but could find no sign of the fugitive.

As soon as he departed, the lady of the house happily announced to the living room at large: "They've gone—They're far down the street—you can come out now." That was the signal. Her hoop skirt started to move as if by itself, or so it seemed until a male leg appeared, and then another. Finally a head and two arms: and then the smiling major in person. His manner displayed mixed emotions about having had to leave the unexpected comforts of his hiding place, into which had crammed his six-foot-four-inch frame. They were married the following year, and Coffin became a leading citizen of Saint John, the owner of a grist mill and lumberyard. After winning accolades commanding the New Brunswick Fencibles during the War of 1812, he was rapidly promoted to full general's rank. He retired to New Brunswick at the close of hostilities, and served as a member in the colony's House of Assembly. (Each of the British colonies in what became Canada boasted an elected legislative assembly.) He served as chief magistrate of King's County and a member of the Province's Council. To keep from being bored, he fought a duel with a Colonel Campbell in 1783 and was wounded in the groin. But he never forgot his dramatic arrival in his intended's underskirts.

IN THE SPRING OF 1777, Stephen Jarvis was in British-controlled New York as Washington regrouped in Morristown, New Jersey. Thousands of Loyalists, many of whom had been viciously persecuted, flocked to the British haven in New York City, where most of them were to remain for the next six years. In November of 1776, at a ceremony at City Hall, a large contingent of the faithful publicly swore their "loyalty to our Sovereign against the strong tide of oppression and tyranny, which had almost overwhelmed this Land."

The city's population swelled to twelve thousand, and then nearly tripled again by 1780. Among the multitude were runaway slaves and black freedmen, who found safety and security under British protection. As the war outside the city roared on, thousands of soldiers, mercenaries, and pro-British fighters came and went —"Waldeckers in their gaudy yellow-trimmed cocked hats, huge mustachioed Hessians, kilted and tartaned Highlanders, [and] black-capped Anspach grenadiers"—together with about sixteen thousand New Yorkers who joined Loyalist regiments. These men and women—such as Lorenda Holmes, a courier who was captured by the rebels and tortured, though she survived even after her foot was burned in a fire of hot coals—strengthened British resolve in New York City, turning it into "the Gibraltar of North America," as it came to be called.

For a time the military presence sparked the city's economy. The British needed an abundance of supplies; the officers and their wives expected to enjoy as much luxury and comfort as was permissible in the colonies. New York's many artisans and merchants could not keep up with demand.

If you were lucky enough to be included in the social circle of General William Howe, commander-in-chief of the British forces, there were fox hunts, golf, cricket matches, saltwater bathing parties, concerts, and horse racing on Hampstead Plains to enjoy. There were also lively dances at the City Tavern on Broadway, where eligible and gallant British officers courted the young New York girls and most everyone revelled in the production of *Tom Thumb* at the newly christened Theatre Royal that before and after the revolution was known as the John Street Theatre.

The gap in lifestyle and extent of liberty between New York's haves and have-nots was impossible to ignore. For thousands of less-well-off New Yorkers, the British occupation ranged from challenging to disastrous. Under martial law, otherwise loyal New Yorkers were subjected to obnoxious bullying from drunken troops and military authorities who usually ignored the flood of complaints. Food prices skyrocketed and decent shelter was hard to come by. Raging fires in September 1776 and August 1778 destroyed houses, shops, and even streets and districts. Soon thousands of homeless refugees were living "like herrings in a barrel" in "Canvas Town," crammed together in "makeshift tents that sprawled west from the foot of Broad Street." Others found shelter in churches. Greedy landlords raised rents in some of the more habitable areas by 400 percent. Corruption and prostitution flourished. The sixty-year-old British commandant, General James Robertson, was hardly a role model; according to his fellow officer General Henry Clinton he was guilty of lining his pockets, keeping a mistress, and "smelling after every giddy girl." American POWs got the worst of it. Locked in dilapidated buildings, the foot soldiers—Patriot officers were allowed to remain in boardinghouses or private homes—were denied food and basic care, which ensured that disease and even minor plagues were rampant.

The two British officers largely responsible for this deplorable situation were Commissary Keeper Joshua Loring, who sold off provisions intended for the prisoners and pocketed the money, and

Provost Marshal William Cunningham, who had come to New York in 1774 to face Patriot wrath. He wanted to exact revenge—and did. In 1791, after Cunningham was back in England, he was convicted of committing forgery and sentenced to hang. Before he was sent to the gallows, he confessed that during the war he had deliberately starved more than two thousand prisoners "by stopping their rations, which I sold" and executing 275 American prisoners. "A guard was despatched to forbid people to look out from their doors or windows on pain of death," he recalled, "after which the prisoners were conducted, gagged, at midnight, just behind the upper barracks, hung without trial and then buried."

The war was indeed brutal, as Stephen Jarvis also discovered. He decided that a "military life" best suited him, especially after he received news that his father had been killed in Danbury. That rumour proved to be false; the Patriots had not killed Stephen Sr., but his property had been plundered. In any event, young Stephen's ire was sufficiently stimulated to pledge that he would stop the Americans. After a few brief false starts, in late April 1777 he found his rightful place as an officer of the Queen's Rangers, a crack attack regiment that terrified Yankee Patriots. His cousin William Jarvis from Stamford joined the same year, though evidence is scant on whether they served together. William was later injured at the battle of Spencer's Tavern (or Ordinary) in Virginia at the end of June 1781—while Stephen moved to Norfolk. William was promoted from ensign to the rank of cornet (equivalent to a second lieutenant) near the end of the war. William and Stephen did meet in Stamford once hostilities ceased and both faced the wrath inflicted by the victorious Americans on their former Loyalist associates.

Among the many Loyalist corps, the Queen's Loyal Rangers were the most effective troops, a magnificent agency of destruction that won its spurs as the most active support regiment of the war, taking part in twenty closely fought battles. (The regiment still exists in Toronto as the Queen's York Rangers.)

The Rangers' first leader was the provocative Robert Rogers, a veteran of the French and Indian War who served as commander of a scouting (or ranger) unit that commendably supported British regulars. After the war ended, he returned to England and wrote two books about his exploits, partly to cover his substantial gambling debts. Back in North America in 1766 with an appointment as a commander, he later ran afoul of British military authorities, who suspected him of passing British secrets to the French. "He is wild, vain, of little understanding, and of as little Principle," according to General Thomas Gage, who especially disliked him. "But with that he has a share of Cunning, no Modesty or veracity and sticks at Nothing. . . . He deserved Some Notice for his Bravery and readiness on Service and if they had put him on whole Pay to give him an Income to live upon, they would have done well. But, this employment he is most unfit for, and withal speaks no Indian Language. He made a great deal of money during the War, which was squandered in Vanity and Gaming."

In late 1767, Gage charged Rogers with treason, though the evidence was circumstantial and Rogers was subsequently acquitted. Once the revolution began, Rogers acted as a free agent, first offering his services to the Patriots. Washington, however, did not trust him and arrested him. He soon escaped and returned to the British side. He was promoted to lieutenant-colonel and raised the Queen's Rangers, mainly with Loyalists from Virginia, New York, and Connecticut.

On September 11, 1777, the Rangers and Jarvis fought in the Battle of Brandywine in Pennsylvania, one of the most dramatic confrontations of the entire war. Brandywine was the only battle in the revolution in which George Washington's men fought directly against General Howe's army. It was also the first time that the Stars and Stripes flew over the Continental troops.

Howe planned to march through Maryland to capture Philadelphia, the largest city in the Thirteen Colonies. He put the German General Wilhelm von Knyphausen in charge of eight thousand men who marched towards Washington's forces at Chadds Ford, a serene and picturesque setting of hills and forests on Brandywine Creek in the heart of Pennsylvania's Quaker community, about fifty kilometres southwest of Philadelphia (and centuries later a popular locale for artists such as Andrew Wyeth, who grew up there). Meanwhile, Howe took the balance of his army north and circled back on the Continental Army's position.

"The Queen's Rangers led the Division of General Knyphausen," Jarvis later recorded. "We came in sight of the enemy at sunrise. The first discharge of the enemy killed the horse of Major Grymes, who was leading the column, and wounded two men in the Division directly in my front, and in a few moments, the Regiment became warmly engaged and several of our officers were badly wounded. None but the Rangers and Ferguson's Riflemen, were as yet engaged; the enemy retired, and there was a cessation for a short time." Jarvis and the other Rangers drove the Patriots from the forest into an open field. Their commanding officer had the men hide behind trees as they fired upon the rebels. Then the Rangers were required to charge the enemy. "At this instant, my pantaloons received a wound," recalled Jarvis, skipping the details, "and I don't hesitate to say that I should have been very well pleased to have seen a little blood also. The enemy stood until we came near to bayonet points, then gave us a volley and retired across the Brandywine." The regiment then took shelter on either side of the creek and waited for Howe to commence his attack on the right flank of Washington's main army.

The fighting continued on into the afternoon, and the booming sound of the cannons frightened Quaker schoolchildren twenty kilometres away. A rebel battery fired deadly grapeshot at the Rangers "which did much execution." Nevertheless, the Rangers waded into Brandywine Creek; the water that reached chest level "was much stained with blood." While Jarvis commended the Loyalist soldiers who fought next to him, he was not always pleased with the actions of his own officers. "After the Regiment had crossed and was charging the enemy," he noted, "Lieutenant Close found it more safe to take shelter under the walls of the battery, where he fell asleep until he was discovered by the Provost Marshal, and reported to the Regiment as killed."

From a hill, Jarvis and his fellow soldiers witnessed Howe's attack. The battle lasted until nightfall, when the Americans finally retreated. Both sides paid a high price in this battle. An estimated 1,300 American soldiers were killed, wounded, or captured, about twice as many as the British. Among the British casualties were 75 of 250 of the Queen's Rangers. With victory at the Battle of Brandywine, the British army marched into Philadelphia, forcing the members of the Continental Congress to relocate west to York, Pennsylvania. With the capital of the rebellion having fallen, Jarvis had every reason to believe that Washington and his men would soon be defeated. The British just had to keep pressing their advantage. And yet, by March of 1778, victory seemed to be evaporating before the Loyalists' eyes. "We were continually engaged with the enemy more or less," Jarvis noted, "and had General Howe during the winter, instead of gambling with the officers every night, to the utter ruin of many of them, attacked General Washington at Valley Forge, where he might have done, the event of the War would have been very different." There was one significant change for the Rangers following the battle of Germantown, a month after Brandywine. The regiment's commander, Major James Wemyss (who had taken over from Rogers), was severely wounded and Howe appointed Major John Graves Simcoe, then serving with the 40th Regiment, to assume command of the Rangers. Within fourteen years, the crusty Simcoe would become the first lieutenant-governor of Upper Canada and be fondly remembered in Canadian history as an idealistic reformer, risk-seeking adventurer, and Toronto's proud founder.

SIMCOE WAS BORN IN 1752 at Cotterstock, England, north of London. His father, John, a naval officer, ferried troops to General James Wolfe during the war over Quebec and died from pneumonia prior to the British victory at the Plains of Abraham in September 1759.

His legacy to John Graves and his brother Percy was a guide to an ordered and disciplined life entitled "Rules for Your Conduct," a list of nineteen tenets that they should follow. It included the patriotic, religious, moral, and military principles that guided John Graves Simcoe's future behaviour and actions as a military commander and political official.

Once in charge of the Rangers in 1778, Simcoe reorganized and immediately expanded the Rangers with thirty Highlanders plus Stephen Jarvis. A fair but tough leader, Simcoe tolerated no disobedience or transgressions: the war was not to be used as an excuse for crime or immorality. Plundering and abusing civilians were forbidden, and he later sentenced two of his men to death for raping an American woman. Once he was in command of the Rangers, "he gave little attention to formal drill," noted the historian Stanley R. Mealing of Carleton University and one of Simcoe's biographers, "but insisted on physical fitness, rapid movement, bayonet fighting, and, most particularly, discipline in the field."

If the Loyalists ever had an informal but influential leader, it was Simcoe, a giant among the pygmies who lost the war. A diehard contrarian as always, Simcoe got into the habit of sending messages to his armed opponents with lifesaving warnings. An enemy sentry in a particularly vulnerable spot about to be strafed by his regiment's musket fire received a message that he would be shot if he didn't move. He once shouted at a threatened Yank officer: "You are a brave fellow. But you must move away." At a time when tradition was everything and his stellar but occasionally bizarre style of bravery was frowned on, Simcoe made his own rules.

At the same time, both Jarvis and Simcoe continued to be frustrated by the ineptitude of their European commanders. Instead of immediately chasing after Washington's army and eradicating the rebel military, Howe and his troops made themselves comfortable in Philadelphia. Howe could have led his army up the Hudson River to secure that strategic valley with General John Burgoyne's British troops. The latter had been marching toward Albany from Canada throughout the summer and fall. Had this strategy been successful, the revolution would probably have ended in the fall of 1777, the rebel forces crushed by two well-equipped British armies.

At the two Battles of Saratoga on September 19 and October 7, 1777, Burgoyne and his men, Brits and Hessians, were on their own in the fight because the expected British reinforcements from the south never arrived. The British and German troops were outmanned (three to one) and outmanoeuvred. Burgoyne had no choice but to surrender to General Horatio Gates, a rebel officer. On one hand, this utterly unexpected British defeat was crippling to Loyalist morale, and on the other the American victory also made France sit up and take notice. Hence, Saratoga long has been regarded by historians of the American Revolution as "the turning point of the war." Within months, the American Patriots welcomed England's archrival, France, as an ally. The outcome of the revolution was now less certain.

As commander-in-chief of British forces, General Howe was blamed for the debacle at Saratoga and was recalled to Britain. In the spring of 1778, he was succeeded in the American campaign by General Henry Clinton, shortly after France formally entered the war as the Americans' ally. Fearful of being surrounded by Patriot troops and facing a defeat like Burgoyne's, the entire British complement in Philadelphia—ten thousand British soldiers strong—evacuated the city in June of 1778, heading through Monmouth for Sandy Hook, New Jersey. From that point they would be ferried to New York City. Jarvis and the Queen's Rangers brought up the "rear of the line of the march."

On June 28, in 38 degrees Celsius heat, the rebel army attacked Clinton's rear guard at Monmouth. Although the Continental Army was initially successful, Clinton's counterattack was so aggressive that General Charles Lee decided to retreat. Washington, his superior officer, was furious with the decision, stopped the retreat, and continued his attack on the British foes. The overwhelming heat exhausted both armies, and the battle ended up as a draw. Being the last great battle of the revolution to be fought in the North, that was a significant outcome.

As an eyewitness to history in the making, Jarvis told the story in these words:

Nothing of moment took place on our route until we came to Monmouth, where on the morning of the 28th of June, the Queen's Rangers met at daylight the advance army of the Americans under the command of General Lee. We had a smart brush, and Col. Simcoe was wounded. We took some prisoners and returned and joined the Army at Monmouth Court House. Sir Henry Clinton, with five thousand of his army attacked Lee and drove him the whole day—took and killed a great many of his men until we fell in with General Washington's whole Army, when we retreated, leaving our wounded in the enemies' hands. On commencing our retreat we had to oppose a large body of the enemy, and one of our field pieces was abandoned, and the enemy gave a shout. Lieutenant Shaw with the Highland Company wheeled about, charged the enemy, and brought off the cannon, which was ever after attached to the Regiment. We continued our retreat during the whole night and came up with the main Army at Middletown, where we halted to refresh ourselves for the first time in twenty-four hours. The day of the battle was one of the hottest I ever felt, and we lost more men by drinking cold water than were killed by the enemy. I bore the fatigue of the day very well with only having again a shot through my pantaloons, leaving the mark of the ball on the skin, or rather the powder without drawing blood. The Army continued its march, the Rangers bringing up the rear. The Army crossed over on a pontoon bridge to the lighthouse island, the Queen's Rangers embarked in flatboats and rowed up to New York and landed at Bloomingdale above New York, where we remained for some time and then crossed over to Long Island and took up our quarters at Oyster Bay.

While at Long Island's Oyster Bay, Jarvis was transferred from the infantry to the cavalry. "From this moment," he remembered, "I became a great favourite with Col. Simcoe." Stephen's hero and patron almost died a year later. The occasion was not one of the memorable bloodbaths of the revolution, but a night raid—the far more typical form of combat between Patriot and Loyalist forces. One early morning in the fall of 1779, the Queen's Rangers, with the cavalry belonging to that regiment and ten light horse under the command of a Captain Stewart, who was stationed on Staten Island, landed at Perth Amboy and proceeded as far as Bonhamtown, New Jersey. When the foot soldiers returned to Perth Amboy, and the cavalry, seventy in number, commanded by Simcoe, advanced to Bound Brook, they destroyed eighteen large flat-bottomed boats and supplies. They then proceeded to Somerset Court House, forty-five kilometres from Amboy, where they released confined Loyalists, set fire to the jail, and destroyed a large quantity of forage and stores which had been collected for Washington's army.

Then there was trouble. While returning to the south side of the Raritan River, within a few kilometres of Brunswick, New Jersey, the Rangers were ambushed by a large group of Patriots who fired on them. Simcoe's horse was shot from under him. He tumbled to the ground and the fall stunned him. His men wrongly thought he had been killed. Jarvis was beside himself when he was told. He tried to convince his comrades to return to the battlefield to rescue Simcoe's body, but it was too dangerous and they refused. In fact, Simcoe was captured by the Patriots and imprisoned in New Jersey. He endured six harsh months as a prisoner before a deal was negotiated for his release. He then resumed his command of the Rangers.

In February 1780, Simcoe plotted to take George Washington a hostage—and Stephen Jarvis was in the middle of it. The winter of 1779–1780 was bitterly cold. Heavy snow and freezing temperatures severely hampered the movement of both the British and the Patriots, and obtaining supplies was difficult. Stephen's cousin Samuel was one of the officers who supervised the transportation of a hundred sleighs with food and supplies over nineteen kilometres of ice through Patriot territory to aid the British soldiers and Loyalists on Staten Island. Despite the weather, Simcoe had formulated a plan to raid Washington's headquarters in Morristown. The American general was staying at the Georgian mansion of Theodosia Ford, the widow of the Patriot Colonel Jacob Ford Jr., while his troops were located about five kilometres away at Jockey Hollow. Simcoe thus believed Washington, who was separated from his men, could be captured. But he would be a hostage to the plans of the Hessian general put in charge of the Queen's Rangers; General Wilhelm von Knyphausen believed that another strategy would work better—that it would make more sense to attack Morristown directly with cavalry. The German general divided his forces, ordering diversionary infantry attacks on two rebel posts, while the Hussars of the Queen's Rangers under Simcoe would attack Morristown. February 8 was set as the date of the raid on Washington's headquarters, but a heavy snowfall and rain halted the plan.

The Queen's Rangers made their next attempt two days later. Fortune, however, smiled upon the rebels and not Simcoe's men, one of whom was Stephen Jarvis. "The time arrived and we crossed over to Elizabethtown Point," he recalled, "and after marching some distance in the country, returned back without making any attempt, and thus the affair ended, much to my disappointment, for I had set my heart on this expedition, as I was to have taken charge of the General after he had fallen into our hands." A winter storm had stopped Simcoe's otherwise overwhelming and un-opposable numbers. The roads leading to Morristown had been made impassable by the earlier snowstorm. A layer of sharp ice cut the fetlocks of the cavalry's horses. Had the Queen's Rangers been successful on February 10, 1780, Washington would have been a captive of a Loyalist regiment, the Continental Army would have been in disarray—at least temporarily, since Washington was a commander not easily replaced—and the outcome of the Revolutionary War might well have changed. And Stephen Jarvis could have laid claim to having once been responsible for guarding a prisoner named George Washington.

STILL IN HIS early twenties in 1780, Stephen Jarvis experienced the war in a personal way, not fully contemplating the larger and geo-political issues at stake. And that included how the British-American conflict had entangled the lives of Aboriginals like Molly Brant. "In Indian country," wrote British American historian Colin G. Callo-way, "the American Revolution often translated into an American civil war. While British regulars and Continental troops fought campaigns in the East, in the backcountry—which usually meant the Indians' backyards [the area "bordering the Appalachian Mountains, the Ohio River Valley, the southern Great Lakes region, and the interior hin-terlands near the Gulf of Mexico"]—whites killed Indians, Indians killed whites, Indians killed Indians, and whites killed whites in gue-rilla warfare that was localized, vicious, and tolerated no neutrals." Mary "Molly" Brant would have concurred with that assessment.

Like a majority of North American Aboriginals, Brant did not care much about taxation and representation, but like other members of the Mohawk Nation, one of the tribes of the Six Nations or Iroquois Confederacy, she did care a lot about land rights and British treaty pledges. In the Royal Proclamation of 1763, the British had guaran-teed Aboriginal rights to a huge swath of North America west of the Appalachians. And in any battle between the British and "land-hun-gry" American colonists, who resented that provision, Brant was de-termined to ensure that the British honoured their agreement. Her bargaining chip was Six Nations' military support.

Molly Brant was born in the wrong century to the right parents. She overstepped her Aboriginal mandate, but had the knack of put-ting at ease visitors to the aristocratic mansion whose drawing room she turned into stage productions where she expanded the impact of her presence. As chatelaine to Sir William Johnson, one of the richest and most powerful landowners in pre-revolutionary America, she acted as both his executive director and—in her post-mistress period—the love of his life. The uppity guests may have felt various degrees of condescension in trying to deal with this wild Mohawk in their midst. But that was their loss. She was also a vital influence in keeping the Mohawks on the Loyalist side of the several wars that would decide the American subcontinent's future. As McGill University historian Elizabeth Elbourne explains, Molly "played an important role in Iroquois diplomacy, in keeping with the prominent participation of women in Iroquois politics. As a clan matron she was able to speak at Six Nations Council Meetings, for example. Her relationship with Johnson raised her status among the Mohawk in particular. She became the head of the clan matrons over the course of the partnership, while her brother [Joseph Brant, Thayendanegea] was created war chief."

Raised and nurtured at local academies, Molly was fluent in English, which enhanced her status as a key link between her Aboriginal community and the British. She mastered the arts of housekeeping early, determined to take advantage of civilized life, should it come her way. The introduction to her future partner was typical. She literally rode into history. During a military muster held at Sir William Johnson's luxurious spread in New York State, the host watched young Molly demonstrate her spirit and agility by vaulting on the back of a galloping horse in response to a dare by its rider, a laughing young army lieutenant. Her red blanket flying, eyes flashing, jet black hair trailing behind her, they capered around the field to their host's delight and aroused interest. "Becoming enamoured of her person," reported a fascinated visitor, "the Colonel brought her to his house." No run-of-the-mill paramour, she eventually became a permanent guest with privileges.

As superintendent of Indian affairs and colonel of the Six Nations, Johnson was one of North America's most powerful resident tycoons. Through several astute property acquisitions, he owned an estimated 400,000 acres spread out across the Mohawk Valley in northeast New York in the region between the Adirondack Mountains and Catskill Mountains, and he built a grand Georgian mansion dubbed Johnson

Hall, where he was attended to by African American slaves and white indentured labourers.

There is debate as to whether Johnson was ever legally married. In his will, he identified as his wife Catherine Weissenberg, an indentured servant from New York City and the mother of three of his children, who died in 1759. That same year, Molly, then twenty-three years old, gave birth to the first of the eight children she had with Johnson. Eventually she was recognized as the supreme hostess in her era and area, as well as business manager of Johnson's and chief advisor of his many ventures. Sir William made few decisions without consulting Molly, which was doubly valuable because she retained and expanded her Native power base, making her an indispensable pivot point of Johnson's expanding empire. They were married Mohawk fashion for more than twenty years: inseparable, ecstatic to share one another's life-forces—separated only by Sir William's unexpected death at the age of fifty-nine in the summer of 1774.

Molly was so obsessed with protecting the personal confidences that even when hosting domestic receptions for her partner, she seldom used either of her real names (Mary Brant—or Koňwatsi'-tsiaiéňni in Mohawk) but presented herself as just plain "Miss Molly," which hardly did her justice. The assembled companies seldom realized that this luminescent presence in their midst was one of America's most impressive—and elusive—contemporary characters: an early North American feminist who made an impact on current events profound enough to move history her way. Miss Molly took charge of every social situation, seizing and altering perceptions. As a Mohawk drawing room warrior, she specialized in a rare frontier commodity. In a wilderness setting where most decisions were re-enforced by spitting gun muzzles, everyday honesty—instead of being taken for granted—amounted to a profound moral commitment. She dealt in plain truths, however uncomfortable they might be. It was her manner—as decisive as an unsheathed tomahawk—

that endowed her with authority. She somehow exuded both the vulnerability that comes with open wounds and the spontaneous joy of being a rain-dancer who had just created her own downpour. That unlikely combination burnished her appeal. She almost always got her way. If not, she would switch to her "witch" mode. "Molly was flesh and bones, blood and guts, truth and physical beauty, wry intellect—her importance surpassed that of other women," noted the admiring Indian poet Maurice Kenny. "She may, by the violence of her temper, be led to create mischief," warned a veteran army camp commander. Both observations were accurate.

There is a highly questionable theory that beauty can be a burden to women, since it raises unfulfilled expectations. That Brant was stunning to behold had to be a word-of-mouth verdict, since there were no authentic paintings of her and photography had yet to be invented. Her natural beauty was best caught by Alice Lavers Clark, the author from Old Fort Niagara, who described her as having "a softened version of the Iroquois almond-shaped dark eyes, with a fullness between the brow and the eye lid, an aquiline nose, high cheek bones, pale copper skin . . . a lithesome, beautiful, young Indian woman, her face framed by black hair down to her shoulders." Equally striking in looks and mind, she created her own world, regardless of the fact that in terms of both race and gender, she was clearly from the wrong side of the tracks during her time.

Merciless with her enemies, generous with herself, Molly was above all gloriously gutsy, intrusive beyond the call of duty. In a lifetime of fronting idealistic British/Canadian causes, she lost more than she gained in terms of possessions but never tried to hide her true thoughts or circumstances. She celebrated her glories and accepted her losses, always playing down her bred-in-the-bone assertiveness. Her few soul-mates were well aware that she existed on an emotional teeter-totter fuelled by the tumults of her own making.

————

SIR WILLIAM JOHNSON'S DEATH in 1774 coincided with the British House of Commons' implementation of the Quebec Act that instituted the first permanent Canadian administration and permitted French speakers unfettered freedom, including restoration of civil law. They were now free to populate or perish; they opted for the former. American colonial leaders were outraged when the British Parliament nullified their land claims as part of the Quebec Act, as the burgeoning empire extended its boundaries southward to the Ohio River and westward to the banks of the Mississippi. At the same time, concessions in favour of Roman Catholicism produced profound resentment among American Protestants, encouraging the onset of the revolution. Molly was given most of the credit for keeping all but one tribe, the Oneida, among the Six Nation Confederacy loyal to the British flag during the ensuing war. "One word from her is taken more notice of by the Five Nations than a thousand from any white man without exception," opined Daniel Claus, a high-ranking British Indian agent, who was married to Nancy, the daughter of Sir William Johnson and Catherine Weissenberg. Molly fearlessly cast her fate with the Loyalists who defended the London connection— even when the Brits turned out to be the losing side. In the summer of 1777, as payback for Molly's work on behalf of the British—she had provided intelligence that led to a British attack on American and Oneida troops near Fort Stanwix in the Mohawk River Valley in upstate New York—Oneida warriors attacked and pillaged her home at Canajoharie (New York), where she had moved following Sir William's passing.

In this Loyalist quest, she was ably assisted by younger brother Joseph Brant, Thayendanegea, who had been mentored by Sir William. In the months before Johnson died, he ensured that Brant was selected as a Mohawk chief. In 1775, accompanied by Johnson's successor as superintendent, Guy Johnson, his son-in-law (in 1763 he had married Sir William's youngest daughter, Mary, or Polly), Brant travelled to London to confer with British officials. He was feted and sat for a painting, wearing full Indian dress, for the artist George Romney. He also met noted author James Boswell, who later said that Brant "was struck with the appearance of England in general; but he said he chiefly admired the ladies and the horses."

Joseph's mission—the same as his sister's—was to ensure Mohawk land rights were respected. He was assured by Lord George Germain, secretary of state for the American colonies, that those rights would be administered fairly, provided the Six Nations remained loyal to the Crown in any "dispute with the king's rebellious subjects." Brant accepted that stipulation and once he had returned to North America helped his sister's campaign by convincing the Mohawks to fight for Britain. For the duration of the Revolutionary War, Brant commanded Indian fighters and fought the Americans alongside Loyalists Major John Butler, his son Captain Walter Butler, and their feared group of Rangers. In November 1778, Walter Butler and Joseph Brant led a contingent of 520 Rangers, regulars, and Indians in an assault on the village of Cherry Valley, New York, west of Albany. Despite the best efforts of Butler and Brant to maintain discipline, the Seneca warriors who accompanied them were out for blood and slaughtered at least thirty of the defenceless inhabitants. The Cherry Valley Massacre was widely reported in Patriot newspapers with stories of scalpings, burnings, and other atrocities, unfairly tainting the reputation of Butler, Brant, and all First Nation Loyalists.

At the conclusion of the war in 1783, Molly, who could not bear to live under American rule, eventually moved to Kingston, where she was granted 116 acres of prime land and an annual pension of £100. The British were grateful for her devotion. Quebec governor Frederick Haldimand told Joseph Brant his gratitude "of the early and strong attachment of your Sister Mrs. Mary Brant, and of the zealous services manifested by Her and Her Family to the King's Government." Molly did return—only once—to the Mohawk Valley, following American independence, and she was invited to move back with a pledge of serious compensation. Perhaps for the first time, she insisted on being quoted. "The answer is No!" she wailed. "With the utmost contempt, I say . . . NO!" Following a brief illness, she died at the age of sixty and was buried in an unmarked grave in Kingston's St. Paul's churchyard.*

In September 1794, two years before she died, Molly found herself aboard the *Mississauga*, a steamship that connected Kingston to Niagara, and spoke briefly with Elizabeth, the wife of John Graves Simcoe, then Upper Canada's first lieutenant-governor. In her subsequent diary entry, the governor's wife dismissed her fellow passenger with the curt comment: "Molly speaks English well, is a civil and very sensible old woman."

The Mohawk poet Maurice Kenny came closest to capturing the elusive woman warrior. "Molly certainly knew violence in her time," he wrote. "Knew blood, knew war from first hand. To her inherited prestige, greater than her brother's, she added a formidable will, keen mind, pointed eloquence and a powerful mystique." That was Molly.

THE FINAL YEARS of the war for Stephen Jarvis were spent largely in the southern colonies. British fortunes seemed to be on the rise. In December of 1778, Savannah—and with it, all of Georgia—was captured by the British. Instead of an enemy of thirteen colonies, there were now only twelve fighting against the Crown. The attempt by the French navy to recapture Savannah in October of 1779 was another great defeat for the Patriot cause. For once it was a great time to be a Loyalist.

After a six-week siege, the King's troops seized Charleston, South Carolina, on May 12, 1780, though Jarvis and the Rangers mainly did reconnaissance work. The city would remain in British control until Loyalists and soldiers evacuated it in 1782. The loss of Charleston

---

* Molly's life was celebrated by the issue of a commemorative Canadian post office stamp, and a full-length opera staged several times in Kingston by professional casts.

and the capture of 5,500 Continental Army troops was a heavy blow to the Patriot cause. After the siege on Charleston, British troops left great destruction in their wake, local Loyalists took up arms, and southern Patriots began brutal guerilla warfare against their loyal neighbours and the British invaders. The words "decimation" and "massacre" occurred more often in the descriptions of the conflicts that followed Charleston's fall.

Jarvis returned briefly to New York from Charleston at the end of June 1780. During the voyage, he discovered two stowaways, a man and woman, both escaped African American slaves. While most of the regiment had joined General Knyphausen in New Jersey, Jarvis permitted the slaves to be sold with permission from a "Mr. McGill," one of the few officers in the barracks. When Simcoe, who vehemently opposed slavery, later learned of what had transpired, he was angry and Jarvis's actions were investigated by a Court of Enquiry. Jarvis was unwilling to inform on McGill, making Jarvis appear guilty in Simcoe's opinion. He publicly and severely reprimanded Jarvis, telling him, as Jarvis recalled, "that I had lost my promotion and his countenance forever." He returned to his duty "more dead than alive." In time, Simcoe learned about the role McGill played in the sale of the slaves and Jarvis was forgiven.

First in Richmond and then Norfolk, Virginia, Jarvis served as quartermaster in a Rangers' troop commanded by Captain John Saunders (who was later the chief justice of pre-Confederation New Brunswick). In preparation for another journey farther south, the young Loyalist recruited soldiers, bought clothing, procured saddles, while Captain Saunders raided local farms and towns for horses. "We embarked for Charlestown, myself, men, stores and horses in one vessel and the Officers in another," Jarvis remembered. "On our leaving Norfolk, Captain Saunders had plundered more horses than he was allowed to put on board. He, therefore, distributed them to his Officers and among the rest, gave me a very fine horse. At sea we had very boisterous weather, our vessel sprang a leak—never so crazy a vessel went to sea. To save our lives, I threw thirty fine horses overboard, but saved every Officer a horse." Eventually, they arrived safely into port. Although Jarvis came to Charleston after its capture, he was there for the many smaller violent battles. On June 3, 1781, he felt he was certain to die. The occasion: the Battle of Snipe's Plantation. Jarvis remembered,

> Captain Saunders . . . made an excursion into the country and attacked a body of the enemy at Snipe's Plantation. We approached the place at sunrise in the morning, found the gate leading to the house secured with a large ox chain, and the fences each side made very strong, which it took some time to demolish under a heavy fire from the enemy. . . . We at last succeeded, and the enemy retreated back into a large rice field, where they were over taken and very few of them escaped with their lives, and only one man taken prisoner, who was so shamefully mangled that we could not bring him away—one of the enemy, who had nearly gained a wood, discovered that no person was following him but myself, waited for me, and when I had got at a certain distance, levelled his rifle. I expected at least he would have killed my horse. To turn from him was to me certain death. I therefore dashed towards him. He fired and missed me and my horse and before he could raise his rifle he was a dead man.

It was kill or be killed, but the young Loyalist officer drew the line at some actions. "Only one man was taken prisoner and he was ordered to be killed, by Captain Saunders. The most disgraceful thing I ever heard of a British officer," he wrote. "The poor fellow was severely hacked, but whether he died of his wounds or not, I do not know. I once pulled out my pistol to put the poor fellow out of his misery but I had not the power to discharge, and said to myself. 'This blood shall not be charged to me.' I do not know but have reason to believe that as many as twenty were killed."

Despite a number of British victories in South Carolina over the next few months, the American Revolution came to an abrupt end on October 19, 1781. Unbeknownst to anyone in the South, it was all over when General Charles Cornwallis surrendered to the French and Patriots at Yorktown, Virginia. All that was left was the protracted treaty negotiations, which took another two years to finalize. With the evacuation of British troops from the southern colonies in 1782, Stephen Jarvis set sail for St. Augustine, Florida, where he and his fellow Loyalists performed garrison duty until peace was declared in the spring of 1783.

A generation later, Lord Tennyson, ever a student of human behaviour, noted, "in the Spring a young man's fancy lightly turns to thoughts of love." This was especially true for Stephen Jarvis, Loyalist soldier. It was time to go home. Home to Amelia.

<h1 style="text-align:center">5</h1>

ESCAPING FROM NEW YORK
TO THE PROMISED LAND

The Great American Dream was the tale of "the huddled masses" landing in New York Harbor and a chorus of fairies springing unbidden from a bush garden, singing about the milk and honey that would characterize their landfall. The Loyalists had the misfortune of realizing that dream backwards.

THE BRITISH DEFEAT at Yorktown in 1781 marked the moment when what seemed like an eternal conflict was essentially over. But at the time the Loyalists thought otherwise, and there was violent fighting right up until the Peace of Paris was signed two long, bloody years later. In the interim, the biblical law of "an eye for an eye" governed the actions of both Patriots and Loyalists. During the spring of 1782 in upstate New York, Mohawk chief Joseph Brant led war parties against Patriot outposts at Fort Herkimer and Fort Dayton, both east of Syracuse, New York, spreading destruction. The American settlers in the area, however, were warned ahead of time by scouting parties and the majority were able to escape and find refuge. Still, some settlers were killed and their livestock was plundered by Brant and his men.

The Patriots outdid that with a massacre of civilians at Gnaden-hutten, Ohio, on March 8, 1782. By all accounts, it was the worst slaughter of the entire Revolutionary War. A band of Pennsylvania militiamen captured nearly a hundred Delaware Moravian or Lenape Indians, who they insisted had participated in raids on American colonists. The Indians, who followed the pacifist teachings of the Moravian missionaries, denied any involvement. Nevertheless, the angry Patriots, led by Lieutenant Colonel David Williamson, insisted they were guilty as charged. The Patriots decided to slaughter the Indians in a most horrific and systematic fashion. The victims—men, women, and children—were ordered into a "killing house," where they were first struck by coopers' mallets, then scalped to death. Before the Patriots departed, they burned the village to the ground. News of the massacre trigged further attacks on Patriots by Indian Loyalists. But nothing was resolved.

In April 1782, Philip White, a Loyalist from Monmouth County, New Jersey, was also murdered by Patriots. A few days later, in retaliation, his Loyalist supporters—members of the Board of Associated Loyalists, a ruthless self-defence group, whose godfather was William Franklin, the former royal governor of New Jersey—executed Joshua "Jack" Huddy, the commander of a New Jersey Patriot militia unit. Huddy had been captured during an attack on a small Patriot garrison at Toms River, New Jersey, at the end of March and imprisoned in New York City. He was released to Captain Richard Lippincott and his Loyalist band on the pretext of being involved in a prisoner exchange. That was a ruse. Instead, Lippincott and his men, without written permission from his superiors (their actions might have received verbal approval), took him to Sandy Hook, New Jersey, and hung him from a tree, leaving his body to dangle at the end of a rope with a pointed message pinned to his chest: "We, the Refugees, have with grief long beheld the cruel murders of our brethren, and finding nothing but such miseries daily carried into execution; we therefore determine not to suffer without taking vengeance for the numerous cruelties, and thus begin, having made use of Captain Huddy as the first object to present your view, and determine to hang man for man, while there is a refugee still existing. Up Goes Huddy for Philip White."

Furious at this brazen act, George Washington demanded the perpetrators be handed over to him—if not, he threatened to execute another Loyalist prisoner, British regular Charles Asgill, the nineteen-year-old scion of a prominent London family. The American commander only backed down after the case became an international incident. Asgill's distraught mother, Lady Theresa Asgill, the daughter of influential French Huguenot émigrés, wrote a heartfelt letter to Charles Gravier, comte de Vergennes, the French foreign minister, pleading for assistance. The case of young Asgill was brought to the attention of King Louis XVI and Queen Marie Antoinette, who ordered de Vergennes to advise Washington that Asgill should not be harmed. Moreover, since Asgill had been captured at Yorktown, his life was protected by the Articles of Capitulation that protected prisoners of war. Congress, with Washington's full support, opted to adhere to the French royals' wishes as well as respect the surrender documents, and Asgill was permitted to return to England in December 1782.

INTO THIS MAELSTROM stepped six-foot-tall Sir Guy Carleton, who replaced Sir Henry Clinton—who was blamed for the British defeat at Yorktown—as the British commander-in-chief in North America in March 1782. It was another difficult challenge in Carleton's mixed military and civil administration career that had started forty years earlier when he had been commissioned as an ensign at the age of seventeen. During those four decades, he had spent more of his time in North America than Europe and had fought with distinction alongside his friend and supporter General James Wolfe on the Plains of Abraham in 1759. As lieutenant-governor and administrator of Quebec, Carleton had instituted the Quebec Act of 1774. It was hailed by the French Canadian elite and Catholic clergy for its implied acceptance that the 1763 British policy of Anglicization was a failure, but was reviled by the American colonists because it set geographic boundaries for colonial western expansion. At the outset of the revolution, Carleton, who could be pedantic and distant but effective at the same time, feuded with British officials about military strategy. He eventually returned to England in 1780, only to be praised by George III a year and half later as the leader who should replace Cornwallis. "The Country will have confidence in a new man, and I believe that without partiality that the Man who would in general by the Army be looked on as the best officer is Sir Guy Carleton," the King wrote to Lord Germain, the secretary of state for the colonies, in mid-December 1781.

Carleton left England on April 8, 1782, and he reached New York City on May 5. He immediately aimed to end the violence and one of his first acts was to abolish the Board of Associated Loyalists. Yet he also realized that in this civil war, as he wrote to Washington soon after his arrival, "the same spirit of revenge had mutually animated the people of New Jersey and the Refugees under my command, both are equally criminal and deserving punishment." As the victor, Washington did not see it that way, believing, as Benjamin Franklin firmly did, that the Tories had few legitimate rights to anything—and that included their land, property, and slaves. As the peace negotiations in Paris were about to begin—with Franklin a key member of the American delegation—Carleton began the arduous task of evacuating British soldiers and the Loyalists from the former Thirteen Colonies.

THE TRAGIC TRANSFORMATION of the Loyalists into prime targets of persecution and forced exile was the American Revolution's darkest moment. Numbering a quarter of a million iconoclasts, facing a nation of smug Patriots gone stir-crazy, the Loyalists survived, but not without buckling under the Patriots' plunder, confiscations, and occasional executions. They faced the harshest of choices: either to betray the loyalty that for many had become their mission from God, or to pick up what they could pack overnight—leaving behind their homes, goods, memories, favourite shaving brushes—and escape into the night to occupy the vacant lot that would eventually become Canada. They left with their skins intact but most of their earthly goods forfeited.

The southern regions were first, where a mass exodus from Savannah and Charleston (called Charles Town until 1783) was organized starting in mid-June 1782. Thousands of Loyalists, many of whom were well-established land- and slave-owners, were put into an impossible position. They were shocked at what some regarded as abandonment by the British. In their view, one shaped by years of war and turmoil, it was hard not to see it as the ultimate betrayal by the Mother Country, even if that was not quite an accurate assessment. Yet, they could not stay since the Patriot governments in Georgia and South Carolina made it clear that they were traitors whose lives would be endangered if they remained. With great reluctance, but little options, the majority boarded British ships for East Florida, still a British possession, where the Loyalists could at least keep their slaves. Others ventured to Port Royal, Jamaica, to start new lives. (In 1783 present-day Florida was divided into two British-controlled colonies. East Florida was the bottom half of the current state, from about St. Augustine to the south, while West Florida was the northwest area of today's state that extended from the Gulf of Mexico into southern Alabama and Georgia.) On many escaping ships, African American slaves outnumbered white passengers.

The evacuation from major centres like Charleston took much longer than the British authorities wanted. The main problem was the lack of a sufficient number of ships to transport the British officers, troops, Hessians, and the Loyalists and their slaves. The whole operation, with ships dropping off soldiers and Loyalists as far away as New York and Halifax and then returning, took about six months, from mid-June to mid-December 1782. For many weeks during that period, thousands of Loyalists and their slaves were forced to wait for transports to arrive at British camps on Tybee Island at the mouth of the Savannah River. There was a lack of food, mainly because the American military would not permit local farmers and merchants to sell provisions to the British without Congress's approval, and that was not forthcoming.

Charleston was caught up in the commotion of the evacuation. "It is impossible to describe, what confusion people of all denominations, seem to be in at the thought the Approaching evacuation," wrote one Loyalist in late November. Desperate, many of the Loyalists tried to sell their remaining property and furniture, while others took the opposite approach and accumulated more goods, hoping to take these possessions with them. Still others attempted to collect outstanding debts owed to them, with little success.

The last of the British troops departed from Charleston on December 14, 1782. The British commander, Major-General Alexander Leslie, was concerned that his men would be fired upon by the Americans. He told the American commander, General Anthony Wayne (his courage and feistiness had earned him the nickname "Mad Anthony"), that if the American troops came within two hundred yards of the British soldiers, he threatened to "lay the town in ashes" and destroy it. Wayne abided by the request and more than sixty ships left on schedule, most to St. Augustine, St. Lucia, and Jamaica, while another twenty, carrying 506 army officers and a contingent of Loyalists, headed back to England.

Thus by late 1782, a total of approximately twenty thousand Loyalists, slaves, and soldiers had vacated their homes and quarters in the southern colonies. Little could they have foreseen that within a year these Loyalists would be forced to relocate again after Britain, as part of a separate Anglo-Spanish peace treaty, ceded East and West Florida to Spain. From a diplomatic and economic standpoint, this concession made sense, but most Loyalists in East Florida felt that their King had abandoned them yet again. "We are all cast off," bemoaned John Mullryne Tattnall, a young Loyalist from Georgia. "I shall ever tho' remember with satisfaction that it was not I who deserted my king, but my King that deserted me."

The hundreds of Loyalists who, for one reason or another, opted to remain faced the wrath of the Americans. More than a hundred Loyalists were arrested in Charleston and put on trial for treason, while dozens more were terrorized. "Whenever we found any Tories we would surround the house, one party would force the doors and enter sword in hand, extinguish all the lights [and then] commence hacking the man or men that were found in the house, threatening them with instant death," James Collins, who had served in the South Carolina militia, later recalled. The object of this attack, Collins added, was intimidation rather than murder. "There were none of the poor fellows much hurt," he wrote, "only they were hacked about their heads and arms enough to bleed freely." The Loyalists quickly fled after this altercation, which was precisely what Collins and his fellow Americans wanted.

Carleton's task became even greater and more demanding in New York City when news arrived that the British had agreed in principle to American independence. Most Loyalists were stunned. Lawyer William Smith wrote that he was shocked "as much as the Loss of all I had in the World & my Family with it." William Bayard, a New York merchant, who soon made plans to return to England, was as succinct but more bitter: "God damn them. What is to become of me, sir? I am totally ruined, sir. I have not a guinea."

Once the Treaty of Paris was finalized in March 1783, there was even more resentment. The Americans, especially Benjamin Franklin, wanted to severely punish the Loyalists, and the British did not have the gumption or resolve to fight back. The Loyalists' interests were sacrificed in the name of peace and London's cowardice. The U.S. Congress was to "recommend" to the state legislatures "to provide restitution of all estates, rights, and properties" belonging to "British subjects," but there was no sanction if the states refused. And refuse they did. New York State already had in place the Confiscation Act that permitted state authorities to seize land belonging to Loyalists and redistribute it; the Citation Act, which made it next to impossible for a Loyalist to collect debts owed by Patriots; and the

Trespass Act that allowed Patriots who lost their properties as a result of the war to collect compensation from Loyalists for occupation or damages. There was to be no quarter granted the Loyalists and, in fact, New York authorities confiscated even more land from them after the treaty was signed.

This nasty treatment was more or less the norm across the other colonies. During the war and its immediate aftermath, every state had enacted legislation aimed at punishing the Loyalists. In May of 1783, merchant David Black returned to his home in Boston and attempted to recover debts owed to him. He was arrested and jailed for the next eleven months. Other Loyalists in Massachusetts only had to pay fines and endure a few hours in the stocks before they were permitted to reintegrate into society. In North Carolina, South Carolina, and Georgia, confiscation acts permitted the wholesale seizure and sale of the Loyalists' property (or property which had been seized earlier). New Jersey's state legislature ruled that any Loyalist was "incapable forever" of holding any public office. Physical attacks on Loyalists and destruction of their property were frequent as well. Within a few years, the bitter attitudes towards the Loyalists in the southern states and elsewhere somewhat softened. Partial compensation was offered in South Carolina and Georgia for lost property, and other harsher measures were ultimately abolished.

On the day the terms of the Peace of Paris were read aloud to a crowd outside New York City Hall, there were "groans and hisses" from the Loyalist audience along with "bitter reproaches and curses upon their king, for having deserted them in the midst of their calamities." One angry Loyalist published a poem on what he regarded as the reprehensible terms of the Treaty, writing cynically:

'Tis an honor to serve the bravest of nations.
And be left to be hanged in their capitulations.

Another pointed out that while thieves and murderers were "faithful to their fellows and never betray each other," England had "betrayed and abandoned their loyal American subjects." Almost immediately, Loyalists in New York began divesting themselves of as much of their property and goods as was possible. Speculators from as far away as Philadelphia took advantage of the opportunities presented, enriching themselves. Loyalists living in houses taken over from absentee Americans were dunned for back rent or damage deposits. New York shops and auction houses promoted sales of fine dishes and "Genteel furniture" at drastically cut prices. "No News here but that of the Evacuation," a less than sympathetic New York correspondent wrote in the *Providence Gazette*. "This . . . occasions a Variety of physiognomic, laughable Appearances. Some look smiling, others melancholy, a third Class, mad. To hear their Conversation would make you feel merry: Some . . . represent the cold Regions of Nova-Scotia as a new-created Paradise, others as a Country unfit for any human Being to inhabit."

Americans looking for a more advantageously situated store, home upgrade, or investment rental property could purchase Loyalist estates for as low as one twentieth of their value. Interestingly, the American statesman Alexander Hamilton worried precisely about this sort of behaviour. He had cut his teeth in trade with the Caribbean and worried about the economic effect of ignoring the available opportunities. "Many merchants of second class, characters of no political consequence, each of whom may carry away 8 or 10,000 guineas have, I am told lately, applied for shipping to convey them away."

New York was indeed a city on the edge during the summer of 1783. Harassment and physical attacks against Loyalists were common and hardly noted. Those who dared to venture outside the city in an attempt to reclaim their former homes in nearby towns and villages quickly learned that they were most decidedly unwelcome. A Poughkeepsie newspaper published a widely circulated declaration by a writer who called himself "Brutus" (who was most likely

William Malcolm, a future New York assembly representative) with this ominous warning: "To all Adherents to the British Government and Followers of the British Army commonly called Tories who are present within the City and County of New-York. Your feelings must be callous indeed. . . . Flee then while it is in your power for the day is at hand, when, to your confusion and dismay; such of you as reject this seasonable admonition, will have nothing to deliver them from the just vengeance of the collected citizens." An assortment of other pamphlets and missives targeted various prominent Loyalists, specifically threatening their lives if they remained.

The adage "what goes around comes around" proved true for Oliver De Lancey (or DeLancey), a member of a wealthy and influential New York family of Huguenot descent. In early February of 1749, when he was thirty-one years old, De Lancey led an attack on a Jewish merchant and his wife who had recently arrived in the city from Holland. New York governor George Clinton, who disliked the De Lanceys, reported that the mob, with their faces blackened, "broke all the Jew's windows, and afterwards broke open his door, entered his house, and pulled and tore everything to pieces." The intruders "then swore they would lie with the woman," because De Lancey claimed that she looked like Clinton's wife, "and as he could not have her, he would have her likeness." This story was all the more curious because De Lancey was married to a Jewish woman whose family had disowned her when they found out about the union. Perhaps his actions were a backlash against his in-laws' treatment of his wife. It was that kind of deteriorated social climate.

In any event, years later De Lancey got the same treatment he had inflicted on the Jewish couple. Throughout the war, De Lancey had remained a staunch Loyalist. In 1775, he had organized and outfitted at his own expense De Lancey's Brigade, three Loyalist battalions numbering more than 1,500 fighters, which he commanded as a brigadier-general. During the conflict, his mansion in Westchester was seized and later disposed of by the Americans for a sizable profit. According to the disposition De Lancey sent to Carleton, he was assaulted in the spring of 1783 "in a most violent manner" and advised that he should "run to Halifax, or to his damned King, for that neither he nor one of his breed should be suffered to remain in the Country." He soon departed New York that year for England where he died in October 1785.

STEPHEN JARVIS ALSO LEARNED firsthand that there was no going home—at least not permanently. At the beginning of 1783, Jarvis was stationed in St. Augustine, Florida, far from his home in Danbury, Connecticut. It had been seven years since he had seen either his family or his fiancée, Amelia Glover. Peace was declared at St. Augustine in April. With all the speed that he could muster, Jarvis sailed up the coast to New York, and then, with the written permission of the Patriots of Danbury, travelled home with his brother for an emotional reunion. "It is impossible to describe my feelings on again embracing those who had always been so dear to me," he later wrote. "Immediately on my arrival, my father sent for Miss Glover, who happened to be in town. I shall leave the reader to judge of the ecstasy and the joy that filled our breasts. Immediately preparations were set on foot for our marriage."

As might be expected by now, Stephen and Amelia's wedding did not work out as planned. Two men warned Jarvis that a mob was coming to arrest him. Turning to his bride-to-be, Jarvis pompously declared, "Miss Glover, good-bye, I can die—in no place more honourably than this—you shall see that I can die bravely."

There was no need for hara-kiri, but suddenly, a crowd of Patriots filled the Jarvis home, demanding to see Stephen. He calmly reminded them that they had given him permission to return to Danbury, and that if they harmed him, they put their friends at risk who had been given similar safe passage in British-held New York. A local Patriot officer promptly promised to have his squadron protect Jarvis from any harm, yet Stephen could see that it would be best if he left Danbury as soon as possible—but not without his beloved Amelia.

Pointing out the danger of staying in town for even another day, Stephen urged his father to let him marry that very evening. His father consented, but it took more persuasion to bring Amelia around. Doubtless, she was upset that her long-anticipated wedding was to be such a rushed affair. The family sent for a minister, everyone gathered in a large room in the Jarvis home, and, within the hour, Stephen and Amelia at last became husband and wife.

The mob outside the Jarvis house dispersed following the wedding. A sergeant and twelve dragoons prepared to guard the house through the night. However, early the next morning during the changing of the guard, the local sheriff forced his way upstairs into the newlyweds' bedroom and demanded payment for an old war debt. Jarvis stood up to him with such defiance that the sheriff fell down the stairs. Unhurt, he returned to the Jarvis house with a posse, but by this time the squadron had returned to its station. Seeing that his reluctant bodyguards might have to fight against their neighbours, Jarvis decided to endear himself to the soldiers. "I threw them a dollar, desired they would get something to drink to the Bride's health, which they did, and before they had finished the bottle I had won them all to my side." Suddenly, the mood of the guards changed. The soldiers claimed that Stephen "had got one of the best of women for a wife in the world; that I was deserving of her, and that they would defend us as long as they had a drop of blood in their veins" (and, one assumes, available booze).

Recognizing that Stephen's quick wits had won the day, the posse withdrew. The newlyweds enjoyed a comfortable breakfast, but did not sit still for long. A mob of disgruntled citizens had gathered down the street. Trading his Loyalist uniform for his brother's overcoat, Stephen slipped out the back door and met his brother in a nearby field. He rode off to the home of Amelia's sister where seven years earlier he had safely hidden from the Patriots. The new Mrs. Jarvis joined her husband the following day, and the couple promptly set off for New York.

Soon after their arrival, they met up with friends from Stamford, including Stephen's cousin William Jarvis, who was soon to go to England, for a day of leisure on a nearby island. The group invited Stephen and Amelia to return by boat with them to Stamford, when the war intervened in their lives once more. "In the morning a mob collected," Stephen later related, "fell upon the boat's crew, beat them unmercifully, and threatened us also, and particularly Mr. William Jarvis . . . who was a native of the place. As I was a stranger to them I took the task of appeasing their wrath, to allow us to go off peaceably." The Patriots let the Jarvis party go on their way, but later came after them again when they realized who Stephen really was. Stephen, William, two of their friends who were British officers, and the boat's captain prepared themselves for a fight, only to breathe easier when the mob backed off. Stephen and Amelia returned to New York the following morning.

AT ABOUT THIS SAME TIME, Governor Carleton was determined to ensure that before he pulled out with his troops—a garrison of approximately twenty thousand men—every Loyalist who wanted to leave would be given the opportunity to do so, and in as safe and secure manner as possible. The departure of so many people in such a short period was not quite akin to the Hebrew exodus from Egypt, but it was close. Carleton and his officers kept control of this organized chaos as much as they could, and it succeeded.

By the end of the year, an estimated 35,000 Loyalists, many from New Jersey, Pennsylvania, and Connecticut, had boarded ships that took them north to new beginnings, especially Nova Scotia, where the British, at Carleton's urging, had offered them free land grants.

The Great American Dream was the tale of "the huddled masses" landing in New York Harbor and a chorus of fairies springing unbidden from a bush garden, singing about the milk and honey that would characterize their landfall. The Loyalists had the misfortune of realizing that dream backwards. They departed New York to view their milk and honey from safer ground in Halifax and the mouth of the St. John River. At the docks, carts piled high with household goods and furniture—an ambitious emigrant even tried to move a two-story house onto one of the departing ships. The subjects of general conversation on the street corners were the worried inquiries as to when the British would finally vacate. The dilemma facing every Loyalist was lampooned by a Patriot poet in "The Tory's Soliloquy" that appeared in the *New York Morning Post* on November 7, 1783:

> *To go—or not to go—is that the question?*
> *Or stay and cringe to the rude surly whigs,*
> *Whose wounds, yet fresh, may urge their desperate hand*
> *To spurn us while we sue—perhaps consign us*
> *To the kind care of some outrageous mob,*
> *Who for their sport our persons may adorn*
> *In all the majesty of tar and feathers;*
> *Perhaps our necks, to keep their humour warm,*
> *May grace a Rebel halter!—There's the sting!*
> *This people's, the bleak clime, for who can brook*
> *A Rebel's frown—or bear his children's stare*
> *When in the streets they point and lisp "A Tory?"*
> *The open insult, the heart-piercing stab*
> *Of satire's pointed pen or worse,—far worse—*
> *Committee's rage—or jury's grave debate*
> *On the grand question: "shall their lives forsooth*
> *or property—or both—atone their crimes?"*
> *Then let us fly, nor trust a war of words*
> *Let's lose our fears, for no bold Whig will dare*
> *With sword or law to persecute us there.*

Sarcasm aside, there was thus relief, but sadness as well. "The Loyalists have faces as long as my arm," reported one Patriot New Yorker who watched this mass movement. In one case, a mother "kidnapped her daughter to keep her from going off with her Loyalist husband to Canada." Sarah Frost, a young wife and mother from

Stamford who was also seven and half months pregnant, and whose husband, William, had fought the Patriots during the war in a Loyalist brigade, boarded a ship bound for Nova Scotia at the end of May. She, William, and their children then waited for two weeks until all of the passengers were ready to depart. "Our women all came on board with their children and there is great confusion in the cabin," she wrote in her diary on June 9. "We bear with it pretty well through the day, but at night one cries in one place and one in another whilst we are getting them to bed. I think sometimes I will go crazy. There are so many of them; if they were as still as common there would be a great noise amongst them. I stay on deck tonight till nigh eleven o'clock, and now I think I will go down and get to bed if I can find a place for myself."

Sarah and her ship, *Two Sisters*, were part of the Loyalist armada of thirteen vessels (frigates and brigs) that had left New York on June 9. Other ships in this fleet included *Amity's Production*, *Hopewell*, *Litttledale*, *Tartar*, and *Thames*. As soon as the flotilla reached Staten Island two days later, however, bad weather once again delayed the departure for another five days. Much to Sarah's delight, the fleet weighed anchor early in the morning of June 16. There was a light breeze and the flotilla was able to keep sight of each other. On the *Two Sisters*, Sarah and the other passengers dined on fresh mackerel. "I had never saw one alive before," she recorded. "It is the handsomest fish I ever saw."

When the winds were decent, the ships travelled eleven kilometres an hour, and by June 21 the Loyalist fleet was 386 kilometres from Nova Scotia. A misty fog had set in and the ships communicated with each other via bells. On the *Two Sisters*, as Frost noted, many passengers came down with measles, though that does not seem to have caused a major problem. On June 26, she caught sight of the banks of Cape Sable Island at the tip of Nova Scotia. "There is general rejoicing," she recorded. "At half after six we have twelve of our ships in sight. Our Captain told me just now we should be in the Bay of Fundy before morning. He says it is about one day's sail after we get into the Bay to Saint John's River. How I long to see that place, though a strange land." A month later, on July 30, with William by her side, Sarah gave birth to another daughter, Hannah.

The June fleet that had brought the Frosts was the second to evacuate Loyalists from New York. In fact, there had been some difficulty securing an adequate supply of ships. By March 1783, the Loyalists who had poured into New York City had strained the facilities. On April 26, the inaugural spring fleet of twenty vessels carried seven thousand newcomers out of New York City and on May 18 landed about half of them at Parrtown at the reversible mouth of the St. John River (in 1785, Parrtown, also spelled Parr Town, merged with the adjacent community of Carleton and was incorporated as the city of Saint John). The other half made their way to Port Roseway (soon renamed Shelburne), south of Halifax. As a gesture of goodwill, Nova Scotia governor John Parr offered newcomers in Port Roseway wooden planks to construct their houses, though it took some time. The fleet returned to transport others—including the June fleet that transported Sarah and William Frost—and by the end of September, eighteen thousand Loyalists had arrived, with twelve thousand more expected.

Polly and Fyler Dibblee had been among the throng, with Fyler working as a deputy agent facilitating travel for Loyalists desperate to flee the U.S. The Dibblees left New York aboard the *Union*, the flagship of the first Loyalist evacuation (spring) fleet, at the end of April with two hundred other Loyalists bound for their new home in Parrtown. Most were like the Dibblees, from Connecticut, but there were also Loyalist families (as well as three widows, one spinster, and several bachelors) from Rhode Island, New York, Massachusetts, New Jersey, and Pennsylvania. More than half the passengers were children. The weather was good and the journey uneventful, which everyone on board the ships no doubt appreciated in light of the many hardships the Loyalists had endured for the past seven years or more. Travelling with the Dibblees were their two black servants, Tom Hyde, a free Black Loyalist, and nine-year-old Sukey, who was indentured. Fyler's legal skills seemed to guarantee a bright future.

Polly's brothers Munson and the troubled John Jarvis with his drinking problem, and their families, also journeyed from New York north to Parrtown. But Munson was understandably bitter. Forced into exile, he and his wife, Mary, had to abandon land and goods at his Stamford home worth nearly £600. He later submitted a claim to a British government commission for Loyalist restitution and was compensated with a payment of £250, or less than half of what he had lost. It was not surprising that he viewed the revolution "as one of the blackest scenes of iniquity that ever was transacted," as he wrote in 1788 to his brother William's father-in-law, Reverend Samuel Peters, who had fled to England just as the conflict had begun. "We have fought a good fight (temporal), if we have not overcome the thirteen United States," Munson added, "yet we overcome one of the great (I won't say good) allies, the devil and all his works."

Two other brothers of Polly's, Samuel and William, decided to go to England before they both eventually joined the rest of the family in New Brunswick and Upper Canada. Before he left New York, Samuel had acquired a black indentured servant named Zimri Armstrong. The contract between the two stipulated that after two years of labour, Armstrong would be free from his obligations. Samuel agreed that he would then provide Armstrong with provisions and clothing and, most importantly, purchase the freedom of Armstrong's wife and children, slaves he had left behind in the United States. Instead, two years later, Samuel, without informing Armstrong, sold his contract to his brother John (who was then living in Saint John). And, far worse, after travelling to the U.S., Samuel bought Armstrong's family and then inexplicably sold them to another master. Loyalist or not, as a black man, Armstrong was powerless. He appealed to the authorities, but no one would help him, despite the clear breach of the contract by Samuel Jarvis—and his abysmal treatment of Armstrong's family. It is unknown what happened to Armstrong. At some point, he was released by John Jarvis and might have ended up in a town in Pennsylvania where he was reunited with his family.

BACK IN NEW YORK Carleton struggled to deal with the dicey issue of the many African Americans, free and former slaves, who were anxious to leave. They had fled to New York seeking refuge, yet Article VII of the peace treaty stipulated that Britain would vacate its military forces "with all convenient speed, and without causing any destruction, or carrying away any Negroes, or other Property of the American inhabitants." That put African Americans like Boston King, who had escaped slavery in South Carolina, in a dangerous situation. A rumour circulated in the city that the runaways were to be returned to their former owners. It caused "inexpressible anguish and terror," King later recalled, "especially when we saw our old masters coming from Virginia, North Carolina, and other parts, and seizing upon their slaves in the streets of New York, or even dragging them out of their beds."

Carleton's prudent solution was to permit African American refugees to leave on British ships, provided they could prove they had resided in British-occupied territory for the past year. Proof of military service was even better. Yet establishing residency or having proper documentation was problematic. Ever officious, Carleton set up a commission of British and American members to judge each individual case and determine if the African American in question met the departure criteria. For many it was a matter of life and freedom as Black Loyalists—formerly enslaved Africans who had been set free for their service to the Crown during the revolution—or beatings and servitude as slaves again. For the lucky ones like Boston King and his wife, Violet, who were pioneers of Birchtown, the black Nova Scotia settlement near Shelburne, the commission decided in their favour. They were then given a travel certificate from Brigadier-General Samuel Birch, the British commander of New York City—a moment, King remembered, that "dispelled all our fears, and filled us with joy and gratitude"—and their names were entered into the "Book of Negroes," a record of every African American who departed from

New York Harbor. Within a few months, 3,000 names had been re-corded—1,336 men, 914 women, and 750 children—with the same detail as was listed for slave sales.

Needless to say, George Washington, the defender of American liberty and a devoted slave owner who regarded African Americans as his personal property, was not happy about Carleton's actions. At a meeting in May, he expressed his anger that Carleton had violated the "letter and spirit of the treaty." The British general stood his ground, insisting that everything had been done openly and with American knowledge. "The negroes in question," he asserted in his reply to Washington, "I found free when I arrived in New York, I had therefore no right . . . to prevent their going to any part of the world they thought proper." Carleton was no abolitionist, but as a respectable gentleman and officer, he held firmly that assurances made to Loyalists, white or black, had to be honoured.

Carleton waited until the end of November to order his troops out of the area. By then, he was fairly confident that every Loyalist had departed who wanted to leave. Evacuation Day, a New York City holiday for years, was on November 25 as crowds gathered to bid the British farewell—and good riddance. As soon as they marched to the city docks, American troops, led by Washington and George Clinton, the chief executive of civilian government, entered the city and the festivities began. At Cape's Tavern on Broadway, the patrons toasted Washington. "In this place, and at this moment of exultation and triumph," they proclaimed, "while the Ensigns of Slavery still linger in our sight, we look up to you, our deliverer, with unusual transports of Gratitude and Joy." Formal banquets and celebratory dinners followed during the next few weeks.

By sheer coincidence, this was the day Stephen Jarvis returned to the city. Some months earlier, he had had to leave Amelia again to travel to Florida in order to fulfill his final obligation to his reg-iment. His last duty to his men was to see them safely evacuated to Halifax from St. Augustine, which now belonged to Spain. Following their arrival in Halifax, the regiment was disbanded. Jarvis's military career had come to a temporary end and he looked forward to becoming a civilian once again.

"Here I took my leave of a set of as brave fellows as ever existed, which I had led in many hard fought battles, and who were as much attached to me as children to their Father," he wrote. "So much so when I left them they carried me in their arms to the vessel in which I took my passage for New York."

He had arrived in New York on November 25, hardly a good day for a recently decommissioned Loyalist officer to arrive. "The question with me was, shall I, or shall I not proceed; or shall I go back to Halifax?" he pondered. "At last I determined to proceed; I must go some time and the sooner the better."

Jarvis waited a week for the festivities to die down, and when it seemed safe enough, he headed for Fraunces Tavern, Washington's new headquarters. If he was going to get safely back to Amelia, he reasoned, he might as well go "right to the top." "So I proceeded to the City and made my appearance at General Washington's Headquarters, and reported myself to General Hamilton," as he recounted. "I was directed to call the next morning at nine o'clock."

One had to admire the audacity of the twenty-seven-year-old Loyalist. He and Washington had almost met on two previous occasions—the first instance involved the British victory at the Battle of Brandywine in Pennsylvania and the second was the failed kidnapping attempt in Morristown, New York—and if the general had been aware of those circumstances, he might not have been so willing to see Jarvis.

But the two men did finally meet—the future first president of the new republic bade farewell to a young Loyalist officer who would one day be part of the vanguard of a northern nation. Had Congress not only just disbanded the Patriot army on December 4, Washington would have been able to give Jarvis the much needed paperwork that would have provided free passage through Patriot-held Connecticut. Remembering how the revolution had imposed long separations from his own wife, Washington took compassion on Jarvis. Drawing

A light infantryman and Hussar (*left*), rifleman (*right*), and grenadier of the Queen's Rangers (*below*). The regiment was named in honour of Queen Charlotte, the wife of King George III.

Although infamous for his role as the commander of the Continental Army during the American Revolution, George Washington lost more battles than he won in his military career. *National Portrait Gallery, Smithsonian Institution; acquired as a gift to the nation through the generosity of the Donald W. Reynolds Foundation.*

Thayendanegea, also known as Joseph Brant, was the younger brother of Molly Brant, the influential Mohawk intermediary. Joseph's English-style education provided him opportunities to take on many roles throughout his life —interpreter, translator, war chief, statesman—and become a prominent Mohawk leader in his own right. *Romney, George, "Joseph Brant (Thayendanegea)," 1776, Acc. #8005. Photo © NGC.*

The Battle of Wyoming—captured here in a painting by Alonzo Chappel—took place in Pennsylvania in 1778. The hour-long battle saw British troops, along with their Iroquois allies, defeat the Patriots. After the encounter, however, American propaganda enflamed the public with fabricated claims that the Iroquois warriors had committed atrocities on the prisoners and fleeing Patriot soldiers; Joseph Brant took much of the blame for these actions, despite the fact that he wasn't present at the battle. *Chicago Historical Society, Accession Number X38.*

John Trumbull's *Surrender of Lord Cornwallis* shows the British general surrendering to American and French forces at Yorktown on October 19, 1781.
General Benjamin Lincoln accepts the surrender, while General George Washington watches from his horse in the background. *Library of Congress.*

Sir Guy Carleton, the British commander in chief in North America following the Revolutionary War. Carleton was responsible for evacuating the thousands of British troops, Loyalists, and freed black men and women in New York at the end of the hostilities. *Library and Archives Canada, Acc. No. 199781.*

Although Loyalists fled to many British colonies, from the Caribbean to the United Kingdom to other parts of what would become Canada, a great number of them landed in Halifax, overwhelming the resources of the sparsely populated Nova Scotian capital when they first arrived. *Library and Archives Canada.*

Loyalist evacuees were staggered over a number of armadas. Shown here in a painting by C. H. J. Snider are just a few of the ships in the British naval force on Lake Ontario: the schooners *Mississauga* and *Bear*, the sloop *Caldwell*, and the schooners *Onondaga* and *Buffalo* (*left to right*). *Courtesy of Toronto Public Library, JRR 1157.*

on his experiences of placing disguised intelligence agents within enemy lines, Washington gave Jarvis some ideas on how he might slip into Connecticut.

Acting on the retired general's advice, Jarvis bought "a stock of tea and sugar" and departed New York City. These supplies may simply have been bought as luxuries for Amelia, or they may have allowed the young Loyalist to pass himself off as a New York peddler heading off to Connecticut to sell his wares. Whatever the reasoning, Stephen safely arrived in Redding, Connecticut, and was at long last reunited with the love of his life, Amelia. The joy of their meeting was multiplied tenfold when Amelia told the dumbfounded Stephen that she was pregnant. Somehow, they spent that winter in Danbury undisturbed as Loyalists living in the U.S. But when the snow melted, the threats were renewed and he was given an ultimatum sent to him in writing "to depart or abide the consequence."

Despite an attack on his father's home during which a pregnant Amelia was roughed up, Stephen and Amelia and their baby daughter, Elizabeth (Betsey), born on May 9, 1784, remained in Connecticut for one more winter. This decision was made only because both mother and daughter became ill that autumn "with inflammation," as Stephen described it. Earlier, Stephen had visited Fredericton, procured a lot, and had a house built. He stopped briefly to see his cousin Munson in Saint John and then returned to Connecticut via Long Island on a transport Munson and his brother Samuel arranged. In those days there were no borders and Loyalists, though at risk of being questioned by American authorities, easily travelled back and forth—and would do so until after the War of 1812. In the new year, once Amelia and Betsey had recovered, Stephen and his family finally departed Connecticut for good and their new life in New Brunswick. The horrors of war and the desperations of separation behind them, their arrival in the recently created province would be a rare blessing.

6

CLAIMING THE KINGDOMS
OF THE ATLANTIC

*When the visiting French artist Marc Lescarbot first
glimpsed Nova Scotia's magnificent Annapolis Basin, he
was overwhelmed, and described it as "the most beautiful
earthly habitation God has ever made." Damned if the
hard-case Haligonians didn't accuse the poor fellow of
understatement.*

I N THE LONG SWEEP of Canadian history there have been no
regional boosters more fierce in their patriotism than the ultra-
proud Nova Scotians. It's a case, as former prime minister Lester
Pearson once noted, of "human sovereignty transcending national
sovereignty." Patriotism is a fever in the blood, and it must arise
spontaneously, from the hearts of people who love their country—or
at least that part of it in which they live.

The early waves of Loyalists who arrived in Halifax, desperate
for homes and hearths, belonged to a galaxy of troubled pilgrims.
They were fleeing the American Revolutionary War and their destination was not, like previous escape routes, Upper Canada, Great
Britain, or the West Indies. Instead, an amazing forty thousand of
these upstanding Loyalists decided to launch their reincarnations

in the northern colony of Nova Scotia and its adjoining territories. That human tsunami flooded the towns and river valleys of the Maritimes, straining tempers, testing facilities, inventing solutions, but also showing the way.

Before the refugee tide washed up on its shores, Nova Scotia had only ten thousand European settlers and three thousand Native inhabitants. The arrival of the new wave utterly overwhelmed the colony's infrastructure and drained its available resources. Compounding the demands of keeping body and soul together were the new social tensions forced upon the refugees. They came from every one of the rebellious Yankee colonies, having belonged to all strata of society and representing dozens of ethnic backgrounds. One out of every ten of those refugees was a Black Loyalist. They came with the highest expectations for a new life. Free at last to live exploiting their freedom of choice as a right instead of a privilege. Could these former hostages to fortune find their feet and turn themselves into the vanguard of a new nation?

That was an open question, but there were some uncharacteristically cheerful British observers who felt that Nova Scotia would, in fact, become the envy of the erstwhile rebels in the United States. Home Secretary Lord Sydney was decidedly upbeat when he projected the future of their Maritimes settlement. His vision made Massachusetts refugee Edward Winslow almost feel giddy.

> Lord Sydney's declaration quoted in your letter, "That he will make Nova Scotia the envy of the American States" has excited a kind of general gratitude; I cannot describe it. Other ministers and Great men have by their patronage of new settlers, relieved individuals from distress, and rendered services to their country, but it is a Godlike task that Lord Sydney has undertaken. Such an event as the present has never happened before—perhaps never will again. There are assembled here an immense multitude, (not of dissolute vagrants such as commonly make the first efforts to settle new countries) but gentlemen of education, independent

farmers and reputable mechanics, who by the fortune of war had been deprived of their property. They are as firmly attached to the British constitution as if they had never made a sacrifice, chanting: "By Heaven, we will be the envy of the American States!"

The home secretary's final phrase became the Loyalists' mission statement for settling the Maritimes. Winslow made it his personal anthem: "Yes—by God! We will be the envy of the American states, when the people of the neighbouring states shall observe our operations. When they see us in the enjoyment of a regular system of Government—protected by the mother Country—not saddled with enormous taxes and compare their state with ours, Will they not envy us? Surely they will." Bless you brother.

Within a year of the Loyalists' arrival in the Maritimes, the British Empire's cartographers were obliged to redraw their maps. Receiving only a few hundred American refugees, the map of the island of St. John (later Prince Edward Island) remained unchanged. However, the repercussions of the Loyalist diaspora arriving in western Nova Scotia's Sunbury County gave birth to North America's first colony of war refugees—in fact, the first Loyalist colony within the British Empire: the newly minted province of New Brunswick. Once simply Nova Scotia, by 1784 it had morphed into three colonies: New Brunswick was carved out of its western portion; Cape Breton was made out of its eastern extension; and a smaller Nova Scotia remained on the shores of the Atlantic. It would be seven years before Upper Canada, the next Loyalist colony, would come into existence.

THE LOYALISTS' TRANSITION to their new northern homes was fraught with difficulties and setbacks, especially during their first winter in the Maritimes. When the first Loyalist refugees made their way to Fredericton in 1783—the settlement was called Ste. Anne's Point until the name was changed in 1785 in honour of King George III's second son, Prince Frederick Augustus, Duke of York—the shoals prevented their ship from going any farther up the St. John River. Disembarking at Maugerville, they were given the choices of trudging twelve miles through the wilderness or waiting for a turn in one of a handful of rowboats that shuttled back and forth between Oromocto and Ste. Anne's. When the refugees finally made landfall at Ste. Anne's, they set right to work to build houses for their first winter.

Some were more resourceful and luckier than others. At Ste. Anne's, fathers and sons travelled great distances "with toboggans through wild woods or on the ice," to find food for their families. Without proper shelter, many lived in canvas tents built into the snow: "There were times," one Loyalist old-timer later remembered, "when strong proud men wept like children and lay down in their snowbound tents to die."

Newcomer Mary Fisher, whose husband, Lewis, fought in the Loyalist brigade the New Jersey Volunteers during the Revolutionary War, told her granddaughter, Georgianna Fisher, that some "wicked" men were so desperate for food that they "killed, roasted and ate [a] cat." Heavy snow fell on November 2. Mary and her family pitched a tent in the woods. "We used stones for fireplaces," she related. "Our tent had no floor but the ground. The winter was very cold, with deep snow, which we tried to keep from drifting in by putting a large rug at the door. The snow, which lay six feet around us, helped greatly in keeping out the cold."

Reflecting on those trying times many years later, Mary did not know how they had survived that first terrible winter. "There were mothers that had been reared in a pleasant country enjoying all the comforts of life, with helpless children in their arms," she continued. "They clasped their infants to their bosoms and tried by the warmth of their own bodies to protect them from the bitter cold. Sometimes family members had to remain up during the night to keep the fires burning to keep them from freezing. Many women and children, as well as men, died from cold and exposure. Graves were dug with axes and shovels near the spot where our party had landed, and there in stormy winter weather our loved ones were buried. We had no minister, so we had to bury them without any religious service, besides our own prayers."

Writing in 1825, merchant and early New Brunswick historian Peter Fisher, who came as a youngster from Staten Island, described the ordeal in a similar fashion:

> The privations and sufferings of these people almost exceed belief. The want of food and clothing in a wild, cold country, was not easily dispensed with or soon remedied. Frequently in the piercing cold of winter a part of the family had to remain up during the night to keep fire in their huts to prevent the other part from freezing. Some very destitute families made use of boards to supply the want of bedding; the father or some of the elder children remaining up by turns, and warming two suitable pieces of boards, which they applied alternately to the smaller children to keep warm; with many similar expedients.

The situation gradually improved for some Loyalists. Eleven-year-old Hannah Ingraham, who arrived with her family in Ste. Anne's Point a year later in the fall of 1783, recalled that her parents received "flour and butter and pork" from the government. "A good fire was blazing on the hearth," she wrote, "and mother had a big loaf of bread with us, and she boiled a kettle of water and put a good piece of butter in a pewter bowl, and we toasted the bread and all sat round the bowl to eat our breakfast that morning, and mother said, 'Thank God, we are no longer in dread of having shots fired through our house. This is the sweetest meal I have tasted for many a day.'" On the other hand, in January 1785 a Loyalist in Port Roseway wrote dolefully that "all our golden promises are vanished in smoke. We were taught to believe that this place was not barren and foggy, as had been represented, but find it ten times worse. We have nothing but his Majesty's rotten pork and unbaked flour to subsist on. . . . It is the most inhospitable clime that ever mortal set foot on."

For a time, the Ingrahams lived that first year in a tent before her father constructed a log house. "One morning," she remembered,

> when we waked we found the snow lying deep on the ground all around us, and then father came wading through it and told us the house was ready and not to stop to light a fire then, and not mind the weather, but follow his tracks through the trees, for the trees were so many we soon lost sight of him going up the hill; it was snowing fast, and oh, so cold. Father carried a chest and we all took something and followed him up the hill through the trees. It was not long before we heard him pounding, and, oh, what joy to see our gable end. There was no floor laid, no window, no chimney, no door, but damned if it didn't boast a roof at last.

In those early years, even if a Loyalist was wealthier, their wooden homes were fairly primitive. Edward Winslow, for example, was hardly poor, but the log house he built for his family in Granville, Nova Scotia, in 1783 was basic in design and comfort. It was, as he described it, "divided into two rooms, where we are snug as pokers." He was able to expand it so that in 1785 when he contemplated selling it, his somewhat exaggerated advertisement read as follows: "The elegant House . . . consist[s] of four beautiful rooms on the first floor, highly finished. Also two spacious lodging chambers in the second story—[with] a capricious dry cellar with arches."

This dwelling was more than the average Loyalist could afford. In most cases, Loyalists, like the Ingrahams, lived in a log cabin with one room, perhaps two. "Its dimensions," noted historian W. Stewart Wallace many years ago,

> were as a rule no more than fourteen feet by eighteen feet, and sometimes ten by fifteen. The roofs were constructed of bark or small hollowed basswood logs, overlapping one another like tiles. The windows were often as not covered not with glass, but with oiled paper. The chimneys were built of sticks and clay, or rough

un-mortared stones, since bricks were not procurable; sometimes there was no chimney, and the smoke was allowed to find its way out through a hole in the bark roof. Where it was impossible to obtain lumber, the doors were made of pieces of timber split into rough boards; and in some cases the hinges and latches were made of wood. These old log cabins, with the chinks between the logs filled in with clay and moss, were still to be seen standing in many parts of the country as late as fifty years ago. Though primitive, they seem to have been not uncomfortable; and many of the old settlers clung to them long after they could have afforded to build better. This was doubtless partly due to the fact that log-houses were exempt from the taxation laid on frame, brick, and stone structures.

Some Loyalists did manage to bring furniture with them. "Here and there a family would possess an ancient spindle, a pair of curiously-wrought fire-dogs, or a quaint pair of hand-bellows," Wallace added.

But these relics of a former life merely served to accentuate the rudeness of the greater part of the furniture of the settlers. Chairs, benches, tables, beds, chests, were fashioned by hand from the rough wood. The descendant of one family . . . described how the family dinner-table was a large stump, hewn flat on top, standing in the middle of the floor. The cooking was done at the open fireplace; it was not until well on in the nineteenth century that stoves came into common use in Canada.

THE EXPERIENCE OF Polly and Fyler Dibblee and their six children during their first few years in New Brunswick was thus fairly typical, though the Dibblees did not seem to have prospered as other Loyalists did in the years after. As they tried to stay warm in makeshift cabins during the bone-chilling winter of 1783 in Parrtown, the Dibblees were forced to subsist on a steady diet of washed potatoes. This was a far cry from the wholesome and plentiful diet the family had become accustomed to before the war. Fyler was appointed one of the province's first magistrates and an agent for Loyalist settlement. At first, he wrote a glowing report to his father about the prospects for his new life. But then reality set in, and within a year his property losses in Connecticut and the limited chances for success in his new country caused devastating psychological stress. He soon wrote his father to report that his family was settled "to their unspeakable satisfaction."

As Polly's brother William Jarvis later explained to British authorities, Fyler became depressed about "the dreary prospects arising from the Climate, Soil and his debts . . . he concluded that he must go to Gaol for his Debts and there [he would] die; [while] his Family would inevitably starve and Perish. The Result was that Mr. Dibblee grew Melancholy and which soon deprived him of his Reason, and for four months could not be left by himself." Fyler was forced to borrow money from his brother-in-law Munson, and that troubled him further. One of the few happier moments was when the Dibblees' eldest child, Walter, married Hannah Beardsley, the daughter of an Anglican clergyman, the Reverend John Beardsley.

Eventually, it was all too much for Fyler. On May 6, 1784, as his family sat down for their evening meal, Fyler slipped away from the table, picked up his shaving razor, closed the curtains that surrounded his bed, lay down, and ended his life by slashing his throat. He was forty-three years old.

Polly was naturally devastated. Although she had two brothers in the colony, the new widow must have realized that they could not give her much assistance. The burden of supporting six children was ultimately Polly's to bear. She could not even sell their house and land, having been compelled by one of Fyler's creditors to surrender the Dibblees' property as payment for all that the lawyer owed him. Worse still, within six weeks of Fyler's suicide, a fire swept through Parrtown, burning the Dibblee home to the ground with all of its "goods and effects."

Adding shame to injury was the reaction to Fyler's suicide back in their hometown of Stamford, Connecticut. Neither Polly nor her brother Munson Jarvis had relayed the news of Fyler's suicide in one of the many letters that made up the regular correspondence between the separated members of the Jarvis family. But when Polly's mother, Martha Jarvis, heard of her son-in-law's death, word soon spread throughout the town.

It became the accepted theory among the Patriots of Stamford that Fyler had killed himself, not because of a severe depression, but because of "the goading of a guilty conscience" for abandoning the rebel cause. The death of her father and the Dibblees' economic predicament must have been especially stressful for Polly's daughter, seventeen-year-old Peggy, whose wedding almost became a casualty of her dire circumstances.

Several months after she was widowed, Polly was given a grant of land about fifty-six kilometres north of Parrtown near Kingston (New Brunswick). Saint John, as Parrtown was then called, was on its way to becoming New Brunswick's largest settlement. Nevertheless, Polly opted for a fresh start in Kingston. She already had family in the area—her brother John Jarvis and his wife, as well as Fyler's brother Frederick Dibblee, a teacher and lay reader to the Anglican congregation, all lived there—so relocating to Kingston made sense. Polly and her children built a log cabin and had sufficient resources to hire a young Aboriginal girl as a servant. Then, Polly's daughter Peggy, her husband, John, and their first child moved to Kingston in 1786; Polly was a grandmother at forty years old.

Just as things seemed to be improving, the Dibblees endured yet another setback: their servant girl accidentally set their log cabin on fire, burning it to the ground. The family built a second cabin, though by now Polly had exhausted her money and could not properly complete its internal structure. At the Dibblee house, there was no chimney nor floorboards, prompting Polly's brother Samuel, visiting from Saint John, to comment on her "miserable habitation, a scene of absolute poverty and distress." Moreover, as a Loyalist, Polly could not collect any funds from the sale of her father's Stamford estate, because Connecticut refused to forward bequests to any Tories. And the British were of no help either. While her brother Munson had received £250 as partial compensation for the losses he suffered in the revolution after an official hearing in Saint John, Polly was initially given nothing since all of the legal and land documents verifying her claim had been destroyed in the fire. In fact, Polly really did not have much of a chance: the British officials overseeing Loyalist claims generally were not as accommodating to women, particularly if, like Polly, they lacked the relevant property papers.

The desperation and panic Polly experienced was evident in the heartfelt letter she wrote about her dire situation to her brother William in November 1787. "I dare not let my friends at Stamford know of my calamitous situation lest it should bring down the grey hairs of my mother to the grave," she wrote him, "and besides they could not relieve me without distressing themselves should I apply—as they have been ruined by the rebels during the war—therefore I have no other ground to hope, but on your goodness and bounty." William was not unsympathetic and immediately sent his sister a trunk from England filled with used clothes, brushes, and other household items. This was soon followed by a loan of $60 so that Polly and her children could buy a variety of food, rather than trying to survive on those damn spuds. "Pour soul, she has suffered beyond the ability of human nature to bear," William commented about his sister's predicament. "How she has lived to me is a mystery."

In 1788, Polly's brother-in-law, Frederick, relocated two hundred kilometres northwest to the town of Woodstock on the banks of the Meduxnekeag and St. John Rivers to administer a school for Indians. Within three years, he was ordained as Woodstock's first Anglican vicar, a promotion that bumped his annual salary from £30 to £50. Next to depart for Woodstock were Polly's daughter Peggy and her husband, John Bedell. He was appointed the town's commissioner of roads, overseer of the poor, and town clerk. Two of Polly's sons, William and Ralph, soon followed their sister.

In Kingston, Polly still had her brother John to lean on, yet he had his own personal problems. The success of their brother Munson, who prospered in Saint John in business and local politics, was an anchor for other Jarvis clan members as they struggled to build up their personal finances. Munson had bought John and his family a house, yet John suffered from his, by now ingrained, alcoholism—or, as Munson described, "liquor has got to be his master." John's shattered life stretched out for ninety-two long and lonely years. His obituary described him as having come to New Brunswick "at first settlement, sacrificing home and all to his attachment to the British Constitution." His glowing, but erroneous, obituary illustrated how quickly the children of the Loyalists began to fabricate myths around their parents and their lives.

In the fall of 1788, Polly, who missed her mother terribly, decided to return to Stamford. A short day before she was set to depart, however, William Jarvis, who was in England, had written her and advise her to remain in New Brunswick. At the time, he was attempting to secure restitution for Polly from the British government and was concerned those efforts would be for naught if she returned to Connecticut. Polly agreed to stay in Kingston. In England, William's friendship with his old Queen's Rangers commander, John Graves Simcoe, paid off. Within four years, he was to return to North America as a member of Simcoe's administration in the new colony of Upper Canada. William networked within the émigré community in London and learned how to contact powerful government administrators. In 1788, his personal connections and lobbying efforts finally secured Polly adequate compensation from the British authorities of £350. With additional funds generously given to her by Munson, Polly was able to pay off Fyler's debts and still have almost £200 to "make a tolerable life of it," as she put it. Still missing her mother, she travelled from Saint John Harbour on a ship bound for Stamford in the spring of 1789.

As a Loyalist, Polly was not welcomed back with open arms. At the same time, the extreme bitterness felt about each other—Patriots and Loyalists—had somewhat subsided. When Nova Scotia Loyalist Gideon White visited his former home in New Hampshire in 1787, he later commented that his one-time neighbours were all "very polite, friendly and social." Other Loyalists expressed similar sentiments. Reverend William Clark, an Anglican minister, who had found refuge in Digby, Nova Scotia, travelled to Boston in 1789. He explained the easing of attitudes with a story: "In times of Rebellion or public Commotion, the Body politic resembles a man under the Delirium of a Fever, who when he gets well and returns to his natural Temper, is quite a different man." Many Loyalists, not surprisingly, forgave nothing. Exiled in London, Jonathan Sewall, the former attorney-general of the Massachusetts colony and a contemporary of John Adams, railed against Patriots as "sanctified hypocrites" and "rebellious, ungenerous, ungrateful sons of bitches." There were even, heaven forbid, marriages between Loyalists and Americans.

This was the last time Polly was in her hometown and the United States. Her mother, Martha, died in Stamford in 1803 without seeing Polly again. The visit with her was brief and before the end of the summer, Polly was back in New Brunswick. There, she stayed for a time with her son Walter and his wife, Hannah, in Maugerville, before returning to Woodstock in May of 1791 to live with her son William, a lifelong bachelor. At last, in her mid-forties, Polly found some peace. "She became the mistress of her son's home," writes Stephen Davidson, her talented biographer, "and for the next thirty years Polly busied herself preparing their meals, tending their garden, and running their household."

To pursue her trail of ill luck, she suffered another setback in 1799 when her son Ralph, only twenty-nine years old, died, leaving a wife and two young sons. Family correspondence noted that Polly was "overwhelmed in trouble for the loss of her son . . . and was greatly distressed." Polly gradually recovered and by the 1820s, had a reputation in Woodstock for being a "well preserved old lady" who enjoyed knitting. "The last recorded memory of Polly Dibblee," Davidson added, "was put to paper by one of her former neighbours.

The frail widow took a moment to show a five-year-old boy how to roast an apple over an open fire. Polly suspended an apple from a string and twirled it over the flames so that it would bake equally on all sides." (Contrary to her usual luck, the apple didn't burst into flame and burn her house down.) The little boy grew up to become the father of Reverend W. O. Raymond, one of New Brunswick's earliest historians of the Loyalist period. Polly Jarvis Dibblee died in early May of 1826 at the age of seventy-nine, much loved, but seldom blessed with good fortune.

DURING THE FIRST DECADES of settlement, the refugees' estimation of the Maritimes would careen back and forth between Polly Dibblee's Hell that encompassed sufferings "beyond all possible description" and Edward Winslow's heavenly Utopia with its "regular system of government—protected by the mother Country." Most of these newcomers were civilian Loyalists by conviction and temperament. Some were disbanded soldiers who had demonstrated their courage in taking up arms against the rebels. Among the latter were Hessians who had deserted their regiments to settle in Nova Scotia. Some moved to towns established either by New Englanders, Germans, or Swiss Protestants twenty years earlier; others spread out into the colony's uninhabited river valleys and sheltered harbours to establish purely Loyalist enclaves. By the end of 1783, veterans of dozens of the elite Loyalist provincial corps had been disbanded in Nova Scotia, adding useful trades.*

This core of war-hardened veterans would stand the northern colony in good stead—and did, during the War of 1812, just three

---

*They included the Queen's Rangers, the King's American Regiment, Detachment of Garrison Battalion, the New York Volunteers, the 1st De Lanceys, 2nd De Lanceys, Loyal American Regiment, 2nd Division, 3rd Division, the Prince of Wales American Regiment, the Pennsylvania Loyalists, the Maryland Loyalists, the American Legion, the Guides and Pioneers, the Detachment of King's American Dragoons, and the Detachment of North Carolina Volunteers.

decades away. Fortune still played havoc with the Loyalists even though they were far removed from Patriot attacks. With shiploads of refugees still arriving, Nova Scotia politicians in Halifax felt it was a "most unlucky season" to try to accommodate so many people. It was going to be difficult to "get them under cover before the severity of winter sets." Having survived seven bloody years of civil war, the Loyalist settlers barely endured the winter of 1783–84. But life continued, and within a matter of months the Nova Scotia government appointed a host of Loyalists as justices of the peace. One of this number, Sampson Salter Blowers, became the colony's attorney general—with happy results. By November 1784 the first Loyalist member of the Nova Scotia House of Assembly, Stephen DeLancey (the nephew of Oliver De Lancey), had taken his seat. Uncomfortable with having to deal with a colonial government in far-off Halifax, the Loyalists who settled along the St. John River in the summer of 1784 persuaded Britain to create the new colony of New Brunswick. This decision, though significant in reshaping the map of North America, was seemingly arrived at with little discussion. Officials in London and Halifax fully supported it and there were few complaints from Loyalists in Nova Scotia. New Brunswick was named for the ancestral home of George III—small comfort to a monarch who had lost most of his country's most valuable overseas holdings.

For Edward Winslow, a Harvard grad whose family had come over on the *Mayflower*, and others who were fierce proponents of a Loyalist homeland, New Brunswick presented an opportunity to create a different kind of colony—one that was neither Massachusetts nor Canada. However, the Loyalists' vision and that of the empire did not entirely coincide, something the refugees discovered after the arrival of their new lieutenant-governor, Thomas Carleton. Two months before Carleton (Sir Guy's younger brother) set foot in freshly minted New Brunswick, the Privy Council in London approved a great seal for the Loyalist colony. It showed a ship sailing up a river (the refugees' means of arrival) and had the motto "Spem

Reduxit" ("Hope Restored") affixed to it. While this phrase reflected the Loyalists' dreams, the empire had other ideas.

Before 1784 was over, Thomas Carleton would sense this growing tension, particularly in Saint John (or Parrtown), where he heard emotional speeches from those who proudly described themselves as "His Majesty's Exiled Loyalists" from different parts of the American continent now resident on the St. John River. Others complained of being "oppressed and insulted." By Christmas Eve, Carleton had received the Huggeford Petition, which was the first detailed list of Loyalist grievances. That was when the governor realized for the first time that these new recruits behaved like perky freelance Americans and not fawning, tea-guzzling British types. Free speech, a free press, and representative government were all part of the "amenities" that Loyalists expected to enjoy in their new locations. And they did. At least, nobody was being tarred and feathered.

Carleton's choice of Fredericton as the Loyalist colony's capital had upset the citizens of the newly incorporated city of Saint John. It also helped galvanize its refugee settlers to hope that the tiny community would soon become a thriving centre of government, commerce, and military stability—which it did in spades. On the municipal level, as reflected in Saint John's royal incorporation charter, the electorate had been granted a touch of democracy. But Governor Carleton and his close circle of advisors made sure that they were the ones who appointed like-minded exiles to the key jobs as mayors, sheriffs, recorders, and clerks "for the preservation of order and securing a perfect obedience." When it came to governing the Loyalist colony, Carleton asserted, "It will be best if the American Spirit of innovation not be nursed among the Loyal Refugees by the introduction of Acts of the Legislature, for purposes for which, by the Common Law and the practice of the best regulated Colonies, the Crown alone is acknowledged to be competent."

But the "American spirit" of the Loyalists would not be quelled. The first provincial election ignited political riots in Saint John. In the words of one contemporary, it was a contest that pitted "government men against those who had not been admitted to privilege." The voters' reaction to the election results was so violent that troops had to be sent into the streets to restore order. Rather than recognizing that the loyal refugees wanted a more democratic form of government, Carleton interpreted the riot as a signal that he had to "hold the reins of government with a straight hand and to punish the refractory with firmness."

Having filled the colonial House of Assembly with those who were the "enemies of faction" and opponents of "violent party spirit," Carleton got down to the business of trying to develop a New Brunswick that, in the words of his advisor Edward Winslow, would become "the envy of the American States." Even before the Loyalists had set foot in the northern colony, they had appealed to the government for the founding of a university. The Reverend John Beardsley, the former rector of the Anglican church in Poughkeepsie, New York, and chaplain to the Loyal American Regiment (and Walter Dibblee's father-in-law), was among eighteen other scholars and ministers who met to create a "Plan of a Religious and Literary Institution for the Province of Nova Scotia." These Loyalists were quick to recognize that if Britain did not provide higher learning in their home state, their sons would have to travel to the new United States to receive higher educations, flavoured by foreign ideals. Consequently, the far-seeing Loyalists drew up a plan to present to the government in Britain urging it to found "a College . . . where Youth may receive a virtuous Education" in such things as "Religion, Literature, Loyalty, & Good Morals." That didn't sound like much fun, but just two years after their arrival in late 1785, the Loyalist institution, which would one day grow into the University of New Brunswick, was established in Fredericton, though it did not start holding classes for several more years. Refugees from the revolution had created the empire's oldest English university outside Great Britain. Two years later, Loyalists in Nova Scotia established a school that would become the iconic University of King's College. At last count, Nova Scotia had nine universities—there were almost as many intellectual outlets as sushi bars.

Colonies that were to become the envy of the Patriot republic needed a strong economic base. A key element in creating such an opportunity was trade with the West Indies. Following the American Revolution, the British government assured the Loyalists who settled along the northern Atlantic coast that they would become heirs to this lucrative trade triangle that also involved home ports in England. What had once been the driving engine of the Thirteen Colonies' economies would now fuel the growth of both Nova Scotia and New Brunswick. That was certainly the hope of Munson and William Jarvis, who counted on making "a very great profit . . . upon this circuitous route."

Looking at a chart of the Atlantic Ocean, the traffic pattern seemed straightforward. Ships brought captured slaves from Africa to the West Indies. Sugar and rum would then fill the now empty holds and would be delivered to Britain—or traded for timber and foodstuffs in British North America. The ships then docked in England where they loaded up with trade goods to use for rounding up and purchasing slaves in western Africa. Sugar and, sadly, the slave trade turned out to be the lifeblood of the British Empire. With the Maritimes expecting to benefit from what the Thirteen Colonies had lost, hope was more than restored—it was replaced by certainty. Not for long. It turned out that Saint John didn't quite eclipse New York, and Halifax did not quite outshine Philadelphia.

At first, Nova Scotia enjoyed the glow of prosperity. Of all the British North American colonies, it bore the brunt of the Loyalist diaspora's arrival, all of whom required housing, feeding, and the means to create new communities. Petitions and complaints from the new American immigrants would dominate government correspondence for years. The hopeful dreams of the "Old Settlers" of Nova Scotia—Scots, Germans, Acadians, and New Englanders—were lost in the strident din of Loyalist demands.

For a time, it looked as if the Loyalist settlement at Shelburne would supplant Halifax as the new provincial capital. With twelve thousand residents by 1784 it was not only the largest city in British

North America, but also the fourth most populous metropolis in the entire continent, ranking just after New York, Philadelphia, and Boston. Located inside a notch of the province's southwest coast- line, Shelburne indeed boasted a spectacular, well-protected deep- sea harbour, the shape of an open straight razor—which was why it was first named Port Razoir and later dubbed Port Roseway by the early Loyalists. That turned out to be highly prophetic. Promoted by a New York investor group whose leader had never been ashore, the settlement experienced a rapid rise and an even more rapid fall. Nearly all of its proud residents got free haircuts as the value of their properties quickly plummeted to zero. Isolated and nearly impos- sible to reach overland, Shelburne had no natural reason for being there, and by the 1820s its population was down to three hundred. Abandoned except for a small shipyard, the pretend city much later turned out to be the perfect film backdrop, with *Moby Dick* (starring William Hurt, Donald Sutherland, and Gillian Anderson), *The Scarlet Letter*, *Virginia's Run*, *Wilby Wonderful*, and most recently the CBC and Black Entertainment Television miniseries *Book of Negroes* (based on the novel of the same name by Lawrence Hill) among its productions. But the real city never existed as a functioning entity.

Before its decline, however, the Shelburne settlement started out with much more promise, though there were serious challenges be- cause some of the Loyalists were so destitute. Merchant Benjamin Marston, a cousin to Edward Winslow, who had been hired in early 1783 to survey the township, was shocked when he saw the first load of Loyalists disembark in mid-May, before they had an opportunity to construct wooden houses from the planks they were given. "These Poor People are like sheep without a Sheppherd," he recorded in his diary. "They have no men of abilities among them." His first impression of them was soon reinforced as he witnessed their at- tempt to survive in "makeshift tent villages," which quickly became "a brewing, stewing, smelly place, littered with ashes and waste, and rudimentary taverns every few hundred paces." In Marston's view, "the Devil is among these People."

Marston was besieged with complaints about land allocation, since friends of the New York investor group had access to the best lots. Many other questions were raised about how Port Roseway—renamed Shelburne by Nova Scotia governor John Parr following his visit in July 1783—was to be administered. A Loyalist with Tory pretensions, Marston quickly identified the same problem that was later evident in Saint John: "Too much Liberty." The Loyalists might have been downtrodden refugees, yet they were still bravado Americans. "This curs'd Republican Town Meeting spirit," he wrote, "has been the ruin of us already & unless checked by some stricter form of Government it will overset the prospect [which] now presents of retrieving our affairs." Nevertheless, Shelburne initially grew at a rapid pace; by the end of the year Parr could report to the town's namesake, the Earl of Shelburne (who had been ousted as British prime minister in April 1783), about the eight hundred homes which had been built, with more on the horizon, and a population of twelve thousand inhabitants. "I have not a doubt," Parr added, "of It's [*sic*] being, one day or other, the first Port in this part of America."

The other main group of Loyalists arriving in Shelburne were former black slaves such as Boston King and his wife, Violet. And they quickly learned that loyalty to the Crown did not eliminate white prejudice towards them or discriminatory treatment. Perhaps as a way to keep matters civil, the Earl of Shelburne had ordered Marston to establish a settlement exclusively for African Americans. The adjacent community to the northwest, called Birchtown, was about five kilometres from Shelburne and reached via a crude trail through the forest. The land allotments for Black Loyalists were considerably smaller than those granted to white Loyalists in Shelburne—the average farm in Birchtown consisting of thirty-four acres as opposed to the typical seventy-four in Shelburne—the food provisions distributed were even more restrictive, and the resources more limited. Nonetheless, that first year, a feeling of community and camaraderie linked the community in common cause. "Every family had a lot of land," Boston King recalled, "and we exerted all our strength in order to build comfortable huts before the cold weather set in." That, in fact, proved impossible and many settlers survived the winter living in mud bunkers. Still, Birchtown endured; by 1784, the Shelburne-Birchtown area's population was 1,485, making it, as Harvard historian Maya Jasanoff pointed out, "one of the largest free black settlements in North America." There were also approximately two thousand black slaves the white Loyalists had brought with them.

A powerful bond in the community was the presence of religious institutions. Moses Wilkinson, aka "Daddy Moses," a former slave from Virginia, was a popular Methodist preacher who saved, among others, Violet King "from evil tempers." "It pleased the Lord to awaken my wife under the preaching of Mr. Wilkinson," Boston remembered. "She was struck to the ground, and cried out for mercy; she continued in great distress near two hours, when they sent for me." Similarly, David George, who had fled with the British from Charleston, laid the foundation of the Baptist Church in Nova Scotia. George decided to build his church closer to Shelburne on land made available to him by a white Loyalist.

Old hatreds remained firm, however. Unable to subsist on the meagre crops they could grow on their mediocre plots of land, many Black Loyalists in Birchtown were compelled to accept menial jobs working for white Loyalists. Paid low wages and exploited by white farmers, many of whom owned slaves, these free blacks became indentured servants. In the fields, it was impossible to tell them apart from the slaves. In a bitter twist, the Black Loyalists were then accused by discontented and unemployed former Loyalist soldiers of stealing jobs from whites because they accepted paltry wages. On July 26, 1784, tempers boiled over and a "Great Riot," as Marston deemed it, ensued. Angry soldiers went on a rampage and destroyed the property of David George and other free blacks in Shelburne. Brave and stubborn, George tried to stand his ground, until the mob beat him with clubs and "drove me into the swamp," as he later described his ordeal. This attack was rated as the first race riot in North America.

The bleak situation for the Black Loyalists grew worse in 1786, after the British government stopped supplying the refugees with food. Two years later, William Dyott, a "sometime general" in the British army and aide-de-camp to King George III, visited Birchtown at the end of August 1788 and was shocked at the state of life there. "The place is beyond description wretched, situated on the coast in the middle of barren rocks, and partly surrounded by a thick impenetrable wood," he recorded in his travel diary. "Their huts miserable to guard against the inclemency of a Nova Scotia winter, and their existence almost depending on what they could lay up in summer. I think I never saw wretchedness and poverty so strongly perceptible in the garb and the countenance of the human species as in these miserable outcasts." In order to survive, many of them were forced to sell "their property, their clothing and even their very beds," Lieutenant John Clarkson, a notable opponent of the slave trade, recorded in his journal in 1791. (Clarkson's brother, Thomas, an abolitionist leader in England, advised him that when he arrived in Nova Scotia he should not call the Black Loyalists "Blacks or Negroes," but "Africans as a more respectable way of speaking of them.")

Boston King, too, remembered that during this "famine" some of his friends "killed and ate their dogs and cats and poverty and distress prevailed." King himself had to leave Birchtown to seek employment wherever he could find it. At one point, weak from having nothing to eat, he fell on the ground and "expected to die." He did not and believed that the "Lord" had "delivered" him from "all murmurings and discontent." Though King eventually found enough work to sustain him and his family, he had had enough of the hardship and abuse. By early 1792, he joined about 1,200 other Black Loyalists on a journey to Sierra Leone, the "promised land," on board fifteen ships that sailed from Halifax. This second exile had been arranged by John Clarkson, who became the governor of the new colony of Freetown on the coast of Africa.

IT HAD BEEN Nova Scotia's hefty and aging governor John Parr—in 1783 he was almost sixty years old and weighed 250 pounds—who had overseen the transition of the Loyalists from refugees to the nation's vanguard. Parr, historian Peter Burroughs concluded, "did not display the degree of solicitous sympathy the Loyalists felt they deserved, although much of their criticism of Parr reflected despondency, frustration, and anger at strained circumstances." The Loyalists of Nova Scotia had every hope that better days were ahead of them when it was announced in 1792 that London had appointed John Wentworth as the colony's new lieutenant-governor (in 1786, with the appointment of Guy Carleton as governor general of British North America, Parr had been demoted to lieutenant-governor). Having been the provincial surveyor for years, Wentworth knew Nova Scotia, quite literally, like the back of his hand. A man of amiable personality and proven Loyalist principles (he had been New Hampshire's last royal governor before the revolution), Wentworth was an ideal successor to the harried Parr. His appointment made him only the second Loyalist to govern a British colony. The nine-year gap between Wentworth's status as a political refugee and his designation as lieutenant-governor was a remarkable turnabout in fortunes.*

Wentworth's rise in fortune was gradual. Upon being appointed Nova Scotia's surveyor-general, he left his wife, Frances, in England where they had first found sanctuary. By 1784, Frances was reunited with John in Halifax. The two had wed in New Hampshire in 1769 after the death of her first husband, Theodore Atkinson, who was a cousin to both Frances and Wentworth. Frances was not a fan of life

---

*It should be noted that New York Loyalist Edmund Fanning was appointed the lieutenant-governor of Prince Edward Island (then the Island of St. John) in 1786, making him the first Loyalist to govern a colony within the British Empire. Although he promptly gave refugee friends from New Brunswick and Nova Scotia government appointments, he was nonpartisan enough to address the needs of the island's non-Loyalist settlers. During his career he was, in historian J.M. Bumsted's words, "perhaps the most successful of the breed."

in Halifax, especially because Wentworth travelled so much of the time. Bored and lonely, she welcomed the attention and advances of young Prince William Henry, King George III's senior son, during his visit to Nova Scotia in 1786. William made it a habit to bring his ship, HMS *Andromeda*, to Halifax for repairs and supplies. At the age of forty-one (the Prince was twenty-one), Frances was widely considered to still be stunning and dressed at the height of fashion, retaining the sophistication she had gained in England. She became Prince William's mistress and the affair was renewed when the Prince made a second visit to Halifax the following year. Frances described her husband, who knew about her dalliance, in a letter as "the most diffident of men." Or perhaps it was because Wentworth himself also engaged in extramarital affairs. As historian Judith Fingard observed, this episode "illustrates the liberalized relationship [Frances] and John maintained . . . in a style typical of the most civilized as well as the most debauched of Georgian aristocracy in England." Frances's dresses were the talk of the town. As one admirer rhapsodized: "At one ball she appeared in a gown richly interwoven with gold and silver, and trimmed with Italian flowers and the finest silk lace; the gown's train was four yards long, and in her hair and on her wrists was a profusion of diamonds. At the many balls and assemblies she was always the most 'observed' lady present."

In 1791, John and Frances Wentworth sailed from Halifax back to England. When the reconciled couple was in London, John Parr, the governor of Nova Scotia, died, and, having friends in high places in both Halifax and London, Wentworth was named lieutenant-governor of Nova Scotia. He maintained a summer home and farm in the Preston area, a community to the east of Halifax that had been settled by Black Loyalists. There he met an attractive woman named Sarah Colley, a Jamaican Maroon (of African descent). She became his next mistress and bore him an illegitimate son named George. While Frances was back in England, Wentworth also took up with Bridget Lowe, and, as was the custom in the eighteenth century, part of his contract was to arrange for her to marry one Fergus Lowe, who promptly vanished from sight following the ceremony. It gave Halifax something to talk about, but that was only the start of that busy family. When Harriet Colley, one of Sarah's descendants, died at age ninety-eight, in 1991, she left 149 grandchildren, 316 great-grandchildren, 86 great-great-grandchildren, 45 great-great-great-grandchildren, and 6 great-great-great-great-grandchildren. (One of Wentworth's classmates at Harvard was future U.S. president John Adams.)

Wentworth's sixteen-year term of office as Nova Scotia's lieutenant-governor had more than its share of controversy and disappointment, as might have been expected. Just three years after he took the reins of power, the British government abandoned its plans to limit the West Indies trade to the long-suffering Loyalists of the Atlantic coastal colonies. Since 1783, there had been increasing tension between Britain and the United States over outstanding debts, as well as disagreements over boundary lines and the continuing British military presence in the Northwest on disputed territory, among other lingering issues. There was even talk of another war between the two countries. In late 1794, U.S. Chief Justice and special envoy John Jay and Lord Grenville, British foreign secretary (and the son of George Grenville who became prime minister in 1806), negotiated the Treaty of Amity, Commerce, and Navigation between His Britannic Majesty and the United States of America—more commonly known as Jay's Treaty—which was proclaimed in February 1796. By the terms of the treaty, American vessels were given limited access to the lucrative sugar markets of the Caribbean. In an effort to placate its former rebellious colonies, Britain ignored the best interests of its loyal Americans, seriously harming the prospects of both Nova Scotia's and New Brunswick's oceangoing commerce. With the loss of the triangular trade, the Maritime Provinces fell back to harvesting more hope than reality. Still, merchants in both colonies remained supportive of British decisions on foreign policy. Meanwhile, in Upper Canada, the settlement of the U.S. boundary dispute led to the construction of military roads linking Amherstburg, London, Niagara, York (Toronto), and Kingston.

The real hostility to the treaty bubbled up in the United States where diplomat John Jay—who in 1789 had been appointed by President George Washington as the first U.S. Supreme Court chief justice—was accused of caving in to British demands and getting little for Americans in return. Jay's Treaty was roundly castigated in the press as "a pact with the British Satan," and Jay was burned in effigy at protests in New York and Boston. Thomas Jefferson believed the treaty was "a monument of venality" that was sure to damage American relations with France. Jay defended himself by declaring that he had averted a war with Britain, and "to do more was impossible." The president agreed and the U.S. Senate, following two weeks of raucous debate, ratified the treaty.

Given this economic setback, it was miraculous that within two years John Wentworth managed to wipe out Nova Scotia's debt and pull the colony out of economic stagnation. This was mainly accomplished with the introduction of an excise tax on imports; duties on rum, the beverage of choice for Royal Navy seamen and just about everyone else in the colony, proved especially lucrative. "Taxes on rum," Wentworth's biographer Brian Cuthbertson adds, "provided the mainstay of government revenue and wages were often paid in part with it. Rum was the currency of Nova Scotian economic life." But despite his Loyalist principles, Wentworth's background favoured a government run by an aristocracy. He had not, after all, been brought up in the democratic traditions of New England town halls. His father, Mark Hunking Wentworth, was a prominent second-generation New Hampshire merchant whose profitable business depended on good relations with the British. John was born in Portsmouth, New Hampshire, in 1737 and attended Harvard College before joining his father's law firm. In the early 1760s, the younger Wentworth spent time in London representing his father's interests and hobnobbing with influential British politicians. By the time he returned to Portsmouth in 1765, he did so fully supportive of the once-despised Stamp Act and all subsequent British measures to manage the colonies.

In Halifax, Wentworth surrounded himself with like-minded administrators and paid as little attention as he could to the House of Assembly. He feared that the forces unleashed by the American Revolution would undermine the status quo. Like Thomas Carleton in neighbouring New Brunswick, Wentworth's "enemies within" presented a threat, be they American Loyalist refugees or radical descendants of Nova Scotia's New England settlers. Any opposition to His Majesty's government was perceived as disloyalty, rather than simply dissent. Wentworth's final years of his administration were filled with head-on confrontations with the decidedly democratic William Tonge. An ambitious son of New England settlers, Tonge challenged the supremacy of Wentworth's executive council. Under his leadership, the Nova Scotia assembly passed bills that thwarted Wentworth's attempts to interfere in financial matters, especially the lucrative contracts for roads and bridges. Wentworth reacted by rejecting the assembly's nomination of Tonge as its speaker. He further asserted his power by declaring that only he had the authority to decide the outcome of contested elections. Ever the Loyalist aristocrat, Wentworth believed that in fighting the forces of democracy he was only following the playbook for how the British government wanted its colonies to actually be governed.

This tension between the democratic aspirations of the Loyalists and the fear of repeating the events of the American Revolution held hostage every decision made by British North America's colonial governments. It would take many decades for the empire to recover from the loss of those thirteen American colonies, and it was the Loyalists who bore the brunt of the blame for that trauma. The faithful refugees saw it as a matter of banking the fires of democracy until their dearest political aspirations could be achieved. While colonial politicians went head-to-head with their empire-appointed governors, most Loyalist settlers were consumed with simply surviving in their new environs. The empire had given them sanctuary and supplied them with food and building materials, but what of the losses they had sustained in the revolution? Wasn't the new

United States government supposed to compensate them for all the property and possessions that they had seized or destroyed? This subsequent anger was valid, as was its cause, built upon the false notion that the thirteen states in the new republic had been promised such favourable treatment by the Treaty of Paris. Yet without legal compulsion, the state governments simply ignored the "suggestion."

Britain ended up paying the penalty for not hiring more capable negotiators. In 1783, Parliament created the Royal Commission on the Losses and Services of American Loyalists. Initially, the commission held its hearings at Lincoln's Inn Fields in London. It took a while for the Royal Commission on the Losses and Services of American Loyalists to realize that with the majority of Loyalists living in North America, it made little sense to hold their hearings an ocean removed. The victims who most needed compensation could not afford the long ocean voyage to claim it. Between the years of 1785 and 1789, the commissioners held hearings in the major cities of British North America. During that time they examined claims amounting to $40 million but ordered that only $19 million be paid out. The British administrators may have had great intentions and the scale of the compensation was unprecedented at the time. But from the perspective of the Loyalists, the arithmetic involved was criminal.

Whenever news of the commission reached their backwoods settlements, the Loyalists of the Maritimes (and even a handful from Bermuda) made the arduous journeys to Halifax and Saint John. Some, who had been living near Annapolis Royal, decided to attend the hearings in Saint John rather than Halifax. As their ship neared the New Brunswick coast, it ran aground. All but seventeen of the Loyalist castaways died of exposure in the woods where they had sought shelter from the icy winds. Joshua Chandler, who had journeyed to England for compensation in 1784—as well as his daughter and son—were among the victims. On another occasion, a group of forty-four settlers (with seventeen witnesses in tow) from Nova Scotia's Cumberland County sailed down the Bay of Fundy to petition the commissioners, only to be told that a dozen of their number were not considered worthy of compensation.

The commission was ostentatiously parsimonious when it came to doling out compensation to their loyal Americans who had suffered so much for the empire. After John Lyon risked his life to return to Connecticut to acquire the necessary paperwork to demonstrate his £1,390 in losses, the commissioners awarded him a measly £270. Some Loyalists denounced the whole procedure as little more than a tight-fisted inquisition. Munson Jarvis summed up these feelings in a letter to his brother William in England: "I must confess that people in general are much dissatisfied with the small pittance allowed them and that it is much short of what they expected." While the process was disappointing for merchants like Munson Jarvis, it was, as noted, utterly devastating for his widowed sister, Polly Dibblee.

STEPHEN JARVIS, who had finally arrived in New Brunswick with Amelia and their little daughter Betsey in June of 1785, decided not to appear before the royal commission, even though it was just a day's journey down the St. John River from his home in Fredericton. The stories of futility retold by his cousins Munson and Polly dissuaded him. His name, however, made it into the official transcripts. Stephen came to the aid of Eli Benedict, a fellow Danbury Loyalist, by writing a deposition on his behalf, testifying that Benedict's father was "a Loyalist and possessed the lands before mentioned." In the end, it was this solidarity in the face of misfortune that would see the Loyalists of the Maritimes through the difficult decades of settlement.

Stephen had brought some dry goods with him to start his own business in Fredericton. By October 1785, Stephen and his family had moved into their "small hovel," where they "thought themselves to be as happy as princes." Among the few things that Stephen and Amelia had packed for their six-week sea voyage was the sword that had been his weapon while he served as a lieutenant in the South Carolina Dragoons. Unbeknownst to either of them, this sword would once again, in less than thirty years, be used to defend loyal British subjects against Americans.

Because they had delayed their departure from Connecticut, Stephen and Amelia had missed that first miserable winter in the Maritimes. Stephen's first memories of their new home thus lacked the desperation of the settlers of 1783. "On the 15th of June, 1785, I landed at Fredericton with a wife, one child and a guinea only in my pocket, with one year's half-pay to draw from and with this I had provided for our future existence. Government allowed the soldiers and refugees three years' rations, and even with this bounty many families suffered greatly for the want of provisions, and had not the forests abounded with moose, many families would have perished."

The house that Jarvis had commissioned a year previously had still not been built, but instead of tents embedded in snow, they rented "a small hovel" for £10. "We found it impossible to remain, for the proprietor had during the preceding winter made a ceiling of slabs and bark overlaid with plaster or mortar or clay, and which he had disturbed in the spring so that every wind that blew our floor was covered with dirt. In this situation we were obliged to live for several weeks before I could possibly find another place to shelter us from the heat," he remembered. "The only difference in the two houses was that we could eat our food without it being flavoured by quite so much dirt as in our first habitation. I commenced building, and in October we got into our new house, and thought ourselves as happy as princes."

Thanks to the "small assortment of goods" that his cousin Munson Jarvis had advanced to him during their stay in Saint John, Stephen "commenced business." The son of a Connecticut farmer and war veteran now tried to establish himself as a merchant in Fredericton. Over the next nine years, Jarvis managed to make ends meet in the tiny colonial capital. By 1797, he and Amelia had four more children: Frederick Starr, Frances, George, and Rachel.

Family and business matters were not the only events that occupied the Loyalist veteran, though. Jarvis never got over the thrill of wearing a uniform, riding a horse, or preparing for battle. His memoir noted, "I was of an ambitious disposition and fond of Military life, and held during the time I remained in the Province, from the year 1785 until the year 1809, the following commissions in the Militia, viz., Captain, Major, Major of Brigade, Deputy Adjutant General, and Lieutenant Colonel, independent of the office of Postmaster, and for sixteen years the great part of the summer was employed in disciplining the Militia of the county, without any other remuneration than the thanks of the governor, with great promises, but his leaving the Province all those expectations failed."

One high point in Jarvis's career as a militia commander was the day his local corps lined the road into Fredericton to welcome Prince Edward, the King's son, as he rode in his carriage to Government House. The Loyalist who had talked with Washington now beheld a son of King George III—the prince whose daughter became Queen Victoria. One might suppose that this would have been the highlight of a Loyalist's life. At forty, Stephen had established himself as a businessman in a loyal colony's capital, had a handful of healthy children, and was a commander in the local militia. But, in retrospect, Stephen dismissed his years in Fredericton in just two sentences: "Nothing of any particular interest happened for many years. I went on a progressive way, building and adding to my convenience."

Considering that he was often in debt, it is easy to see why in later years Jarvis wanted to forget what was almost a quarter century spent in New Brunswick. However, those years included near-death experiences, politics, and a visit to Connecticut as well as his appointment as Fredericton's postmaster.

On August 21, 1798, he recorded the following incident:

> Mrs. Jarvis and self retired to rest last night with a candle burning by our bedside. We had scarcely fell asleep, when a sudden gust of wind forcing through a broken pane of glass blew the

window curtain to the candle which instantly took fire. When I awoke, I found the window curtain all in flames and in an instant more, must have communicated with the curtains round the bed, as they touched that of the window. However, I had just time to snatch the flaming curtain from the window, and with the assistance of Mrs. Jarvis, extinguish the flames, with no other damage than being considerably burnt. . . . Mrs. Jarvis was slightly burnt in one of her hands, her breast, leg and foot, and in her confusion either against the table or candle, has much bruised her hip.

Nine months after that incident, the Jarvises' last child, William Botsford, who would eventually rise to prominence in Upper Canada, was born. His middle name honoured a Connecticut Loyalist refugee named Amos Botsford. The latter was speaker of the New Brunswick House of Assembly from 1786 to 1812 and boarded with the Jarvis family during his time in Fredericton. In addition to allowing Stephen and Amelia to reminisce over past times in Connecticut, Botsford's stays with them were an appreciated addition to the family budget. In 1801, Stephen considered letting his name stand for Fredericton's seat in the House of Assembly, but he did not follow through. His cousin Munson was the only New Brunswick Jarvis family member to pursue politics, sitting in the House as a member for Saint John in 1804.

Perhaps the nostalgic conversations about Connecticut brought on a bout of homesickness. Whatever the cause, in the summer of 1801, Stephen and Amelia sailed south and visited with their relatives in Stamford. It had been sixteen years since they had walked the streets of a town once filled with hostile rebels. When Samuel Jarvis Jr., Stephen's cousin, wrote about the reunion, he remarked that Stephen and Amelia "made us all happy in seeing them." Samuel had spent some time in New Brunswick, but abandoned his Loyalist principles and returned home. This did not tempt Stephen. The couple went back to Fredericton. A move was in their future—just eight years away—but it would not be to the nation that had so violently persecuted them.

IN 1805, it looked very much as if an icy river would do what Patriot soldiers and rebel persecutors had not been able to accomplish. While on his rounds as a mail carrier, Stephen Jarvis had to harness his horses and sleigh across the frozen St. John River to the village of Sheffield. Normally, during the cold pit of a New Brunswick winter, the river froze to such an extent that it became one long icy highway, allowing Loyalists from Woodstock to Kingston the opportunity to hop into horse-drawn sleighs and visit one another more quickly than they could in sailing vessels during the summer.

Stephen recounted his adventure in a letter to an acquaintance.

My horses and sleigh slumped through the upper ice, and by a violent plunge of the horses, threw me headlong out of the sleigh. While endeavoring to recover my feet, one of them was caught between the runner and the ice where I was confined until I could break it with the heel of my other foot. The horses were up to their backs in water, and a passenger, Mrs. Bisset was in the sleigh. I was able to get into it and without any other difficulty, drove . . . as fast as I could. . . . My foot and ankle is much swelled and am in the most excruciating pain.

Jarvis was almost vanquished by a river. And yet, this and his other adventures were dismissed as "nothing of any particular interest."

Characteristically for Jarvis, what did have "particular interest" was how he was treated by those in authority. During the revolution, whenever he felt his pride had been tested (read—injured) by his father or a commanding officer, he had reacted strongly, defending his principles with the fanatic conviction of a religious convert. The incident that would redirect his life almost as profoundly as his joining the British in 1777 was his treatment at the hands of the New

Brunswick government forty years later. "About the year 1807, an action took place between one of our ships of war and the American ship *Chesapeake*, and it appeared to me that war would ensue between the two Governments, and I offered my services in case the Militia should be called into actual service, which offer was thankfully accepted, but when it was found necessary to embody the Militia, the command was given to another person. This so far excited my resentment that I immediately made up my mind to quit the Province, and made a visit to Upper Canada." Feeling passed over, Jarvis immediately vowed to leave New Brunswick.

The following year he visited Upper Canada, the colony once governed by John Graves Simcoe (his commanding officer in the Queen's Rangers) where his cousin William Jarvis still held a government position. Stephen stayed with William in their "hospitable mansion . . . where I spent a most agreeable visit, he has a most amiable wife and family." This was a bit of an exaggeration, at least when it came to describing the next generation of the Jarvis dynasty. William's son, Samuel Peters Jarvis, had recently been in a street brawl that involved his classmates and some Native children. One of the latter was almost killed in the fighting, and young Jarvis was going to be brought before the local magistrate.

Delinquent sons of cousins aside, what Stephen Jarvis saw in Upper Canada was so encouraging that he made one of his trademark snap decisions. Upper Canada was where his destiny lay, and that was where he would take his family. Even the impending marriage of Frances would not delay his departure. Leaving his daughter behind in New Brunswick to marry Major John Maule of the 104th Regiment on July 16, Stephen herded a highly reluctant (but compliant) Amelia and their unmarried children into canoes on June 30, 1809, and headed westward for Upper Canada.

Looking back on the trip, Stephen wrote,

> We traversed the waters of the St. John in birch canoes, lying on the beach where there were no inhabitants, much disturbed with

gnats and mosquitoes at night, and crossing the portage from the waters of St. John to St. Lawrence, thirty-six miles, most up to our knees, and black flies to annoy us. We at last encountered all our difficulties, and reached Quebec all in good health . . . after remaining a week, we proceeded to Montreal where we remained one week longer, providing ourselves with such necessaries as would be necessary for commencing housekeeping. We again set off . . . for Kingston. We were fourteen days on our passage to Kingston. I . . . was ordered a passage in one of his Majesty's armed vessels, and arrived at York [Toronto] on the 28th of August, and took possession of a house which had already been purchased for me, and began to make ourselves comfortable.

Having acquired 1,200 acres of land near York and a new job in the civil service with his cousin William, Stephen Jarvis had survived his midlife crisis and was looking forward to a life that would—finally—compensate him for all that he had suffered as a Loyalist. But destiny was far from finished with Stephen Jarvis.

7

THE SELF-MADE GOVERNOR WHO
WORSHIPPED HIS CREATOR

Military hero leads top commando regiment! Becomes founding governor of Upper Canada! Directs armed defence against Napoleon Bonaparte! Just then, another opportunity presents itself.

I F CANADA BOASTED a founding spirit it had to be the crusty colonel and idealistic reformer, risk-seeking adventurer, and Toronto's proud founder John Graves Simcoe. He had commanded the Queen's Rangers during the Revolutionary War with brilliance, grit, and exactness that prompted his men to obey when he spoke. A severe illness had compelled him to return to England just prior to the British defeat at Yorktown in 1781, after which he served briefly as a member of the British House of Commons. But as a military man, he craved more responsibility and much more adventure.

In 1791, the British Parliament passed the Constitutional Act, which authorized the division of Quebec into Upper and Lower Canada, with provision for an elected legislative assembly. This was a geographic alignment of British North America necessitated by the influx of thousands of English-speaking Loyalists into largely French-speaking and Catholic Quebec. This was to be no

American-style democracy, however. The real power was in the hands of Guy Carleton—Lord Dorchester as of 1786—the governor in chief of Upper and Lower Canada, who was based in Quebec City. He was assisted by two appointed lieutenant-governors. Major-General Alured Clarke, who had commanded British troops during the Revolutionary War, became the first lieutenant-governor of Lower Canada and played a key role in implementing the provisions of the Constitutional Act.

For Upper Canada, Dorchester had urged that Sir John Johnson (the son of Sir William Johnson) be appointed the colony's founding lieutenant-governor. Johnson was respected by Loyalists and Aboriginals alike for his work as superintendent general and inspector general of the Six Nations Indians and those in the Province of Quebec. However, the British government felt that Johnson might be too distracted by his many property and commercial interests and instead chose Simcoe, ignoring Dorchester's wishes. Offered the position of lieutenant-governor of Upper Canada, Simcoe accepted the appointment with enthusiasm, despite his unhappiness that Lord Dorchester turned out to be his superior. In his new role, Simcoe established the foundations for both the Province of Ontario and the City of Toronto—which was quickly renamed York by Simcoe as part of his campaign of Anglicization to obliterate any and all Aboriginal designations.

York, where Simcoe reigned, became the centre of his hyperactive administration that created the outlines of a new North-of-America culture. In the process, Simcoe made as many casual friends as dedicated enemies, but led a formidably useful career. His half decade as lieutenant-governor allowed him to innovate and demonstrate both his statesmanship and his frustrations. During the four and half years of his administration (illness forced him to leave the province in 1796 though he did not officially resign until 1798), Simcoe set down the perimeters not only of a city and a province but for a country. It was he who endowed that barely conceived nation with evidences of a founding identity and invested the energy to bring it about. Simcoe's drive and determination, plus an intuitive strategic impulse, helped create a land worth fighting for by well, Canadians, damn it.

Simcoe was wildly both ahead of—and behind—his times. Being a staunch conservative, he advocated the creation of a landed aristocracy and called for the Church of England to become the doctrinaire state religion. At the same time, acting as a courageous reformer, he was the first British statesman to introduce anti-slavery legislation. That was a brave step, considering the prevailing social ethic that then encouraged families in good standing—William and Hannah Jarvis among them—to keep slaves on their farms and in their cellars. His prototype was responsible for the ultimate banning of slavery in the British Empire—and elsewhere.

Simcoe's spirit was troubled by the fact that, unlike some of his contemporaries in the remaining colonies of British North America, he never received any title, which he so coveted (until the wrongly named Lord Simcoe Hotel was opened on King Street West in downtown Toronto in 1956). He was never honoured with a lordship or even a knighthood, which was how ambitious men then measured their status. In his case, this was the litmus test of his disturbing devotion to sponsoring fundamental reforms. Simcoe's baiting of the holders of dug-in privilege and practitioners of social and political entitlements went neither unnoticed nor unpunished.

Simcoe was a self-made man who worshipped his creator. He made history but was never a pleasant hail-fellow-well-met kind of character, dripping bon mots or trying to ingratiate his presence among the embroidered elite of George III's royal court. His job description—if he had one—was to imagine himself as a streak of lightning that illuminates each situation while drastically replacing worn-out infrastructures and challenging the status quo. To place his quicksilver approach into a slightly more contemporary setting: he behaved as if he were an unquiet secular spirit pumped up by a large dose of "uppers" that would not allow him to temper his temper.

"This colony, which I mean to show forth with all the advantages of British protection as a better Government than the United States can possibly obtain," he wrote in January 1791 before he departed London, "should in its very foundations provide for every assistance that can possibly be procured for the arts and sciences, and for every embellishment that hereafter may decorate and attract notice, and may point it out to the neighbouring States as a superior, more happy, and more polished form of Government." Simcoe's legacy helped create the political and social framework for English Canada until it was finally ready to claim nationhood in 1867. No other provincial magistrates had such national impact. As founding lieutenant-governor of Upper Canada, Simcoe came up with a seventeen-point vision statement which he spent eighteen months drafting. In it, Simcoe offered a series of ambitious and unrealistically expensive plans for the force-fed economic, constitutional, religious, and educational development of his new territory. A crucial part of his master plan, namely deciding which church his parishioners could be married in, was thwarted by the Loyalist settlers themselves. It quickly became a dominant issue. He wildly supported an Episcopal establishment, which meant that the bishops were in charge, which in turn considerably reduced the Enlightenment quotient. The harsh realities of the Loyalists' existing denominations and the unwillingness of the Brits to fund the Church of England combined to derail Simcoe's intent. "His strongest personal disappointment came from the refusal of full endowment to the Church of England," wrote his biographer, Stanley R. Mealing. "Anglican Loyalists were never numerically dominant in Upper Canada."

The denominational spat gained purchase when Simcoe revised the Marriage Act, allowing only Anglican ministers to join impatient couples in matrimony. It was the Loyalists themselves who rejected this narrow dictum. The Loyalists and other settlers belonged to dissenting faiths—mainly Methodist, Presbyterian, Baptist, and Congregationalist—and wanted to be married by their own ministers. In many areas there was no resident clergy at all. Marriage services were often conducted by commanding officers of military posts or by civil magistrates. If the legality of these marriages was doubtful, their children were branded as illegitimate and they were prohibited from inheriting property. The Marriage Act passed by the second session of the legislature of Upper Canada in May 1793 provided that past weddings were legally binding, yet stipulated that future marriages must follow the Church of England catechism. As there were now more dissenters than members of the Church of England in Upper Canada, this aroused a tsunami of criticism about a delicate subject. In 1796, the magistrates of the eastern districts asked that ministers of all denominations be allowed to solemnize marriages, but Simcoe would not hear of it, dismissing the idea as the product of "a wicked head and disloyal heart." That was the governor digging in.

If Loyalist children were sent south because of the availability of higher education in the United States, Simcoe prophesized their British principles "would be perverted." Education, he felt, was one of the strongest holds that Great Britain had over its colonies. "Loyalty which glories in the honest pride in having withstood all the tempests of Rebellion, will be totally undermined and subverted by different principles being instilled into the rising generations," preached the ultra-stubborn but immovably faithful Simcoe. That he did not achieve his objectives was due more to the London government's stand-pat attitudes than to objections by his parishioners—the Brits were generally more interested in the development of Lower Canada than investing time and effort in Upper Canada. According to Mealing, "the plan he had laid in England was more ambitious, to control not only the location but also the nature of new settlements. The instrument intended for that purpose was his provincial corps, the second Queen's Rangers, and the model of their proposed operation were the Roman military colonies. Disbanded Rangers would form the nuclei of future settlements; around which immigrants would 'coalesce as British Subjects.' This plan was the most cherished of Simcoe's projects for Upper Canada. He saw it as an antidote to the insidious growth of frontier democracy." His Rangers functioned as defenders of "social cohesion [but they] never received a fair test of practicality, because neither the imperial government nor the commander-in-chief at Quebec could be induced to think of them as anything but ordinary troops." Lord Dorchester finally took charge of the Rangers' work and responsibilities in June 1796. For the next six years, the Rangers were relegated to being employed as . . . oh, the ignominy of it all . . . road builders! At the heart of Simcoe's problem was that he never could persuade the imperial administration that his province should be treated as "a special foundation" instead of as a normal colony.

Some of his reforms were smooth sailing, such as his appointment of Captain Charles Stevenson as deputy quartermaster-general. Stevenson was a trusted family friend and advisor who frequently popped up in Simcoe's wife, Elizabeth's, diary. When Simcoe was told that William Osgoode, a British judge (after whom Ontario's leading law school was named), had been appointed to head Upper Canada's law department as chief justice, he was delighted. "In regard to the legal appointments, the placing of so respectable a Man as Mr. Osgoode at the Head of the law Department leaves me nothing to desire on that Subject, and I shall be well content without the slightest wish for Recommendation in any of the legal situations or vacancies that may happen, provided that secondarily to Integrity & Ability they be filled by such persons as appear to have the most Influence, and exert it in support of His Majesty's Government."

Mealing noted that Osgoode got on especially well with the lieutenant-governor whom he joined at Quebec in June 1792 on his way to Upper Canada. He had lived with the Simcoes at Newark for a spell and wrote periodically to Elizabeth long after leaving the province. Two years following Osgoode's departure for Lower Canada in 1794, Simcoe still found his absence "most severely oppressive." The two agreed on most questions, including their mistrust of merchants as monopolists; but Osgoode never felt the intensity of Simcoe's commitment to the province. His own Toryism was far more rigid. His hostility to Americans was unqualified and more than a little hysterical: he thought of New York as "the very Nest & Hotbed of Turbulence and Disaffection." Nevertheless, Osgoode's measures did regularize and extend the jurisdiction of the untrained justices of the peace and district magistrates who settled most of the legal disputes in the province. Simcoe retained his own ideas about whether attorneys or judges should be on his colonial executive: "I beg to submit seriously to the consideration of His Majesty's Ministers, whether any of the Gentlemen of the Law (excepting the Chief Justice) should have a seat in the Executive, or even the legislative Council. Unless in the latter be necessary to prevent the Judges from being elected in the House of Assembly, as is now the practice in New Brunswick," he maintained.

With utmost faith in eighteenth-century British parliamentary government and its notion that the rule of law was primarily in the hands of wealthy noblemen and landowners, Simcoe established a top-down government in Upper Canada in which power remained firmly within the appointed Executive Council—and the council appointees were all influential cohorts Simcoe trusted. He was convinced that an appointed Executive Council—in other words, a functioning pseudo-aristocracy—was exactly what was needed "to counteract any notions of the Canadians rejecting the King and creating a republic."

But given that he had Loyalist Americans living in Upper Canada with expectations for a more democratic form of government, Simcoe created the structure for a third tier of administration. These were the town councils which recognized that most of the provinces' first settlers had grown up or lived a good part of their lives in the United States and would not be happy unless some form of direct democracy was implemented. Simcoe was certain that the limited powers of these councils would be enough to appease the republican-minded exiled Yanks. That was not always the case. He treated governing as a moveable feast. It didn't matter if the trail to getting his way was bumpy; a detour and others' examples helped pave the way, even if occasionally—very occasionally—he had to sound humble. Hence his diffident request to Henry Dundas, the secretary of state at the Home Department, and Lord Grenville, the foreign secretary, to appoint William Jarvis to a position in his Upper Canadian administration. "I beg leave in the strongest Terms, and which I have heretofore had the Honour of expressing to Lord Grenville & Yourself, to recommend Mr. William Jarvis for the Offices of Secretary and Clerk of the Council, as held by Mr. Odell in New Brunswick." That did the trick.

WILLIAM JARVIS EXPECTED a lot out of life, but he was continually being disappointed. He had risked all for the Crown and anticipated that there would be a certain *quid pro quo*. In the war's aftermath, he journeyed to England to seek opportunity and redress for his family and other Loyalists. This quest for a fortune proved elusive. At first, he had reason to be hopeful; in mid-December 1785, a few months following his twenty-ninth birthday, he married the lovely, twenty-three-year-old Miss Hannah Owen Peters, the daughter of Reverend Dr. Samuel Peters, a Loyalist who literally had been driven out of his home in Hebron, Connecticut—150 kilometres northeast of the Jarvis family home in Stamford. William and Hannah had a lasting marriage that produced seven children, though like her husband, Hannah was never quite satisfied with her lot in in life.

While he was in England, William Jarvis lobbied British officials for higher compensation for his family members, with limited success. In a letter of July 1787, he wrote to his brother Munson that the payments to Loyalists thus far had been so minimal that "some have run mad with despair and disappointment." Ever resourceful, William also worked as a purchasing agent for Munson's business in Saint John, arranging for the shipment of such items as iron bars and pots, knitting pins, steel compasses, rope, twine, and, of course, chamber pots.

Most significantly, he remained close to Simcoe. For Jarvis, this was a smart maneuver. Jarvis was soon on his way back to North

America with a status and position that made him proud—or so that was what he believed when he and Hannah and their growing family boarded the HMS *Henneken* in April 1792 bound for Quebec. The ocean voyage was not an easy one, especially one "awful night," as Jarvis recorded in his journal, when he and Hannah thought they and their children were doomed. But the weather improved and they finally landed in Quebec on June 11, 1792. "Many Gentlemen at Quebec gave a great deal of Attention to me," Jarvis wrote without a drop of hidden humility. This interest, if it was indeed more than a figment of his haughty imagination, was owed entirely to his connection to Simcoe. Jarvis, according to Simcoe, had been a loyal British subject. He had shown a "firm and faithful attachment which at a very early period of his life led him and his family to take up Arms for its protection," Simcoe told Henry Dundas in August 1791. That recommendation led to Jarvis's appointment as the first provincial secretary and clerk of the Executive Council of Upper Canada.

Jarvis was, of course, grateful to Simcoe, but unhappy with the modest annual salary of £300, which could not sustain the high lifestyle he and Hannah coveted. He tried to make extra income registering land patents, but that proved impossible when John White, the attorney general, claimed half the fees but left Jarvis paying all of the expenses of the legal transactions. Once the family relocated to York in 1798, they lived in a log house Jarvis had had built on the outskirts of York (today near the corner of Shelbourne and Adelaide Streets in downtown Toronto) with their six black slaves. "A spacious room in one corner of that served as the office of the provincial secretary," as Loyalist historian Robert Allen described it. "The living rooms of the family were located at the rear and upstairs. On the second floor about the office, and reached by a handsome winding staircase from the main hall, was a large drawing room where parties and balls were frequently held. . . . Horses, cows, sheep and pigs were kept on the property which was surrounded by a solid fence with a high peaked gate."

Jarvis suffered from a bad bout of pretentiousness, which in small-town, gossipy York led to much snickering behind his back. As Allen points out, he was caustically referred to as "Mr. Secretary Jarvis." Some years later, Stephen Jarvis, who worked in William's office for several years after he moved to York, wrote this unflattering assessment to William's brother Munson:

> You will naturally expect that I should say something of your Brother, the Secretary. Sorry I am to say all his flattering encouragements held out to me before my arrival in this country have become illusive, and instead of being of service to me has been of the greatest injury. . . . He is over head and ears in debt, despised by the Government, cannot get credit . . . and nothing but his amiable family retains him in his situation; and in short my dear Sir he has neither Religion, Honor, or Honesty in his Nature. These are hard words, my dear friend, but they are no less true. He neither fears God, Man or the Devil.

Constantly living beyond his means did not help William Jarvis's disposition. In 1795, while he was still based in Newark, he challenged four men to duels—still the foolish way gentlemen settled their differences—when he was accused of maligning their reputations. Three of the challenges were dismissed, but one almost took place until a senior administrator wisely halted it. Hannah Jarvis, too, was as resentful as her husband that things did not always turn in her favour. William frequently bemoaned that Simcoe had not appointed him to the Executive Council. Mrs. Jarvis knew the reason why: the lieutenant-governor, she told her father, was under the influence of "a lot of Pimps, Sycophants and Lyars."

Hannah's bitter jealousy aside, she was not entirely wrong. In appointing a local postmaster, Simcoe kept it simple by picking a youthful roustabout—but it had to be *his* roustabout. "The Office of Printer seems to be of the utmost Importance," he noted. "It has been suggested to me that by annexing the Office of Post Master to that of Printer a sufficient Salary may be annexed to induce some Person to expatriate." Simcoe tapped twenty-one-year-old Louis Roy, an apprentice working at a print shop in Montreal, and hired him as the first King's Printer for the province. Roy lasted exactly a year, then closed his printing business in 1794 and left for New York. The reasons for his departure were "the result of the hardship of frontier life"—plus John Simcoe's temper.

In his *Historical Narratives of Early Canada*, Ontario author William Wilson recorded Simcoe's previous selection of the same sophomore to be the province's first newspaper editor: "His Excellency assumed the editor's good sense and discretion would induce him to give preference to information which was most favourable to the British government and to feature articles of a useful and instructive nature." Simcoe emphasized that the *Gazette*'s primary function was to disseminate government matters, such as his speeches from the throne. Only when there was "a dearth of political intelligence" was the paper permitted to provide its readers with details of local and international interest. Its main mandate was to serve as the government's mouthpiece and its first editor. The newspaper contained a proclamation by "His Excellency Lieutenant Governor John Graves Simcoe" calling for "the suppression of Vice, Profaneness, and Immorality." (That really wasn't news.) It directed all "Peace Officers and Constables" to prosecute to the limit of the law all persons "who shall presume to offend" laws pertaining to the above and to prosecute "all persons who contrary to their duty shall be remiss or negligent in putting the said Laws into execution." (Neither was that.)

Simcoe also appointed Peter Russell as collector of customs, auditor, and receiver-general. According to his biographer, Edith Firth, he

was never considered one of the great men of Ontario. Although later criticism has unjustly charged him with greed for land, his contemporaries objected to his greed for fees and offices. As administrator he was cautious, practical, capable, painstaking—and greedy. Unlike Simcoe he had little imagination, sometimes had difficulty making decisions, and was willing to devote much thought and effort to detail. Russell, however, was a capable administrator. Yet the record of legislation during his administration is impressive, not for great statutes but for those which corrected abuses, improved [living] conditions, or made the machinery of government work more smoothly.

Simcoe's appointment of David W. Smith as surveyor-general was questionable as well. "Smith, who had come to Canada directly from England, was unfamiliar with and unimpressed by the democratic notions the Loyalists had brought with them from the [Thirteen] Colonies," Wilson wrote. "He was contemptuous of the concept of democracy whose public meetings, he declared, were always 'attended by riot and confusion.' Smith related elections not to public policy, but to raucous popular festivals. Despite his disdain for 'this darned election business,' Smith dearly wanted a seat in the Assembly where he would 'take great pleasure in framing laws for the lands I have had so much pleasure in laying out.'"

In 1792, Smith was elected (by acclamation) a member of the first Upper Canadian House of Assembly, for Suffolk and Essex (southwest of Toronto), and returned to office five more times. Then he visited England, though he did not retire from his position until 1804 and collected his salary long after he left the country. It gets worse. Created a baronet in 1821, Smith received the title that Simcoe had so long coveted.

While in office, Simcoe pursued the promise of producing copper coinage for his pragmatic republic, but it remains difficult to discover how well it was received. "It is an object of the utmost Importance to the Country that the Species of small coinage should be circulated amongst the Inhabitants; at present the Farmer has no other means of obtaining such necessaries as he may want, but by bartering the produce of his Land for them with the petty Merchant, who by this means sets his own price on both commodities," he maintained. The fifth and last session of his first Parliament met on May 16 and was prorogued on June 20, 1796. The most important piece of legislation was an act to ascertain and limit the value of current coins (until the 1820s, Upper Canada used coins from Britain, Spain, France, and the United States). The penalty for tendering false coins was one year's imprisonment and one hour in the pillory for the first offence. For the second time around the culprit was adjudged guilty of a felony and executed without benefit of clergy. Eventually, a mint was established under the title of the Copper Company of Upper Canada and a number of half pennies were struck. They were dated 1794 and 1796 but didn't have wide circulation. Later more metallic and paper currency was issued.

THE LEAST DISPENSABLE MEMBER of the lieutenant-governor's entourage was his petite and lively wife, the exquisite Elizabeth Posthuma Gwillim, who supplemented her husband's presence and kept classic diaries that made history. It was perfect casting. The direct heiress to a major fortune, her father (who had served as General Wolfe's aide-de-camp) had died before she was born; her mother died in her childbirth. Elizabeth came from an upper-class Devon family and was very much in tune with the Age of Enlightenment into which she was born. Married at sixteen to a man twice her age, she produced a family of eleven children, and, between births, maintained a classic daily journal that would become better known than her husband. "What is strikingly impressive is how she made it her business to notice everything, to make sense of all that came her way," states Mary Quayle Innis, who edited Elizabeth's diary. Adds Canadian historian Michael Gnarowski: "One places Elizabeth Gwillim readily on a roster of remarkable English women who accompanied their men folk and left a cultural legacy upon which the arts of the New World would be founded."

Her diary entries dovetailed with her husband's more somber professional observations, dwelling on the small but urgent epiphanies of daily life in the wilderness. She turned out to be not only an

incisive observer of her new environment, but also an amateur bot-
anist and watercolour artist whose sketches brought home the only
pictorial record of Upper Canada's evolution. A typically compelling
diary entry:

> We dined in the woods on Major Shanks' farm lot where an ar-
> bour of hemlock pine was prepared, and a band of music stationed
> near. We dined on large perch and venison. Jacob the Mohawk was
> there. He danced Scotch reels with more ease and grace than any
> person I ever saw & had the air of a Prince. The picturesque way
> in which he held a black blanket, gave it the air of a Spanish cloak.
> His leggings were scarlet bands. I never saw so handsome a figure.
> Geese and blackbirds seen which denotes the approach of spring.

Simcoe's stay in Upper Canada was brief but hectic. Sadly, he remains a tragic figure—not because he didn't accomplish enough but
because he was not granted the greatest gift of all: the time to exploit
his talents to the full; to express his enduring paternalistic love of the
country he had tried to civilize. It was indeed tragic that Simcoe died
at fifty-four years of age on his way to Asia, and that he never had the
chance to finish what he had started or to realize his final act as the
newly appointed commander-in-chief of the Indian subcontinent—a
prestigious and powerful posting that seemed tailor-made for his
dramatic ministrations.

Those crucial years in charge of Upper Canada placed Simcoe
in a unique category as one of Canada's essential stepfathers. "In
only a little over five years Simcoe had shaped the future province of
Ontario for good and ill and marked out the military paths by which
the second northward march was to be halted in 1812," so wrote Canadian historian Thomas H. Raddall. "That was monument enough
for any man."

The happy accident that the Loyalist refugees settled in Upper
Canada saved the northern part of the French Empire, first for the
British, and later for Canadians. Having settled into Upper Canada

and the Maritimes, the Loyalists secured these areas for the British Crown. They were soon to be joined by waves of emigrants from the United Kingdom and other parts of Europe who increased Upper Canada's population from about 100,000 in 1815 to 932,000 by 1851. (By the Act of Union of 1840 that combined Upper and Lower Canada into the Province of Canada from 1841 to 1867, Upper Canada was known as Canada West.) Their dominance was a sometime thing. A formative but not frequently mentioned phenomenon, this mountainous wave of migration following the end of the Napoleonic Wars altered the landscape. They came by transatlantic shuttles: the great timber transports carrying ships' masts east, returning with human cargo in their crowded holds. They were escaping the Irish potato famine, religious oppression, jammed tenements, budget-conscious superiors, general cussedness, or just nasty in-laws. Simcoe wasn't there to witness his new country being breech-birthed into life, but he would have approved.

IN MORE SPECIFIC TERMS, it was settlement policies implemented by Simcoe and his immediate successors that determined the course of Upper Canadian development for the next generation. Simcoe gave both expression and impetus to the blend of conservatism, loyalty, and emphasis on economic progress that was to dominate the province before and after the War of 1812. The most persistently energetic governor sent to British North America after the American Revolution, he not only articulated faith in imperial destiny but became its most sympathetic and persuasive advocate. Convincing the Loyalists that their destiny matched his vision, however, was not as straightforward as Simcoe had imagined.

The fleeing Loyalist refugees who populated the lands of the upper St. Lawrence River and the northern shores of Lake Ontario became a useful buffer zone against future American expansion—at least, that's how Simcoe saw it. The officials who were appointed to govern this vast territory had their own visions of how to prevent formation of another republican America. Under Simcoe, the favoured scenario never changed. His aim remained to establish a religious monopoly for the Church of England and to install a permanent elite that would create a countervailing court on the Canadian side of the Atlantic. The farming class and middle-class Loyalists had other expectations. They were, after all, lapsed Americans—even if in exile. Over time there emerged a vision of government that was neither American nor British—and even if it could not yet be called Canadian, that's exactly what it was.

"A Government should be formed for a Country," argued Loyalist Richard Cartwright in 1792. "Not a country strained and distorted for the Accommodation of a preconceived and speculative scheme of Government." Cartwright had grown up in Albany, New York, and following the revolution he became, arguably, Kingston's most prominent merchant (his grandson was the staunch Liberal Party politician, Sir Richard Cartwright, who illuminated Wilfrid Laurier's cabinet). Cartwright imagined a different kind of Upper Canada than Simcoe. The lieutenant-governor wanted to transplant England to the shores of Lake Ontario, while Cartwright and other similarly minded Loyalists supported parliamentary government and British institutions adapted to a colonial setting, not "on copying all the subordinate establishments without considering the great disparity of the two countries in every respect." For this reason, Cartwright, despite his devotion to the Church of England, opposed Simcoe's Marriage Act, quite simply because it ignored the wishes and needs of other Upper Canadian Protestants.

What Cartwright wanted most of all was respect for his views and the views of other Loyalists who had sacrificed so much for the Crown. Appointed to the Legislative Council, he refused to be blindly obedient to each of Simcoe's whims and dictates. He regarded, as he said, his "knowledge of the country and legislation to be most applicable to the situation of the colony; not merely to show my Complaisance to the person at the head of the Government." In short, he and his fellow Loyalists who were called to serve did so willingly and with great reverence, but also with the position that they, rather than officials in England—and that included their appointees like Simcoe—knew what was best for the province. Simcoe could not remain in Upper Canada forever. The province became Cartwright's life and future. "All my prospects, as well for myself as my family," he wrote, "are confined to this province: I am bound to it by the strongest ties, and with its welfare my interest is most essentially connected."

With so much invested, Cartwright, among others, was not supportive of Simcoe's decision to woo disenchanted Americans with promises of land grants. In Cartwright's opinion, Upper Canada was founded as an "asylum for the unfortunate Loyalists reduced to poverty and driven into exile by their attachment to Britain." But Simcoe had insisted that the province's future economic prosperity could only be boosted with an influx of immigrants—even former rebels. Moreover, he was not convinced that they had all succumbed to republicanism. "There are thousands of inhabitants of the United States whose affections are centered in the British Government & the British Name," he had told his friend Henry Dundas in June 1791, "who are positively enemies of Congress & the late division of the Empire; many of the Connections have already taken refuge in Canada & it will be true Wisdom to invite & facilitate the emigration of this description of people into that Country." All that was required to obtain two hundred acres from His Majesty's Government was an oath of allegiance to said Majesty and Parliament. That, plus the payment of six-pence-per-acre property fees, "which rendered land in Upper Canada dirt-cheap relative to the two to three dollars per acre charged by land speculators in New York and Pennsylvania," as historian Alan Taylor noted.

This was too good an offer to pass up. And an estimated twenty thousand of these "Late Loyalists" made their way north, "flocking from the States with all of their property," as John Munroe, a Queen's Ranger, told his former commander. Some, like Cartwright, were appalled at this situation. "Loyalists heard, with astonishment and indignation, persons spoken of as proprietors of townships whom they had encountered in the field under the banners of the rebellion," he declared. This may have not been true in every case—many of these newcomers were Quakers and Germans with no particular affinity for the Patriots—but many, too, brought with them a strong faith in American principles. This demographic shift, though beneficial for the Upper Canadian economy, made the province more American rather than less, a reality that would have ramifications during the War of 1812. This was contrary to Simcoe's blueprint and contrary to the vision that Upper Canada was strictly a Loyalist preserve, though the Late Loyalists did improve Upper Canada's economy.

There was also no denying the profound Loyalist influence on Upper Canadian society. Notwithstanding their affinity for American-style democracy, loyalty to the King and the imperial connection remained essential for many Loyalists in 1790 as it would two decades later. In March 1810, on the occasion of George III's Golden Jubilee, the Upper Canadian Assembly passed the following declaration:

> With gratitude and thankfulness we acknowledge . . . a most special blessing which had accompanied and adorned your Majesty's reign. Attached to Your Majesty's person and government, happy in the enjoyment of that invaluable constitution which we possess and grateful for the bounty which we in this Province have received from Your Majesty's hands. . . . We . . . do most fervently implore the great ruler of Princes, that He may be graciously pleased to preserve Your Majesty's valuable life, and to permit Your Majesty long to be the Father, the Protector, and the King of your people.

Stuff like that.

THAT THE LOYALISTS were able to tame the isolated Upper Canadian frontier is the real miracle of their story. "Twenty-six years ago," Richard Cartwright wrote in 1810, "this province was . . . a howling

wilderness, little known and less cultivated." There had been nothing, he added, "except the movable hut of the wandering savage."
Yet nearly three decades later he noted with pride, "I have seen the
wilderness . . . converted into fruitful fields, and covered with comfortable habituations. I have seen about me thousands who without
any other funds than their personal labour, begin to denude the soil
of its primevall forests, in possession of extensive and well cultivated
farms and abounding in all substantial comforts of life."

Cartwright's assessment was a tad melodramatic, but he was not
far wrong either. A nascent civilization of sorts had slowly taken
shape during the 1790s at Kingston, Niagara, and York, where
amidst "dusty streets" residents could frequent churches, taverns,
and shops which sold a variety of imported goods from England and
the U.S. Most of the houses were made of wood, though Isaac Weld,
an Irish writer, who travelled throughout the United States and British North America from 1795 to 1797, commented on the statelier
homes, constructed of stone and brick, which he found in Kingston.
Anglican Churches sprang up, along with courthouses and jails, both
requiring frequent extensions.

In York, crowds gathered gleefully to watch very special "op-
eras"—in reality public hangings, climaxed by the dance-like limb
movements of the unfortunate victims' death throes as they dangled
in their final spastic agonies. The town's primitive criminal code
listed two dozen capital offences that provided plenty of stars for the
free entertainment. Schoolchildren were given the days off to watch
and the crowds dressed up for each occasion. The first local trial condemned a culprit named John Sullivan who was charged and convicted of minor theft. An anonymous blackguard had forged a bank
draft for three shillings and nine pence which Sullivan had stolen
and had tried to cash. That was enough to earn him a death sentence
with no appeal and no attending clergy to bless him on his way. The
judge concluded his charge with this icy comment: "Although your
crime is great, it does not exceed the boundless mercy of God." Sullivan patiently waited to be hanged but nobody applied for the job.

Eventually a fellow prisoner, serving time for robbery, was hired on the spot to do the deed, in return for a full pardon and 20 guineas.

The most boisterous of these grisly events was the double hanging of two rebels named Lout and Matthews for their part in the William Lyon Mackenzie Rebellion of 1837. Although the town, by then renamed Toronto, had an official population of only 2,500, four times as many gawkers showed up to watch their deadly gavottes. Most of the audience went formal for that special occasion, including compulsory hats. Located southeast of King and Yonge Streets (where the King Edward Hotel was eventually built), the local prison was a primitive square building constructed out of vertical logs covered with clapboard. Although no municipal official admitted it at the time, the strengthened jail was designed to serve as an emergency shelter in case of trouble with the nearby militant Mississauga Indians.

In the 1790s, outside of these nascent urban centres, the province was a harsh and unforgiving frontier environment. The Loyalists were pioneers in every sense of the word and their main focus, each and every day, was on "clearing the land, planting and harvesting, and attending the myriad of tasks necessary to sustain life," in the words of Queen's University historian Elizabeth Jane Errington. "Throughout much of the first twenty-five years of colonial development," she adds, "an individual's community was confined to his or her family and to the few settlers he or she met occasionally at the mill, at work parties, or at social occasions."

More than three decades later, little had changed. Soon after artist Anne Langton arrived in Upper Canada from England, settling on a farm near Fenelon Falls, northwest of Peterborough, she wrote to her sister-in-law, Margaret, who was back in Manchester. "What most strikes me," she noted from her new home, "is a greater degree of roughness in the farming, building, gardens, fences, and especially the roads than I had expected." Still, Langton was impressed that while so much remained to be done to tame the wilderness, "so much has been done." Getting from one place to another in Upper

Canada required a hardy stamina. Samuel D. Purdy, the son of a Loyalist, started the first stagecoach service between Kingston and York in January 1817. The fare for weekly service in a converted sleigh was $18, which was fairly expensive. The long journey, which took at least four or five days over rough mud roads, was a miserable experience. In the winter, passengers had to contend with bitterly cold weather; in the summer they were at the mercy of mosquitoes and blackflies.

LOYALISTS' EXISTENCE WAS based on domesticity—a five-syllable word for being born at home, living at home, working at home, dying at home, and, of course, bundling at home. "Home," as the *Magazine of Domestic Economy* decreed in the 1840s, "is of more deep, heartfelt and personal interest to us than the public affairs of all the nations of the world." In early Canada, most people occupied homes that had no grandeur and less comfort. But it was all they had. Front doors were often a thick plank of wood, fastened by a makeshift latch. According to Walter S. Herrington, an early historian of Loyalist pioneer life, "the latch was lifted from without by means of a leather string attached to it and passed through a hole a few inches above, and when the inmates of the house retired for the night, or did not wish to be molested, the string was pulled inside. The old saying, 'the latch-string is out,' was a figurative method of expressing a welcome, or saying 'the door is not barred against you.' The pioneers had big hearts, and to their credit the latch-string was rarely pulled in when a stranger sought a meal or a night's lodging."

Attics were usually made into second rooms that could only be entered by a ladder though a small opening. Most Loyalists' homes had little furniture except the absolute essentials, since it had been inordinately difficult to transport their chairs, tables, and drawers from their homes in the United States. Beds, such as they were, had mattresses, added Herrington, "made of boughs, corn husks, straw, or feathers, and rested upon wooden slats, or more frequently cords laced from side to side and end to end of the framework of the bed-stead." Cooking initially was done with an iron fry pan resting on hot coals in the fireplace. To bake bread, the settlers used a bake-kettle and then a reflector, "which was an oblong box of bright tin, enclosed on all sides but one. It was placed on the hearth with the open side next to a bed of glowing coals. In it were placed the tins of dough raised a few inches from the bottom, so that the heat could circulate freely about the loaves. The upper part of the reflector was removable, to enable the housewife to inspect the contents."

But even if they were safe houses of last resort, they provided privacy and protection—a place to call their own. "As I remember my people and their friends, they were content but not complacent," wrote Jeanne Minhinnick, the wonderful muse and taste arbiter of Prince Edward County who grew up in precisely such surroundings. "Their houses and furniture changed scarcely at all," she noted. "The atmosphere was busy, lively and stimulating. But we also knew and liked many people who had no education, yet were sharp and observant, practical and resourceful. A variance of speech and accent added flavour and evoked no disrespect. Now, we were all Canadians."

A Loyalist pioneer diet was what you might expect: lots of pork and occasionally fish—bass, pike, pickerel, salmon—which was plentiful in Upper Canada's rivers and streams. Boiled cornmeal sprinkled with brown sugar was a favourite for breakfast, as were cornmeal pancakes. For a long time, Loyalists refrained from cooking American-style johnnycakes, a cornmeal flatbread, because as Herrington writes, "it was regarded as a Yankee dish." The women picked wild strawberries, raspberries, and gooseberries and prepared jams, and they taught their daughters to sew and weave clothes on a spinning wheel. Nearly everything the Loyalists wore was homemade including their leather boots, which involved months of tanning, kneading, and rubbing using solutions of lye and oak bark. Making decent boots was a skill that was much admired and in demand. In the winter, furs from bears, foxes, and raccoons were used for thick hats, and in the summer, rye straw was utilized for straw hats. Neighbours watched out for each other and large tasks were accomplished with cooperative "bees"—everything from logging and stumping to quilting and paring bees.

ONTARIO HAS FORTY-NINE COUNTIES but only one "County." That would be Prince Edward County, within hailing distance of Belleville, which was established by the Loyalists on the windy side of the eighteenth century, claiming its individuality not just as another municipal construct, but as a way of life. Named in honour of Queen Victoria's father, the County still weaves its spell of rural tranquility—its coves, bays, and islands exude the spicy flavour of a northern Cape Cod . . . without the hot dog stands. A twenty-first-century hideaway for wine-growing locals and burnt-out Torontonians living in its two dozen towns, villages, and unnamed house clusters, it trumped the racing urban heart rates and instilled a mood both calming and nostalgic. It was the legendary Loyalists, fleeing the American Revolution, who in 1784 chose to land at Prinyer's Cove in the County, one of many Upper Canadian sweet spots they settled.

Most of the County's current inhabitants trace their roots to this mass exodus, and genealogy remains the County's second most popular indoor sport. Like their forebears, County folk are honest, unaffected, and kind to strangers, who are welcomed—but carefully monitored for a generation or three—sometimes even four, if they get uppity.

First to arrive in their new homelands in the County were members of disbanded Loyalist regiments, moving from New York to Cataraqui (Kingston), the Bay of Quinte (Belleville, Picton), and Oswegatchie (Prescott) via Quebec, Lachine, and Sorel. The newcomers leased land by drawing lots—signing their names on the backs of the allocation tickets to build primitive starter shelters. Former regimental officers who had fought with the British received extra free acreage, according to rank. A few disillusioned Loyalists traded their slice of wilderness for a 26'er of rum and vamoosed to greener pastures. But mostly they stayed and adopted the dependable custom of spreading the work through neighbourly barn-raising bees, and, later, logging bees as well as apple-drying bees. The log cabins they put up were a storey and a half high and eighteen by sixteen feet on the ground. Cracks were sealed to keep out the vermin. They had one window with four small panes supplying light; the rocky fireplace was used for heat, cooking, and lounging. Floors consisted of mud or crudely levelled split logs. But it was home.

CANADIANS, THEN AS NOW, were marked by an ability to endure—to survive a lousy climate and worse politicians. That ability to hang on with minimum complaints has always been our burden. Concentrating too much on survival too often deterred the application of imagination and creativity. It robbed the national will of following those intuitive leaps that allow individuals to reach for originality that creates a buzz.

Yet survivors are the winners in any game, and the Loyalists who flooded into Prince Edward County and the rest of the Canadian colonies a couple of centuries ago specialized in that essential skill set. To these ideologically driven pioneers, history was nothing more than memories refined, the record of collective and individual encounters between character and circumstance. "The peasantry here evince the utmost indifference about everything that is not absolutely necessary to support existence," complained visiting British traveller John Howison. "They raise enough wheat, corn and potatoes to place themselves beyond the reach of want, but rarely increase their comforts." That wasn't always true, but the newly arrived refugees from the American wars joined a loose collection of Lonesome Charlies in a sophomoric land occupied by pioneers with few unifying arcs— except unrequited faith in a distant monarch who didn't know they existed. Canny, sober, and frugal by nature, they had little trouble maintaining the Calvinist creed that the earthly path to salvation is through hard work—and that good men more than earn their keep. That kind of Boy Scout advice was about as useful as establishing a wilderness Rotary Club, but it aptly summed up their gospel. These reluctant heroes occasionally cursed their fate, but they accepted it. They had landed in a vacant land with no visible advantage except size. At first they earned nothing much except blisters, their lifestyle reduced to a bare-bones existence, scratching the untilled soil for sustenance. Having been evicted by political dictate from a society in ascendancy where they had enjoyed a certain standing, they now found themselves pushed to the margins, relegated to the vagrant status of refugees. They were forced to fall back on inbred values and the dubious penance of feeling too insecure to know when to quit. It was a mark of their stubbornness that they lived to tell their tales. While they celebrated few happy endings, their underlying message was clear: survival in this barely explored back lot was not an impossible dream. They had escaped with their skins and noggins intact; now, it was their turn to enlist their energies in the quest for a permanent alternate domicile. And they found it, as they would later discover—out there in the Canada of the future, beyond the farthest mountains, behind the clouds, covering ten million square kilometres of the earth's land surface—waiting to be explored, exploited, and enjoyed.

The realization came quickly to the occupiers of the untouched acres that they had been blessed by the rarest of benedictions: another chance. Their scrubby vegetable gardens provided the settlers with a natural advantage. The soil was hungry for crops. Seeds and roots were traded from farm to farm. The juices of such herbs such as sage, summer savory, dill, chamomile, and marigold flowers were rubbed on wasp stings. Pressed dandelions were a useful liver tonic. Catnip tea cooled fevers. Ladybugs secreted a hormone on flowering grape clusters, which, when smeared on growing grapes, added a peanut butter flavour to the wine. Opium poppies were mysteriously listed as "useful." Most early gardens utilized piles of dead branches for fencing, but the advent of verandahs required more classic innovations. Hardy perennials like Stars of Bethlehem bloomed for decades with no care required. Funerals were compulsory social occasions. About-to-become widows lamented the fact they couldn't get into the room to comfort their expiring husbands because of all the professional mourners who had crowded in. They were women who would keen for the dying with wild unnatural whimpers in a most compelling, primitive way. They made you want to die.

Inside the dwellings, parlours were the forerunners of living rooms. Kitchens remained the family rooms. Often alone, mothers conversed with their stoves. Early forks were not curved and thus unsuitable for lifting food, so most backwoodsmen ate by putting knives into their mouths. Grace was usually performed by grandfathers who, feeling close to future probabilities, included heavenly praise for their repasts in their recitations. ("These creatures bless and grant that we may feast in Paradise with Thee . . . Amen.") Winter and summer kitchens were standard issue in well-equipped households. Eggs were stored in lime and salt in cellars where they would keep fresh all winter.

The great Upper Canadian forests of beech, maple, pine, and walnut, once cleared, gave way to the planting of pigweed, groundnut, wild rice, and Indian cabbage. Boiled tree bark was the emergency diet. Wild turkey (from the marshlands), wolves, lynxes, martins, foxes, minks, and weasels provided Sunday brunch treats. Pumpkin loaves, made of cornmeal and boiled pumpkin, and eaten hot with melted butter, topped the menus. Tea was a luxury but hemlock (in small quantities) and sassafras provided substitutes. The first leap forward was the establishment of flour mills. In 1782, for example, British authorities instructed Loyalist Robert Clark, a militia officer and millwright, to erect a mill in Kingston in anticipation of the mass Loyalist migration to the area. Farmers brought in crops of wheat by wagon (or in sacks carried on their backs) and paid for the milling by leaving one tenth of the grain as a fee. Root vegetables were stored for winter months by being pickled in vinegar or preserved in molasses and maple syrup. Dandelion roots served as a substitute for coffee; or with the addition of half a pint of whiskey and three weeks' storage in a tightly closed stone jar—Voilà!—dandelion wine.

Hannah Jarvis cooked homemade yeast: potatoes that were peeled, boiled, and beaten, with brown sugar. Onetime cures included soda poultices for bee stings; mustard plasters for chest congestion; milk poultices for boils. Clover brew helped control poison ivy; raw beef disguised black eyes; hive syrup cured croup; and Pinkham's Pink Pills were handy for female complaints. Well, not all of them.

Carpets were too expensive but animal furs were useful in their place. Flat desks with pewter inkwells were considered the height of luxury. Kerosene lamps lit the evenings, projecting glib patterns on the white walls. It wasn't until 1850 that washstands—with bowls but no drains—were installed in most bedrooms. Beds were advertised as hygienic, which meant they weren't supposed to be habitats for bed lice. They didn't stay away; warm human bodies were the best hiding places. (Cockroaches cheered along the resident lice, scampering to fulfill their self-appointed missions.) Who knew? Three-point Hudson's Bay Company blankets were the most popular night coverings. Bedtime candles accompanied evening ablutions.

This was the tongue-twisting lesson of the day that mothers end-lessly drilled into their children, to repeat after them: "Wilful waste makes woeful want." The blue paper wrapped around supplies of sugar was kept in case it could be used as a dye. Women wore their best dresses only twice: to be married and to be buried in.

Jeanne Minhinnick's choice of the outstanding rooms and houses in her area and in her time (1903–1985) included: the Belleville home of John Turnbull (agent for the Commercial Bank of the Midland District); John Walden Myers's villa in the same town; Charles Oakes Ermatinger's wilderness spread near Sault Ste. Marie; the Macdon-nell mansion at Pointe Fortune in Prescott; the intriguing Campbell House at Williamstown; William Fairfield's fascinating White House near Collins Bay; Surveyor-General John Macaulay's College Av-enue house in Toronto; as well as Edgar and Rosemary Sexton's stately castle in Brockville. This last is beside Senator George Taylor

Fulford's former mansion (now a museum) built by the fortune he made selling cure-all "Pink Pills for Pale People," composed with, among other ingredients, a touch of cocaine.

Luxury servings at Loyalists' dinners included such delicacies as steak-and-kidney pie, potted meats, treacle pie, and trifle. Silver services dominated, but there was a mixture of tin, antimony, and zinc that produced Britannia jugs that had a finished polish, brighter than pewter and yet modestly attractive—perfect for cloudy day afternoon teas. Toronto's John Beverley Robinson, a leading member of the community, solved his family's need for servants by hiring a small army of helpers: footmen, coachmen, cooks, housemaids, apprentices, gardeners, waiters, needle women, charwomen, scrub women, and Hannah, who was listed with no job description.

TWO OTHER LOYALIST PIONEERS were Stephen and Amelia Jarvis. In June 1809, after leaving their daughter Frances to marry Major Maule, and then paddling, sailing, and trudging westward through river valleys and gnat-infested forests to Upper Canada, the Jarvises and their five exhausted children had finally taken possession of a house in York. Twenty-four years after her experience of having to live in a "hovel" following their first moving to Fredericton, Amelia must have been thankful that Stephen had bought a house which was ready to receive them. It helped diminish the sting of being uprooted from New Brunswick. In addition to earning £100 per annum and receiving half pay as a retired officer, Stephen was also the master of 1,200 acres of land. Still, budgets remained tight.

Frederick Starr (who was addressed by his second name), Stephen and Amelia's twenty-three-year-old son, received a grant of four hundred acres. Following in the footsteps of his Connecticut grandfather, Starr embraced farming and immediately began tilling the land. His younger brothers, in their turn, chose a different destiny, pursuing careers in public office that would launch the Jarvis dynasty.

Encampment of the Loyalists at Johnstown, a New Settlement, on the Banks of the River St. Laurence in Canada, taken June 6 78.
taken from ... marked in the Plan

Upon reaching Nova Scotia and New Brunswick, Loyalists often established encampments—such as the one depicted here by James Peachey—as their first settlements before constructing more permanent lodgings. *Library and Archives Canada, Acc. No. 19892181.*

The early years in Canada were hard on the Loyalists. Scarcity of resources, a lack of infrastructure, and extreme weather all contributed to their hardships. Polly Dibblee knew such struggles all too well, as this local newspaper report attests to: just six weeks after her husband, Fyler, committed suicide, the Dibblees' house was burned down, with all of their effects in it. *Image courtesy of Archives & Special Collections, Harriet Irving Library, University of New Brunswick.*

After leading the Queen's Rangers in the Revolutionary War, Sir John
Graves Simcoe became Upper Canada's first lieutenant-governor, serving from 1791 to 1796. In his role, he introduced many institutions—
from trial by jury to English common law to the abolition of slavery—that
would become the foundations for the colony. *Courtesy of Toronto Public
Library, 927-1 FRA.*

Archives of Ontario, F 47111063

Born to an upper-class family in Devon, England, Elizabeth Simcoe moved to Upper Canada with her husband, John Graves. Her diaries and sketches construct a portrait of the everyday struggles and successes that constituted life in Canada at the turn of the nineteenth century. *Library and Archives Canada, Acc. No. 19721182.*

Archives of Ontario, F 47111072

Archives of Ontario, F 47111039

This scene is a rendition of the opening of Upper Canada's first parliament on September 17, 1792. Simcoe sits proudly atop his horse while his wife, Elizabeth, watches beside the flagpole. William Jarvis, then Simcoe's secretary, is dressed in a green jacket and framed between his superior and the tree, while Chief Justice William Osgoode stands holding a cane on the right-hand side.

Courtesy of the Niagara Historical Society & Museum.

The view in Kingston—or Cataraqui, as it was then known—that would have greeted Loyalists would have been a far cry from that of the bustling New York City they had just left. *Library and Archives Canada, Acc. No. 19892215.*

William Jarvis served as John Graves Simcoe's secretary for many years. Jarvis often suffered from bouts of gout and money problems, but his family still carried on the Jarvis name and legacy—Jarvis Street in Toronto is named after his son Samuel Peters Jarvis. *Courtesy of Toronto Public Library.*

The Queen's Rangers oversee the cutting out of Yonge Street. *Library and Archives Canada, Acc. No. 197226767.*

Troops at Fort George perform daily drills while two soldiers tend to the garrison's mascots—two black bear cubs. *Courtesy of William L. Clements Library, University of Michigan.*

Fort York barracks. Aboriginal families fish in the waters nearby while others arrive to trade with the soldiers, who are busy building new fortifications. *Library and Archives Canada, Acc. No. 19903363.*

Utterly fearless, General Isaac Brock was responsible for defending Upper Canada against the United States during the War of 1812 until his death at the Battle of Queenston Heights. Brock's actions earned him the title "The Hero of Upper Canada." *© 2016 Guernsey Museums & Galleries, States of Guernsey.*

A benevolent Britannia offers comfort and a chance at consolation for exiled Loyalists. The reality, however, was much different. Despite all the Loyalists had been through in remaining faithful to the Crown, the British government ultimately only compensated Loyalists for one-third of the value of the claims that they filed. *Courtesy of Yale Center for British Art.*

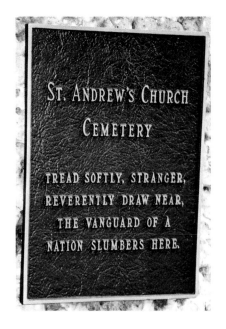

This plaque stands on the gatepost of St. Andrew's United Church in Williamstown, New Brunswick. Taken from the first two lines of the poem "Epitaph on an Early Settler" by Hernward R. Cockin, the lines speak to the Loyalists' sacrifice, their dignity, and their lasting legacy. *Fred H. Hayward UE.*

But no matter how bright the future would be for the Jarvis children, being a Loyalist's wife was no picnic. For the second time in her life, Amelia had been made a hostage to the whim of fortune. In 1785, the animosity of their Connecticut neighbours to her husband's war service and political beliefs had compelled them to become refugees; she had been forced to leave her family and all that she had known to seek sanctuary in the New Brunswick wilderness. Her husband's midlife crisis revolving around his business difficulties and downgraded reputation as a militia officer had propelled them into yet another colonial capital in 1809. Instead of just making ends meet as a merchant and postmaster, Stephen Jarvis was now a member of Upper Canada's civil service, working with his cousin William Jarvis in the office of the colony's registrar. The job, however, did not live up to his expectations and by 1812 he quit, angry at the way William conducted himself.

While Amelia, who had moved to Toronto, could be proud of the fact that her oldest son, Frederick Starr, was finding his feet in farming, she was homesick for Frances, her second daughter, the one who had stayed with her husband in New Brunswick. As the wife of a major in the 104th Regiment stationed in the first Loyalist colony, Frances was not likely to see her parents anytime soon. But where military conflict had separated Amelia from family in the past, the War of 1812 would actually be the cause for a reunion with her far-flung daughter in four years' time. In the interval, Amelia saw to the purchasing of new furniture and watching over her children's transition from New Brunswickers to Upper Canadians. Betsey, born in Connecticut, was now twenty-five years old and in danger of becoming a spinster. Rachel (dubbed "Bell" by the family) was only fourteen and George Jarvis was just twelve, while little William Botsford was only ten. Despite their tender years, both boys would see action in the coming war in just three years' time.

Although Amelia's previous experience as a refugee wife must have, to some degree, prepared her for the move to York, her transition

was made easier by the fact that so many other New Brunswick Loyalists were also making a fresh start themselves in Upper Canada.
Despite the assistance they received from the British government,
many of the Loyalists in New Brunswick found it difficult to put
down roots. Some of them were psychologically ill-prepared for the
rough pioneering life they'd had to endure and drifted away. This
was especially true of soldiers without families who had less of a stake
in establishing New Brunswick as a new Loyalist haven. Others were
convinced that there were always greener pastures elsewhere. A few
moved on to Quebec, and many more, like Stephen and Amelia,
to the new Loyalist colony of Upper Canada where Lieutenant-
Governor Simcoe offered generous land grants. An untold number of refugees returned to the United States, once it was safe to do
so. So debilitating was the exodus that Edward Winslow, under the
pen name "Tammany," cautioned his fellow New Brunswickers in
the *Royal Gazette* of July 1802 against voluntarily surrendering "the
peace, comfort and happiness of their families" to seek opportunities
elsewhere.

Those who did depart for Upper Canada or Quebec sold their
homes and almost all of their belongings to associates, friends, or
other Loyalist families. Little could be brought with them to their
destination, some 1,365 kilometres away. The journey took the trav-
ellers up the St. John River to its source. They then crossed overland
(through an area which is now in Maine) to the St. Lawrence River,
and eventually reached Upper Canada via the Great Lakes. The trip
was arduous and not for the faint of heart. Other Loyalists sailed to
New England and then crossed overland to Upper Canada to settle.

Even travelling from Fredericton to Quebec City, only 595 kilometres (370 miles), was a treacherous journey. Elizabeth Simcoe noted
in her diary for March 4, 1792, that a former member of the Queen's
Rangers, Captain Aeneas Shaw, arrived in Quebec City, where the
Simcoes were staying before they headed to Upper Canada. Shaw's
group "walked on snow shoes 240 miles in 19 days, came up the river
St. John, and crossed many small lakes," she recorded.

Their mode of travelling was to set out at daybreak, walk till twelve, when they stood ten minutes (not longer, because of the cold) to eat. They then resumed walking till half-past four, when they chose a spot, where there was good firewood, to encamp. Half the party (which consisted of 12) began felling wood; the rest dug away the snow till they had made a pit many feet in circumference, in which the fire was to be made. They cut cedar and pine branches, laid a blanket on them, and wrapping themselves in another, found it sufficiently warm, with their feet close to a large fire, which was kept up all night. Capt. McGill, who set out with them, cut his knee in felling wood, and was forced to stay at the Madawaska Settlement [now Edmundston, New Brunswick].

Shaw accompanied the Simcoes to Toronto (York) where he served in the military and became a member of the Executive Council of Upper Canada.

The fortunes of New Brunswick gradually improved, stimulated by the economic impact of more than two decades of warfare in Europe stemming from the viral machinations of Napoleon Bonaparte. During Great Britain's battles with the French emperor, demand for colonial fish, foodstuffs, and timber skyrocketed. Production was further stimulated by the Navigation Acts and the whole framework of mercantilist regulation that gave colonial products preference over foreign competition. Between 1805 and 1812, the exports of fir and pine timber from New Brunswick, Great Britain's preeminent "timber colony," increased more than twenty-fold. Businessmen, many of them based in Greenock, brought their capital, labour, and technology to the shores of the Miramichi and St. John Rivers. Shipbuilding soon emerged as a sideline of the timber trade. By 1815, the year of Winslow's death, New Brunswick's economy was dominated by forest-based industries.

The Loyalist ascendancy over British North America was only about thirty years. After 1820, when the Great Migration began, everywhere that the Loyalists had settled (in the Maritimes as well as

Upper Canada) was flooded with British, Scottish, and Irish immigrants, diluting whatever impact the Loyalists had—or at least making it very difficult to determine their long-lasting legacy. In New Brunswick, for example, Irish immigrants (both Catholic and Protestant) became the majority after the 1840s, bringing their religious squabbles and worldview with them. In Upper Canada, Brits and Scots quickly outnumbered the Loyalists.

Nevertheless, the memory of the Loyalists remained strong, if not precisely accurate. The bitter feuds of the 1780s over land and power and Loyalist departures from New Brunswick to Upper Canada and elsewhere were conveniently ignored. Celebrations in 1883 to mark the centennial of the Loyalists' arrival in the Maritimes reaffirmed the British connection. And, thereafter, correctly or not, they were perceived to be the guardians of Canada's imperialist ties to the British Empire. Even in the context of the Canadian economic debate of the late nineteenth century, the protective tariff, promoted by John A. Macdonald and the Conservatives, was equated with Loyalism, while the freer trade with the United States advocated by Wilfrid Laurier and the Liberals was perceived by many Canadians to be treasonous. By the 1930s, historian Chester Martin of the University of Toronto (who was born in Saint John) drew a direct line between the Loyalists and the achievement of responsible government in the 1840s—a constitutional development that in his view positively impacted on political reform in Britain as well.

The Loyalists provided New Brunswickers with a powerful bond to "what they conceived to be their glorious past and invested characteristics peculiar to the Loyalists in the language of religion, mission, and destiny," suggested historian Murray Barkley in a 1975 article in *Acadiensis*.

> The Loyalist experience provided the one element of glory in New Brunswick's history. . . . History was the chief vehicle through which the Loyalist tradition was expressed, being based on the assumption that the past contained principles to which the present

should adhere, in order to preserve the continuity of national life. Those exalted qualities, principles, and aspirations attributed, with fanatic pride, to the "true founders of Canada" by succeeding generations were . . . more important ingredients in the development of Canadian nationalism than the actual accomplishments or the political and social ideology of the Loyalists themselves.

A YOUNG JOSEPH CARROLL, whose father had, like Stephen Jarvis, uprooted his wife and children for a fresh start in York, remembered his mother's unexpected joy upon moving to the colony's capital.

A few mornings after our arrival, mother made an agreeable acquaintance. A comely young married woman, by the name of Barber, occupied a neat little house across the road from us. They met in the street, and found that both (at least Mrs. B's parents) were from New Brunswick; and as they both knew, or at least knew of, many of the same persons, they began to question each other about this and that individual; and they soon found that they had a common knowledge and friendship of many people, which was, as we all know from experience, a source of pleasure. At length, said mother, as the plot thickened, "I wonder whatever became of Sally Rodney?" At this the young woman burst into tears (the first time I ever saw a person weep for joy,) and said, "Why she's my mother, and is alive, and living out on Yonge Street." Sally Rodney was [the illegitimate] daughter of [Admiral George Brydges Rodney] Lord Rodney, a naval officer, who spent some time in New Brunswick, and lured one of the handsomest young women of the country from the paths of propriety; and Sally Rodney was the result. Sally had married fairly well, and we afterwards often met her. . . . . Across the way from our place, mother renewed her acquaintance with the family of Stephen Jarvis, Esquire, respectable people, from Fredericton. . . . This was solace to her. She and old Mrs. Jarvis were life-long friends and intimates.

In 1812, the lives of both families were turned upside down by the whims of American desires to subjugate those loyal to the British Crown. This time, however, the Jarvises and other Loyalists did not flee or face expulsion. Instead they would fight to defend their new homeland against a much heralded, but carelessly executed, American invasion.

8

1812—THE WAR TO END WARS

The 1812 War was not rationally necessary, except in the bizarre sense that it all seemed to become inevitable . . . once it had happened.

—Welsh author Jon Latimer

THE MOST EMOTIONAL series of public events recorded on Canada's social calendars during the summer of 2012 was the start of national celebrations commemorating the War of 1812, that bizarre contest that was fought two troubled centuries earlier after the Americans invaded Canada. Largely ignored by history, its seventy battles, sieges, raids, and massacres were fought over thirty bitter months of vicious combat. But in the end, not a sliver of territory changed hands. Since this was an epoch when victory depended on capturing new ground, it was not easy to select the winners.

But it was the Yanks, with 11,200 actual war casualties, who withdrew and scampered back home, thus declaring themselves the losers. The puzzling hands-off attitude by the British was summed up by historian William Kingsford who noted that "the events in North America between 1812 and 1815 were not forgotten in Britain—

for they have never been known there." Still, this war to end wars turned out to be highly significant, mainly in its aftermath.

DURING THE WARS with Napoleon in the first decade of the nineteenth century, Britain tried to prevent American ships (though neutral) from trading in Europe, mainly as a way to halt goods from reaching France, its enemy. When the Royal Navy boarded ships from the young republic, they seized whatever they considered to be contraband and forced American sailors into service on British vessels. This might have all been settled by negotiations, but American leaders also resented the fact that the British were encouraging First Nations to resist white expansion into the West.

It came down to a question of honour and the Republicans (technically, the Democratic-Republicans) who controlled both houses of the U.S. Congress demanded justice—despite the fact the nascent U.S. military and navy (such as they were) were hardly prepared or in a position to challenge the British again. Much was at stake, including the unity of the United States and, more specifically, the Republicans' future electoral success against the Federalists (an American political party from the 1790s to 1820 that supported, as its name suggested, a strong centralized federal government). "I think our Doom will be Fix[ed]," Thomas Webb, a concerned Republican, wrote in mid-May 1812, "and we shall become the tame Submissive Vasals of Briton & a Laughing Stock to the World . . . & the Henry Plotters will get the Asendancy & then we may bid a Long farewell to Libberty [*sic*] & Equal Laws."

Republican president James Madison conceded after the fact that he "knew the unprepared state of the country, but . . . esteemed it necessary to throw forward the flag of the country, sure that the people would press forward and defend it." Once the House of Representatives and the Senate voted in favour of combat, he signed a declaration of war against England on June 18. But the immediate prize was much closer—Upper Canada, home to Loyalist refugees for the preceding thirty years.*

On the eve of the battle, the newly anointed United States boasted a population of eight million activists, while Canada only had half a million scattered settlers—300,000 of them being Quebeckers who were not enthusiastically inclined to do battle on behalf of their British cohorts—plus another 100,000 arrivals who were American by birth or descent. Only the modest-circulation *Connecticut Courant* called on its sensible populist roots and precisely predicted the war's outcome, stating that it was "commenced in folly and carried on with madness that would end in ruin." For one thing, it was evident from day one that no one had fully considered the conflict's founding rationale. The unanswered puzzle, even among the war hawks, was the trickiest question facing American strategists: What in hell would they do with Canada, should they win? Prospective Canadians were no help, since they didn't know either. Finally, Secretary of State James Monroe came to the rescue by suggesting that Canada be taken for ransom as a bargaining chip with which to force British concessions on the high seas. At the time, America's secretary of war, William Eustis, was working with a staff that had been reduced to eleven junior clerks. The Yanks seemed unaware of strategic subtleties, not having fought a war since their revolution nearly forty years earlier.

The armed contest pitted not only their weapons but the essence of the combatants' spirit against one another: Canadians remaining loyal to their heritage versus Americans rallying to the quest for independence and self-realization. The Yanks were betrayed by their unwillingness to credit the possibility that they weren't all-powerful. When the Americans originally decided in 1812 to conquer the wilderness that would become Canada, Thomas Jefferson, their

---

*Lower Canada was harder for American forces to reach, requiring an overland march and then a siege on the Fortress of Quebec. British sea power, which then dominated the world's oceans, protected the Maritime colonies.

heavyweight guru who had authored their flamboyant Declaration of Independence and now was strategizing the northern invasion, offered some disturbingly ill-informed advice. Convinced that the scatter of residents north of the 49th parallel would follow the American example of cutting their British colonial bonds, he assumed we would greet his invading troops by spreading flower petals in their path while singing rounds of happy huzzahs. With an absent dose of clarity and good sense, Jefferson predicted that "the acquisition of Canada will be a mere matter of marching and will give us experience for the attack of Halifax next, and the final expulsion of England from the American continent." That boastful sentiment was echoed by Henry Clay, a senator from Kentucky, when he told Congress: "The conquest of Canada is in your power. I trust that I shall not be deemed presumptuous when I state that I verily believe that the militia of Kentucky are alone competent to place Montreal and Upper Canada at your feet." This attitude reached its comic peak when Secretary of War Eustis boldly declared: "We can take Canada without soldiers. We have only to send officers into the provinces and the people, disaffected towards their own government, will rally around our standard."

It was true that some Upper Canadians were unhappy with restrictive British rules and regulations that governed politics and impacted on the economy, and no doubt believed an American conquest might improve their situation. Yet the influential "true Loyalists," as small in number as they were, wanted nothing to do with the Republicans who had threatened their lives—or with Napoleon for that matter, who, it was rumoured, might acquire Upper Canada if the Americans were victorious. One anonymous contributor to the *Kingston Gazette* in the spring of 1812—presumably a Loyalist— summed up the prevailing feeling by pointing out that any invading army organized by the Americans would be "composed of the refuse and scum of the earth, Renegades and Vagabonds of all nations, who having fled from justice in their native land have found an asylum in the United States." Upper Canada had to be defended at all costs, he argued. "Our wives, our children, our property all is at stake and shall we then tamely submit and see ourselves plundered of our well earned property, of property for which we have fought and bled?" The answer to that rhetorical question was clearly "No damn way!" Likewise, Richard Cartwright, also writing in the *Gazette,* urged his "brave and loyal" fellow Upper Canadians to "rally round the Government." And rally round, they did. This particular clash of arms featured the bristling might of a rearmed and rambunctious America determined to conquer and rule over the territory that would otherwise become Canada. To achieve that, they first had to occupy it. In this intention they were stopped in their tracks by the combination of booted and spurred Canadian volunteers bearing arms, who in turn were reinforced by the hardy professionals of the local British garrisons and seriously backstopped by contingents of dedicated Aboriginals, mainly Mohawks.

Three years into the war, the invading Yanks would indeed be on the march—backwards. Beaten and humbled, they would de-camp Canadian territory as fast as they could. The American invaders were bested at nearly every turn, starting with the battle for Detroit, which was won hands down by the smaller Canadian contingent. (The British army and their Native allies suffered no casualties except for two wounded soldiers.) Most of the subsequent confrontations followed that pattern and it was clear that while the Americans fought as a duty, the Canadians were rallying to enthusiastically defend their new mother country. Under the layers of bafflegab and propaganda, there burned a small candle, pointing the way to Canada's eventual independence.

THE WAR OF 1812 produced Canada's first genuine military hero: British Major-General Isaac Brock, the elegant and intuitive commander appointed to defend Upper Canada, a colony that was almost entirely surrounded by American territory. It was a matter of dim record that when Brock was a twenty-one-year-old regimental

captain, he was baited into a duel. As the injured party, he had the
right to choose weapons. He picked pistols to be fired not at the usual
twelve paces, but point-blank, sitting at a table, with the opponents
face-to-face, their weapons hidden behind handkerchiefs. Upon
hearing the rules, Brock's opponent blanched and not irrationally
complained that they could both die. Brock smiled, and cocked his
pistol. His challenger blustered, then quit the field in disgrace.

As a commander, one of Brock's first moves was to recruit respectable youngsters who had volunteered their services and their
horses. Among them was the adventurous fifteen-year-old George
Jarvis, Stephen and Amelia's son, who enlisted in the 49th Regiment
as a Gentleman Cadet. By the end of the war, he was promoted to
private, corporal, and then sergeant. With characteristic (and frustrating) brevity, Stephen Jarvis, in contrast to other Loyalists, spent
little time reflecting on the proclamation of war with the United
States or on York's preparations for the coming conflict. His memoir leaps from describing his family's move to York to detailing his
involvement in the War of 1812. There is no indication of either
excitement at the prospects of facing Americans in battle or of regret at having to take up arms for a second time in his life. At first,
the war provided Jarvis with a means to supplement his income. He
took charge of the property of landowners who left Upper Canada
for the duration of the war. But it was hard to keep an old soldier
at home. With the escalating conflict, Stephen, as he wrote in his
memoir, "was again appointed Adjutant General of the Militia, and
was employed as such until York was taken by the enemy." He was
proud, too, that George had volunteered and Starr, his eldest son,
then twenty-five years old, served with the head of the Waggon (or
Wagon) Department of the 2nd Regiment of York Militia. Starr was
the first of the Jarvis sons to face the American foe because he was the
one who received a treasured family heirloom: the sword that had
been stained with American blood more than thirty years earlier, the
very same weapon Stephen had carried into battle as a lieutenant
in the South Carolina Dragoons. While Amelia may have protested

her son's preparation, she no doubt saw the futility of it all when she remembered that her husband had taken up arms when he was just nineteen years old.

It was young George, however, who had a knack for staying close to the action, as he did on that fateful October 13, 1812, during the fiercely contested Battle for Queenston Heights on the Niagara frontier. His cousins, the sons of William Jarvis, nineteen-year-old William Munson and his older brother, Samuel Peters—who two months earlier had helped Brock capture Detroit as a member of the 3rd York Militia—also participated in the battle.

The conflict at Queenston Heights pitted thirteen hundred British, Canadian, and Native combatants against an invading force of nine hundred American soldiers who hoped to establish a foothold on the Upper Canada side of the Niagara River before winter. Their target was the village of Queenston, which was at the mouth of the Niagara River's gorge. The river at this point was only two hundred yards wide. Queenston itself consisted of just twenty homes and a stone barracks with a smattering of farmhouses. The 49th Regiment of Foot, a company of the 2nd Regiment of York Militia, a detachment of the 41st Regiment of Foot, and a handful of local militia defended Queenston from Lewiston, New York, just across the river. Despite the strong British military presence in Queenston, it was still a tempting target for an invasion.

The Americans began crossing the river early in the predawn of October 13. Leading a reduced force but convinced that a rapid counterattack would prevent the Americans from securing their positions, Brock led the charge against the waves of invading Yanks. As George Jarvis later recalled in his memoir: "On retiring to the north end of the village on the Niagara road, our little band was met by General Brock. He was loudly cheered as he cried 'Follow me, boys!' and led us at a pretty smart trot towards the mountain. . . . At that time the top of the mountain and a great portion of its side was thickly covered with trees and was now occupied by American riflemen."

Glinting sword in hand, wearing a plumed hat and a scarlet coat with twenty golden buttons, outfitted in gleaming epaulettes and a scarf of many colours given to him by his native soul-mate—Tecumseh, the great Shawnee leader—the tall, dashing General Brock was a splendid sight leading his troops into battle. Unfortunately, he was an equally splendid target. When he paused momentarily in his climb to the battlefield, from thirty paces uphill a sharpshooter from an Ohio platoon of Patriots stepped out of ranks and pointed his musket at the illustrious Brock. He aimed between the general's second and third row of jacket buttons. The bullet hit just below Brock's heart. He died instantly.

Young Jarvis vainly attempted to comfort him: "Our gallant General fell on his side, within a few feet where I stood," he later reported. "Running up to him, I enquired: 'Are you much hurt, Sir?' The General placed his hand on his breast, made no reply, and slowly sunk down. The 49th now raised a shout, 'Revenge the General!'" Regulars and militia pressed forward, anxious to follow that yell, driving a superior force up the mountainside to a considerable distance beyond the summit. In recounting this story to grandchildren, George would point out that he was the nearest to Brock at his death. It was a historic moment. The defending army's publicists, anxious to exploit their fallen hero, planned to tell the world that the general's final words—in the Horatio Nelson manner of dying exhortations—had been: "Push On, Brave York Volunteers!" It was the youthful Jarvis who corrected the record and made history, in a small way.

Brock's casket was borne to Fort Niagara through a double line of five thousand clearly devastated Aboriginals and Canadian militiamen, sadly resting on reversed rifles. The salutes, with cannons firing at minute intervals, were echoed by the salvos of American gunners across the river—a rare but moving tribute to a courageous adversary. It was the War of 1812's defining moment.

———

GEORGE'S ADVENTURES did not end with the scaling of Queenston Heights. At one point in the conflict, a group of Americans captured the teenager and took him back to their camp. After enduring a night of taunting and threats of a hanging, George was released and rejoined the 49th Regiment. Stephen Jarvis, ever ready to commit his life (and events of war) to paper, wrote his cousin Munson in Saint John in November of 1812:

> You have, no doubt, with our successes thus far, and as my dear Daughter is in your city I trust that she has informed you of the meritorious conduct of our Brave Boy George, who thank God is exchanged and is again in front of the enemy with his brother Starr waiting an attack, which they expect every day. There has been an Armistice since the Battle of Queenstown and which continues, for what purpose I know not, without it is to give them an opportunity of erecting their gunboats and to attack us more formidably. You will agree with me that it is rather a hard case that my loyalty should make me a beggar which this war perhaps will effect, but we must trust to a Just Providence, and do our duty . . . if the war does not destroy us altogether.

While Jarvis's pride in his sons shines through this letter, he was also concerned that his farm might "go to ruin and our resources must be exhausted." The citizens of York were continually wary of an American invasion, leaving them little time to tend to their properties. Stephen's daughter Frances also felt the impact of the War of 1812. Her husband, Major John Maule, left her with friends in Saint John, New Brunswick, as he and the 104th Regiment marched overland to Kingston. It was a trek of historic proportions, unmatched by any Canadian regiment before or since. Setting off from Fredericton on February 21, the men of the 104th Regiment trudged one thousand kilometres (seven hundred miles) in just fifty-two days through one of the harshest winters on record, the only Canadian regiment "raised to the line" during the War of 1812. Recruited primarily in

New Brunswick, it included men from Prince Edward Island, Nova Scotia, and Britain as well as Upper and Lower Canada. These were Loyalist sons, blacks and whites, with Acadians and Habitants among the ranks, and not surprisingly they used snowshoes—that quintessential Canadian footwear—to march through the woodlands and across the frozen rivers of Lower Canada. With the 104th Regiment garrisoned in Kingston, American commanders felt that the Loyalist settlement was now impregnable, so they focused their efforts on capturing York, which, although a capital city, was only protected by a few troops manning a minuscule fort.

On April 27, 1813, the American army launched its long-feared attack on York. That morning, fourteen ships transporting a combined force of about 2,800 soldiers and sailors appeared in York Harbour. They were met by only three hundred British regulars and an estimated fifty Aboriginals. It was not much of a battle; most of the casualties were the result of an explosion at the garrison as the American troops marched in. The fort's powder magazine blew up, with the flying debris killing many waves of the American soldiers, including their commander, General Zebulon Pike. In the melee, William Munson Jarvis, who was stationed at the garrison, lost an eye—the most serious wound sustained by any young Jarvis.

Stephen Jarvis would later recount, "My son George happening to be then in York, General Sheaffe gave him command of one of the sections of the Grenadier company of the 8th Regiment. He took into the field twenty-five men in his Division and returned with only three, the rest being either killed or wounded." The fighting lasted a mere six hours and Sheaffe, outgunned and outmanned, retreated to Kingston. For reasons that are never given, the Americans made Stephen one of their prisoners once they took the city. In his memoir, he only notes that after he was captured, he "was dismissed from my military duty and applied myself to business." It would be up to his sons and those of his cousin, William Munson, to uphold the Jarvis name in battle. The Americans also temporarily imprisoned William Munson as they did Stephen. The whereabouts of William

Munson's father, William Jarvis Sr., during the American invasion of York are not known for certain. Given that the "principal gentleman" of York retired from the town, it may be that he took his wife and youngest children north along Yonge Street to seek refuge in the woods.

During the four days the Americans occupied York, its citizens—who numbered less than a thousand—were the victims of looting and plundering by U.S. soldiers and rogues from within the community. Penelope Beikie, the wife of John Beikie, the sheriff of York, claimed that "every house [the Americans] found deserted was completely sacked." On the second day of the occupation, an unknown group—possibly "freelancing sailors," as historian Alan Taylor suggests, though no one has ever identified the perpetrators—burned the government buildings on Front Street. It was later claimed that the Americans were angry after they found a scalp "suspended near the speaker's chair" and wanted revenge.

Within two months' time, William Munson, still recovering from his eye injury, was back in action at the Battle of Stoney Creek (today near Hamilton, Ontario). At that fight, with only a small number of their First Nation allies, the British regulars and Canadian militia put the fear of God into the Americans by yelling "like Indians," as one Upper Canadian soldier recalled. The ploy worked. "Indians!, Indians!" an American sentinel shouted in terror. The decisive battle, which the British and Canadians easily won, was over quickly and two of the American commanders, Generals William Winder and John Chandler, were captured.

Meanwhile, George Jarvis—who had just turned sixteen—was busy tending to the needs of a sweet woman named Laura Secord. On that fateful June 22, 1813, Stephen's second son was serving in the 49th Regiment under thirty-two-year-old Lieutenant James Fitzgibbon. Secord, the wife of a Loyalist who had been wounded at the Battle of Queenston Heights, entered the history books as the brave heroine who warned Fitzgibbon of an impending American raid. This information helped the British and their Native allies fend off the enemy at the Battle of Beaver Dams. However, Secord's thirty-two-kilometre walk through American-occupied territory was completely forgotten until 1860, when she finally received compensation from the Crown for her efforts. The myth building (and chocolates) would come later. Were it up to the Jarvis family, however, Secord would have been only a minor footnote. Like any good son of Stephen Jarvis, George kept a detailed notebook of his service in the war, being careful to jot down the year, month, and day of every event. What may disappoint admirers of Laura Secord is that George makes no mention of her dramatic appearance "to warn Fitzgibbon and save the country," even though he was there when she arrived. According to his version, all that Fitzgibbon did after giving Secord a hearing was to instruct young George "to see to the lady's comfort."

In July of 1813, the "business" to which Stephen Jarvis applied himself took him to Montreal. There, for the first time in four years, he saw his daughter Frances Maule and met his two grandsons. Fanny, as the family called her, had accompanied Colonel Martin Hunter of the 104th Regiment to Lower Canada earlier that spring. In later years, Jarvis would proudly write of the fourteen grandchildren Fanny produced, declaring, "It is a matter of surprise that children of their age should be so well educated and so forward—coming from the Land of Savages in America." Jarvis took great delight in both his grandchildren and his sons. On July 29, he wrote, "My hero George had returned safe from the sixth engagement since the war started." Within two days, American forces entered York for a second time that year, plundering and burning the capital. In Stephen's absence, his youngest son, William Botsford, was at home with his mother, Amelia. As an older man—he served as sheriff of the Home District in Upper Canada from 1827 to 1856—William Botsford could still vividly recall his mother's anxiety and his great responsibility as the "man of the family."

The British later exacted their revenge. In August of 1814, a raiding party of four thousand Royal Navy troops disembarked from

British warships anchored in Chesapeake Bay. They broke into the White House, the sparsely guarded sanctuary of American presidents, raided the kitchen, and enjoyed a hearty meal that had been originally set for a state banquet of forty Yank dignitaries. Then the friendly invaders set aflame that hallowed presidential palace as well as the nearby Treasury Building, and left town without ever being challenged by the stunned locals.

That raid was one of the highlights of the war in its daring execution and dramatic results. Having been warned of the attack, American president James Madison and his wife, Dolley, had skedaddled away, barely ahead of the invading commandos. Never again, before or since, had America's chief executive been deprived of his presidential perch.*

There still exist several seriously documented strategies in the secret vaults of American diplomacy for future invasions of Canada. The most specific is the 1934 "Action Plan Red" with strategic details providing for "the widespread destruction and devastation of Canada," specifying "bombing targets in Halifax, Montreal and Quebec City." A subsequent amendment maintained in the Pentagon advocated the use of poison gas, so that "Canada would surrender quickly, saving American soldiers' lives."

There was indeed an element of the absurd in the American side of the war. Early in the conflict, two hundred of the invading Ohio militiamen stopped the invasion of Canada in its tracks by announcing that they had not signed up for service outside American territory, and sat on their weapons.

During the shake-down phase of the contest, the Canadians mostly held back, giving the Yanks plenty of opportunity to demonstrate their dismal planning, accentuated by bad luck. Take the case of Winfield Scott, who was promoted personally by President Madison

---

*The subsequent efforts to repair the damage to the presidential residence with coats of white paint over the scorched walls resulted in the White House gaining its nickname. It was officially designated the White House by President Theodore Roosevelt in 1901.

to the rank of brigadier general—though he was only twenty-eight years old—and placed in charge of four brigades assigned to capture Fort Erie. On the morning of July 3, 1814, Scott guided his brigade across the Niagara River rowing small boats, with him in charge. He tested the depth of the water with his sword and figured he could easily wade ashore. But when he stepped off his boat, he promptly disappeared from view. That can happen—riverbeds are notoriously uneven—but a public dunking was not the leadership image that the new commanding officer had hoped to portray.

One of the least remembered but dramatic aspects of this war was how a tiny contingent of Quebeckers in Chateauguay Valley, which was on the main attack route of the invading Americans, turned them back, setting the stage for the defeat of the main American army at Crysler's farm (close to Cornwall, Ontario) a few weeks later. The French Canadians—who numbered about 460 versus an American force of 4,500—were under the command of Lieutenant-Colonel Charles de Salaberry, and were assisted by the talents of local Abenaki scouts whose rifle shots could blind a squirrel from twenty paces. "It was a well-planned backwoods maneuver, taking the best possible advantage of the differences between the combatants," commented Loyalist descendant Tom Walker. During the battle, the American troops under sniper attack were so disorganized that they accidentally shot at each other. The French Canadians and small number of Indian fighters outlasted the American force until British/Canadian reinforcements arrived to send the disheartened and confused Americans on their way.

Recognizing that they had little time left for a decisive victory, American commanders made a final attempt to take control of the Niagara peninsula. George Jarvis, who had stood next to the dying Brock in Queenston, was now with the 8th Regiment, fending off the renewed American efforts. On July 5, he was part of a disastrous defeat at the Battle of Chippawa. Of the 2,100 men fighting for the British, 108 were killed and 319 were wounded, double the losses of the enemy. Twenty days later, the two forces once again faced one another in the bloodiest of the war's clashes—the deadliest battle fought on Canadian soil—the Battle of Lundy's Lane.

It was not a battle fought at a great distance from the foe. Soldier met solder at close quarters to such a degree that war-hardened British officers were horrified at the carnage. Lieutenant-General Gordon Drummond later wrote, "Of so determined a character were (the enemy's) attacks directed against our guns that our artillery men were bayonetted by the enemy in the act of loading, and the muzzles of the enemy's guns were advanced within a few yards of ours." At the end of the day, while the number of wounded was almost the same for both sides, 84 of the British forces were dead while 171 Americans had been killed on the battlefield. The wounded on both sides totalled more than 1,100, with 110 Americans captured versus 169 for the British who were taken prisoner. "Such a scene of carnage I never beheld," Dr. E. W. Bull, the American surgeon, wrote on July 31. "Red coats and blue and grey were promiscuously intermingled, in many places three deep, and around the hill . . . the carcasses of 60 or 70 horses disfigured the scene." The British surgeons, too, were kept busy day and night in oppressive heat amputating limbs from the suffering wounded with only alcohol to use as an anesthetic.

George Jarvis had been in the thick of it all. Just seventeen years old, George was placed in command of a battalion company when his captain took ill. George fought from two in the afternoon until midnight. He later recalled, "I don't deny that the Americans showed courage, but they had little or no discipline and no confidence either in themselves or their officers. In the woods they were our superiors, but in the open field, they were nowhere."

A week later, Jarvis's commanding officer led his men in a siege of the Americans' Fort Erie in a fight that lasted on and off from August 4 to September 21—the last and longest battle of the War of 1812. In the wee hours of August 15, General Drummond ordered a three-pronged attack. The 8th Regiment, which included young George Jarvis, was part of a large contingent of men commanded by Lieutenant-Colonel Victor Fisher. Fisher and his men attacked the American battery at Snake Hill. Lieutenant-Colonel Hercules Scott of the 103rd, commanding 650 men, was assigned the task of removing the Douglass Battery located between Fort Erie and the lake shore. And the assault on the northern entrenchments was led by General Drummond's distant cousin, Lieutenant-Colonel William Drummond of the 104th. He and his 250 men targeted the main fort. During the attack, William Drummond famously shouted to his men, "Give no quarter to the damn Yankees!" The British and Upper Canada forces caught the Americans by surprise and indeed captured the fort's northern bastion. However, the enemy regrouped and retaliated with a barrage of gunfire, killing—among others—Lieutenant-Colonel Drummond.

A large gunpowder magazine beneath the bastion that was occupied by the Crown's forces was ignited, demolishing both the bastion and the nearby barracks. About two hundred British soldiers were killed while flaming timbers fell on Americans. The bodies of some of Jarvis's fellow soldiers were thrown from the bastion to land on the bayonets of American soldiers in the trenches. When the 104th Regiment collected itself together for the next day's roll call, soldiers could be seen openly weeping over the loss of half of their companions. George Jarvis's obituary, written sixty-four years after the disastrous siege, noted that he was "at the front and called the storming of Fort Erie, perhaps the bloodiest strife of the war." The historian James Croil summarized the siege noting, "From the 29th of July till the 21st September, George never had his clothes off. Every other day he was on piquet (guard duty) and during the whole time under constant fire from the enemy's guns. Nearly every day it rained, and huts, constructed with branches of trees, formed their only covering."

On September 17, at Fort Erie, the Americans captured George and took him within their lines. He eventually escaped, and by November, the 8th Regiment began its march to Montreal, from where it sailed to England. George was the first of Stephen Jarvis's sons to visit England. A Jarvis now guarded Windsor Castle, representing a family that had once carried sword and musket in defence of a United British Empire. In 1816, George's commander interceded on his behalf and had him transferred to the 104th Regiment that was about to sail for Lower Canada. A rotting ship almost succeeded in doing what fighting at close quarters had not done. It took two months for George's ship to cross the Atlantic; during the voyage, it was almost consumed by flames. Upon arriving in Montreal in July of 1817, the 104th Regiment was disbanded and twenty-year-old George was set free to return to York.

George's obituary in April 1878 succinctly recounted his exploits in the War of 1812. "But too few has been allotted in two years, and while under eighteen years of age, to participate in seven general engagements, to be twice taken prisoner, and to escape scatheless mid all the accidents of flood and field." George returned to a York that had been at peace for three years. While he had been doing sentry duty at Windsor Castle in late 1814, British and American negotiators had been meeting in Ghent, Belgium, to finish the wording of the final peace treaty. On Christmas Eve 1814, they declared hostilities to be at an end. After being ratified by Congress in February, the treaty was proclaimed throughout British North America on March 1, 1815.*

The War of 1812 was over. Its repercussions had only begun. The sons of two Loyalists, Stephen and William Jarvis, had survived the

---

*Mysteriously, nature recognized the ending of the War of 1812. On April 15, 1815, when Canada's victory was assured and the disillusioned Yanks had snuck back home, the ice disappeared from the bays around York. This was two weeks earlier than usual, which in turn allowed immense flights of wild ducks and pigeons to revisit their summer nesting grounds early. It was nature's way of saluting the finish of a bloody, brutal war. The birds had not been properly briefed.

War of 1812, and, like the city of York, would rise out of the ashes to accomplish great things. Both city and sons had gone through their test of fire and were stronger for it.

THE FINAL COUNT was that the invading 35,000 Americans were beaten by 5,000 British redcoats, and most crucially, a people's army led by the utterly fearless General Isaac Brock. Details of the War of 1812 are still debated, but out of that overwrought analysis emerged one crystal-clear truth: the terminal victims of the war were the courageous Aboriginal allies who provided the essential buffer state that backstopped the defending troops. Instead of being rewarded, they were deprived of their well-earned recompenses and became minor factors in the country's future. Shawnee war chief Tecumseh was fully as responsible for the Canadian victories as General Brock, and the two fighters worshipped one another. Tecumseh was killed while protecting retreating British troops, and it remains one of the blackest marks in Canadian history that the First Nations were rewarded for their inestimable contributions by having their best land, mainly in the American Midwest, stolen.

The U.S. victory at the battle of the Thames (near London, Ontario), where Tecumseh was killed, marked the effective end of the Indian Confederacy and their hope of rolling back America's settlement frontier. The British might have defended Aboriginal land rights, but, weary of fighting and arguing with the Americans, they took the most politically expedient path and thoughtlessly abandoned their onetime allies. It was that shameful legacy which fully confirmed, once and for ever, the existence of two very different states that split the North American continent into two independent entities with no consideration of Aboriginal dreams of justice.

The War of 1812 brought the United States from a federal union into single nationhood, so it became recognized as having won its independence. Canada, which entered the war defended by a down-home collection of freelance Sunday warriors, emerged as its own master. We moved from colony to nation, both in perception and in reality. "Canada flourished as the result of an invasion being repelled," popular historian the late Pierre Berton wrote in his history of the war. "Out of it, shaped by an emerging nationalism and tempered by rebellion, grew that special form of state paternalism that makes the Canadian way of life significantly different from the individualistic Americans'. Thus, in a psychological as well as political sense, we are Canadians and not Americans because of a foolish war that scarcely anyone wanted or needed, but which, once launched, none knew how to stop."

Canada was not considered a nation when the smug Yanks staged their invasion. By the time the final shot was fired, we had become a brave new home country. The War of 1812 actually became an absolutely invaluable event in Canada's historic march to nationhood. Had anyone predicted that the Yankee invasion would turn out to be a prologue to defeat, they would not have been believed. Yet that was precisely what it turned out to be—and if there are any doubters, let them remember our troops enjoying their celebratory luncheon just before they set Washington's White House on fire.

9

THE ETERNAL JARVIS SAGA

"All I ask from life, is to have been born a JARVIS!"

As the dust of war began to settle around him in January of 1815, Stephen Jarvis took stock of his family and his fortune. His second daughter, Mrs. Frances Maule, was due to leave for England with her husband's regiment; and only two of Stephen's other children, Betsey and Bell (or Rachel Isabella), the two unmarried "girls," still lived in the Jarvis home. The war years had been hard on Stephen's Amelia. Having endured the stresses of the attack on York and anxiety over her two soldier sons, Mrs. Jarvis was in a state of weakened health. In 1815, she had the first of many strokes. Still, the Jarvis family was more fortunate than most as all three Jarvis sons survived the War of 1812.

Frederick Starr Jarvis, the oldest son, twenty-eight years old in 1815, returned from the wagon department to work his family's fifteen-acre land, known as "Brunswick Farm." Within a year of peace being declared, his father sold him Brunswick Farm for $500. Starr soon married Susan Merigold, the eldest daughter of the Jarvises' neighbours, Thomas and Elizabeth Merigold. Thomas was also a Loyalist who had come to Upper Canada via New Brunswick.

Starr and Susan eventually had twelve offspring—eight sons and four daughters. Sadly, two of the children, Henry and Hester, died young.

When George Stephen, the second Jarvis son, returned in 1817 from his two-year station in Great Britain, he took up the study of law in Brockville. Turning sixteen in 1815, George's brother William Botsford Jarvis, who had been the "man of the house" when American troops attacked York, returned to his studies. Within three years' time, he became a clerk in the provincial secretary's office. William Botsford worked alongside his second cousin, Samuel Peters Jarvis. In 1817, Samuel, a lawyer, was appointed clerk of the crown in chancery, an administrative position in the Upper Canadian House of Assembly. He served in that capacity for the next two decades.

Samuel Peters's brother William Munson had also survived the war, though he had returned home having lost the use of an eye. In the years ahead, the four daughters of William and Hannah Jarvis married into successful merchants' families. Prosperity seemed assured for all of the members of Upper Canada's extended Jarvis family except, perhaps, for the elder Stephen. After the battle of York, the old Loyalist soldier retired from military duty, leaving the fighting to the younger members of the clan in favour of pursuing business interests (his experience working with his cousin William had also soured him about employment with the government). Following the advice of friends, Stephen went to Montreal with $500 to buy a variety of goods that he planned to sell at a profit in York. As he later confided in his memoirs, "if the war had continued, I should have done well." But it didn't. "The Peace of 1815," he recorded, "left a very large supply of goods on hand, and the depreciation was of such extent that I was obliged to sell my house and all my real property to get out of debt, and at the close of war, I was reduced to my half-pay only for the support of my large family."

Once again, Stephen was a hostage to the consequences of war. But rather than moving to seek out new prospects as he had done in 1785 and 1809, he only had to wait for a change in the leadership of Upper Canada for his fortunes to improve. In 1817, Britain appointed a new administrator for its triumphant Loyalist colony. Colonel Samuel Bois Smith succeeded Francis Gore. Once before in the Jarvis saga, service in the Queen's Rangers had been the means by which William Jarvis was able to hitch his future to the rising star of John Graves Simcoe. Now, thirty-four years after its disbanding, the Loyalist regiment in which Stephen had served during the revolution came to his aid. Smith, a former officer in the Queen's Rangers, was delighted to be reunited with his old friend Stephen and promptly gave him an appointment in the registry office of the home district. At a salary of £150 per year, the new job gave Stephen a peace of mind he had not known since the beginning of the War of 1812. He also finally achieved the prestige he had long sought in both the revolution and New Brunswick by being appointed to a position within the Upper Canadian House of Assembly. Sometime after he was made provincial registrar, Jarvis became the Gentleman Usher of the Black Rod, a position that his son Starr would later fulfill as well. Stephen Jarvis revelled in being part of a five-hundred-year-old parliamentary tradition. The ebony cane that is the Black Rod is the symbol of governmental authority. The usher of the black rod is the personal attendant of the sovereign's representative as well as the senior protocol officer. He directs the details relating to official parliamentary ceremonies, including the opening of the legislature and the Speech from the Throne.

The historian Dr. Henry Scadding described Jarvis as "the last man in Canada to give up the style of hair-dressing in Perruque that was the fashion in Washington's time. . . . At the ceremony of the Opening of the House, part of his duty was to make several very fine bows, and his appearance, when in his silk hose and silver shoe buckles, with lace ruffles under his chin and about his wrists, with sword in hand and hair tied Perruque, he was the last of picturesque type now unknown. His courtly manners and distinguished bearing made his official bows the despair of all his successors."

Full of confidence in himself, his future, and his children, Stephen decided to make a final journey to Connecticut to visit his aging parents in 1818. Weakened by her strokes, Amelia was not able to visit the colony of her birth. Perhaps it was just as well. Stephen was as exuberant a Loyalist as ever and nearly got himself in trouble. When he shouted "Hurrah for Old England" and drank the King's health in his parents' home, his father was terrified, crying out, "For God's sake, son, you will be mobbed again!" When his first cousin Noah Jarvis invited him over for a drink, Stephen was shown a framed copy of the Declaration of Independence. Noah chided him saying, "There my royal cousin is, I think, a dram bitter enough for you." Stephen replied, "Aha! That's it, is it you damned rebel!"

Word of Amelia's dramatically declining health brought the sixty-two-year-old Loyalist's visit to a sudden halt—and revealed that where his wife was concerned, he was the same impetuous, ardent lover he had been in 1775. As soon as Stephen received the troubling news from Upper Canada, he set off on horseback just an hour before midnight and rode until he reached Forty Mile Creek two hours before dawn. After getting a ride in a sleigh, Jarvis then walked fourteen miles, borrowed a horse, and rode all night until dawn. When he got home, he found Amelia to be better. But her recovery was only temporary. She died within the year.

Although he lost the love of his life, Stephen maintained his devotion to the Crown, a loyalty that had shaped his destiny. To a cousin in 1819, he wrote, "I suppose your government will be looking wishfully towards Canada, since they have got the Floridas, and without the object of the Great Canal into the South Sea should draw their attention, I suspect we must again contend for the possession of the Land of Liberty—our population is increasing fast, my dear sir, and experience has shown what a small number can do in repelling an invading foe—God of his Infinite Mercy prevent a war between the two governments, and may always live and flourish as good friends and neighbours." The eternal Loyalist veteran was upbeat about the future. A corner had been turned in his family's fortunes. In that same year he wrote a relative that he had "been spared to see my children grow up to be respectable and valuable members of society."

Stephen's time in the United States had stirred old feelings. Despite his unwavering loyalty, he was still an American at heart. There were wounds yet unhealed. In 1823, he wrote to a cousin in New York: "What can be the reason that all my relations are so loathe [*sic*] to let me hear from them? Is it because I am so staunch a Subject to the Government under which I was born, and to which I have religiously adhered, that they wish to forget me?" Putting aside the ongoing rejection from the Patriot cousins, Jarvis reflected on his legacy in a gushing letter to a Boston relative four years later. "I shall, however, leave a family behind that will be no disgrace to the name of Jarvis . . . they are valuable members of society and are comfortable in their several stations."

The oldest Jarvis Loyalist had every reason to feel proud. Betsey, the daughter born in the midst of Patriot persecution, had married a widower with a large family. Her husband, the Rev. Dr. Thomas Phillips, later became the first vice-principal of Upper Canada College. The Jarvis influence would be felt beyond the realm of education. George, Stephen's war hero son, had been called to the Upper Canada bar and within two years' time had been made a judge of the Ottawa district. George commanded a cavalry troop during the rebellions of the 1830s and in 1836 represented the Cornwall area as a Conservative member of the Upper Canada legislature. He was a judge in Stormont, Dundas, and Glengarry. In 1850, he was appointed the lieutenant-colonel of the 1st Stormont Militia, which would have made his father especially proud. George's son, Salter Mountain Jarvis, fought for Canada in the Fenian Raids of 1866 and later in the Northwest Rebellion. Interesting careers for a man who would one day become an Anglican minister. Later descendants of the Jarvis family would see action in both world wars.

––––––––––

IN THE DECADE after the War of 1812, York continued to thrive as the centre of Upper Canadian commerce, trade, education, religion, and culture. Upper Canada College started training and moulding the young minds of the province's future leaders in 1829, and Osgoode Hall was opened two years later to educate many UCC graduates as lawyers. York had a general hospital in the vicinity of King and John Streets, though given the primitive state of medicine practiced it was said "that once you entered the hospital you did not come out." St. James Church was severely damaged in the war by the Americans. The wooden church was torn down in 1833 and replaced with a new stone structure that was destroyed by fire in January 1839. It was rebuilt one more time, reopening eleven months later as the St. James Cathedral. Likewise, the provincial Parliament Buildings, which the Americans had ruthlessly burned, were also rebuilt. (The new Parliament Buildings were completed by 1820, then destroyed again in a fire in 1824.) Every issue, no matter how big or small, seemed to revolve around politics and York's status as the provincial capital. "The people of York were all politicians," astutely pointed out Joseph Gould, a young farmer who visited in 1830, "and excitement ran so high that quarrels between neighbours were of frequent occurrence."

A trip to York was not without its difficulties. Travel on George Playter's horse-drawn stagecoach service from Holland Landing to York, sixty-one kilometres south down Yonge Street, took about eight hours over an uneven and treacherous muddy path. The fare was six shillings and three pence, and often the passengers had to help the driver push and drag the coach and horses up steep hills and out of the muck.

It seemed that everyone had an opinion about York, good and bad; it is a theme that runs through Toronto's history. "The Town of York is not like any other I have ever seen and [is] still less like any with which you are familiar—it seems all suburb," Mary O'Brien, who lived north of the city, observed in February 1829. "The streets are laid out wide and parallel at right angles with each other . . . the shops are numerous but [do] not make much show." A few months later on another visit, she found "the streets swarming with people and abounding in carriages. I have never before seen it so busy and gay."

The travel writer George Henry, author of *The Emigrant Guide, or Canada as It Is* (1835), extolled York and its "neat pretty villas, built on handsome construction." He also was awestruck by the newly built bridge over the Don, "the numerous substantial brick dwelling houses," and the "really elegant" stores and shops along King Street. More than a decade earlier, Frances Stewart, an Irish immigrant, was far less impressed by the town. "York looked pretty from the lake as we sailed up in a schooner [from Kingston]," she wrote in 1822 on her first trip there, "but on landing we found it not a pleasant place, as it is sunk down in a little amphitheatre cut out of the great bleak forest. . . . It is not a healthy town (fever and ague are common) and it is said to be much fallen off with the last two years; a deadness hangs over everything." That assessment was particularly true for the lower-class and less well-off residents, of which there were many among the 1,500 inhabitants. Punishment for petty crime was severe—public lashings were frequent—and theft, arson, and larceny were hanging offences. There was little sympathy for the poor or the downtrodden among York's elite who resided in brick mansions near the waterfront and on country-style estates beyond the city's (ever expanding) boundaries, like "The Grange," built for £300 by lawyer D'Arcy Boulton on a lot west of University Avenue and Dundas Street.

Stephen's cousin William Jarvis, the provincial secretary, shared upper-class values even if he did not quite measure up. William suffered from gout and money problems. When he died on August 13, 1817, he was "virtually bankrupt," claimed Toronto lawyer David Jarvis, a descendant of Munson Jarvis. William was not a major figure in York's establishment and was generally disdained for his ostentatiousness. He was certainly not in the same league as such boulevardiers as William Allan, one of the founders of the Bank of

Upper Canada, or John Beverley Robinson, the son of a Loyalist, who served as the attorney general of Upper Canada before becoming chief justice in 1829. William Jarvis did run for office (he lost) and, despite his reputation for being a political conservative, for a time he supported Judge Robert Thorpe in his attempts to shape a more democratic Upper Canada. An Irish immigrant, Thorpe arrived in York from Prince Edward Island in 1805, when he was appointed judge of the Court of King's Bench in Upper Canada. Politically active and opinionated, he argued that citizens would only remain loyal if they enjoyed the rights to which they were entitled under British law—and if they had a cabinet that was responsible to the elected legislature, not the governor. This was certainly a common set of values for loyal American refugees.

The question of power—who held it and how it was wielded—became the focus of the definitive conflict in Upper Canada during the 1820s and 1830s. This constitutional battle, a clash over the province's future, was part of the middle-class struggle for democracy that played out in the early nineteenth century. In England it manifested itself in the fight over the Reform Acts of the 1830s to expand the right to vote, and in Europe it culminated with the less successful, though more violent, 1848 revolutions.

In Upper Canada, the fight came down to a contest between conservatives (Tories) and reformers (Grits). On one side were members of the Family Compact (often called "the court party"), the elite group—many of whom were Loyalists or the sons of Loyalists—who served at the behest of the governor on the appointed Executive and Legislative Councils. And on the other side were reformers, many of whom could also claim Loyalist ancestry, and, as historian David Mills has suggested, "often cited the Loyalists' dedication to principle to justify dissent against what they perceived to be the narrow and self-serving interests of the provincial administration." There were both moderates, such as William Baldwin and his son Robert, who believed "responsible government"—government in which the executive would be responsible to the elected representatives of the people rather than the governor—should be achieved through a peaceful process, as well as radicals, like William Lyon Mackenzie, a newspaper publisher and Toronto's first mayor in 1834, who ultimately concluded that only an armed rebellion could resolve the alleged injustices that ailed Upper Canada.

Mackenzie had immigrated to Upper Canada from Scotland in 1820 at the age of twenty-five, part of the Great Migration from England, Scotland, Ireland, and Wales, a mass movement of people who were pushed to seek new opportunities by the onset of industrialization, the growth of factories, and changes in agricultural practices and land distribution. Upper Canada's population doubled from 1815 to 1828, making the Loyalists a minority in the province, as was the case in New Brunswick. The newcomers brought with them ideas about government and society that challenged, and even posed a threat to, the province's entrenched Loyalist values. In the decade after the conclusion of the War of 1812, being Upper Canadian was synonymous with being staunchly British. No one better epitomized those traditions than Reverend John Strachan, an Anglican clergyman, teacher, and mentor to the members of the Family Compact. As he claimed in a speech on June 3, 1814, even before the war was officially over: "We have shown that the same spirit animates the children of the Loyalists which inspired their fathers to put down treason and rebellion; and to stand up for the unity of the empire. We have given many proofs of our loyalty and affection for our gracious Sovereign; reverence for our laws and constitution, and devotion to our country."

That declaration of faith and devotion in all things British manifested itself in many ways from mourning the death of King George III in 1820 to trying to ban the use of American textbooks in Upper Canadian schools lest they negatively influence the minds of youngsters in York, Kingston, and other villages with objectionable republican values. (On the other hand, some Upper Canadians, like today, grudgingly admired American know-how. In the view of one Kingston writer in 1826, for example, the Americans "are chiefly remarkable abroad for their great good sense, their industry, their plain dealing, their equitable temper, their perseverance, their sound practical morality, cool courage and variety of resources, after the overthrow of any hope whatever.") Preserving the British connection for which the Loyalists had risked their lives was imperative. Thus, someone of William Lyon Mackenzie's ilk and class, who insulted the powers-that-be with his impertinent language—in a newspaper article of May 18, 1826, Mackenzie referred to Strachan as "a diminutive, paltry, insignificant Scotch turncoat parish schoolmaster"— soon wrote favourably of American-style democracy, which was a perceived threat to the Loyalist way of life.

One of Mackenzie's enemies was William Jarvis's son, Samuel Peters, who, as his biographers Douglas Leighton and Robert J. Burns put it, had "a fiery temperament and an impetuous nature combined with a strong sense of family and personal honour." These characteristics were precisely what led to Samuel's infamous duel in 1817 that resulted in the death of eighteen-year-old John Ridout— though Ridout, the son of Surveyor-General Thomas Ridout, was hardly an innocent victim. The two young men had a misunderstanding over money and some badmouthing about the Jarvises by Thomas Ridout's wife and John's mother, Mary. The families lived across the street from one another and their children attended the same schools. The Ridouts charged the Jarvises with failing to repay a debt incurred by Samuel's sister. What precipitated the duel was John Ridout asking Samuel to confirm that he had witnessed Samuel's father signing a document proving William Jarvis was trying to elude his creditors. Samuel threw John out of his office. This was on John's mind a few days later when he assaulted Samuel in the street with a stick in front of witnesses. A duel was the only way to settle their differences. In the exchange of gunfire on a field north of York, Ridout shot first prematurely, but missed. Ridout tried to walk away, but the duel continued at the behest of the seconds. At the count of three, Jarvis fired at Ridout, whose pistol was empty, and killed him. (According to one of Jarvis's descendants, Julia Jarvis,

Samuel tried to fire wide and instead hit Ridout unintentionally. This may be family folklore. On the other hand, purposely firing wide in a duel was interpreted as "an admission of guilt or as an apology.") Ridout lived long enough to shake hands with Jarvis, but then fainted and died. Jarvis was charged with manslaughter, but, like nearly all those guilty of participating in duels, he was acquitted by members of a jury who agreed with the principle that defending one's honour was paramount, even with pistols at eight paces (standard dueling was at twelve paces). Thereafter, as Ridout descendant Godfrey Ridout, a University of Toronto music professor, recalled (in a 1974 exchange of letters to the editor in the *Globe and Mail* with Julia Jarvis about the history of the duel), Mary Ridout stood "on the steps of St. James Cathedral every Sunday after divine service and loudly, as only she could, cursed the Jarvis and Boulton families (D'Arcy Boulton had been Jarvis's second)." Samuel's involvement in this incident prevented him from succeeding his father as provincial secretary, a position he coveted. Once he was acquitted in the killing of Ridout, Samuel did serve briefly as the secretary to the acting lieutenant-governor.

In 1818, Samuel Peters married Mary Powell, the daughter of Chief Justice William Dummer Powell, who had presided over his trial. Despite the notoriety of the duel, Mary's mother, Anne, was not unhappy about the union; only the memory of William Jarvis tainted the wedding announcement. "We can have no personal objections to the connections [with the Jarvis family]," Anne Powell wrote, "but truly regret that an unworthy Father had entailed difficulty upon a Son, who have been perfectly equal to the support of a family; he is Wm. J. the late Secretary of the Province whose unprincipled conduct threatened ruin to his family." Samuel and Mary and their budding family returned to York in 1824.

By then, William Lyon Mackenzie had begun publishing his newspaper, the *Colonial Advocate*, infuriating the leaders of the Family Compact and their supporters with his legendary brazen rhetoric. "It is not . . . to be denied that the government of Upper Canada is a despotism," Mackenzie later concluded, "a government legally existing independent of the will of the governed." John Beverley Robinson once referred to Mackenzie as "a conceited red-haired fellow with an apron"—and that was about the politest comment that was ever made about him.

Samuel Peters Jarvis had zero tolerance for Mackenzie. In June 1826, he led fourteen young men in an attack on Mackenzie's printing shop. (Samuel also had a personal score to settle with Mackenzie. The printer had called him a "murderer" for the duelling death of Ridout.) Disguised as Natives, they planned to horsewhip Mackenzie, but as he was not in his shop, they dismembered his printing press and threw it into Toronto's harbour. Jarvis and members of the Family Compact later paid Mackenzie damages of £625, allowing him to set up a larger operation. Not all of Samuel's recruiting had to do with settling personal grievances. He also organized a group of volunteers to fight on the government's side in the Rebellion of 1837 led by William Lyon Mackenzie. He named this militia the Queen's Rangers in honour of his father's old Revolutionary War regiment.

It was Samuel's cousin, William Botsford Jarvis, Stephen and Amelia Jarvis's youngest son, who was front and centre during the ill-fated Mackenzie rebellion. William filled a number of public offices during his lifetime. In 1827, he became a sheriff of the home district. That same year, he married Mary Boyles Powell—granddaughter of Chief Justice William Dummer Powell and niece of Samuel Peters's wife, Mary Powell—a union which linked him with York's elite. William and Mary moved into the house William had purchased in 1824 (from lawyer John Edward Small) northeast of the town's main business area. Because wild roses grew in such abundance near the four-hundred-acre estate, Mary christened it "Rosedale"—the name later used for the entire upscale Toronto neighbourhood north of Bloor Street, east of Yonge Street, and south of St. Clair Avenue.

Distinguished by bushy sideburns and a thick (Lanny McDonald–style) moustache, Sheriff Jarvis is remembered for freeing the inmates of the debtor's prison to save them from cholera. In the 1830s, he was part of the Provincial Agricultural Association, district and local agricultural societies, the Toronto Agricultural Association, and the Toronto Athenaeum; a municipal politician; a land speculator; and an entrepreneur.

In the first municipal election following York's incorporation as the city of Toronto in 1834, William Lyon Mackenzie was elected an alderman and then chosen by his peers as the city's first mayor. He soon found the job too mundane, despite having to deal with another cholera epidemic, during which five hundred people died. He was elected again to the provincial assembly in the fall of 1834 and did not relinquish his work as mayor (which was permitted in those days) until the next civic election in 1835.

Mackenzie did not set out to resort to violence. But when his appeals to officials in England for redress against the perceived abuse of the Family Compact were ignored, he adopted a more radical position that ultimately culminated with his attempted takeover of Toronto in the failed Rebellion of 1837. After a middling serious rebellion broke out in Lower Canada on October 9, 1837, British troops stationed at Fort York in Toronto were dispatched into Quebec to suppress the uprising.

With most of the regular troops gone, Mackenzie and his motley herd of about four hundred supporters marched into what is now downtown Toronto. On December 4, 1837, his people's army, carrying pitchforks and rifles designed to hunt fowl, tried but failed to seize a Toronto armoury. The encounter between Mackenzie's revolutionaries and the remaining garrison (re-enforced by students from Upper Canada College) lasted less than a day. This was attributed mostly to the unfortunate perception among the rebels that when their comrades in the front ranks bent down to reload, they were thought to have been hit by enemy fire. In less than an afternoon the confrontation was over, and the rebel forces retired to various taverns to celebrate. Local Tory supporters later burned homes and farms of the known rebels but everybody else went back to work. (Since this was, after all, a Canadian revolution, the former rebels were compensated by the Canadian government for their lost property.)

During the altercation, William Botsford Jarvis had taken a handful of men and stationed them in a cabbage field to await the arrival of Mackenzie and his rebel soldiers. He ordered the firing of the single volley which broke up the rebels' march on Toronto. In his day, Jarvis was sometimes referred to as "the saviour of the city." William Botsford Jarvis became a member of the St. Andrew's Masonic Lodge, the St. George's society, the Toronto Turf Club, the Toronto Club, and the Toronto Boat Club (which later became the Royal Canadian Yacht Club). In 1845, he was a commissioner who oversaw the construction of the Provincial Lunatic Asylum—one of the many examples of his efforts to try to improve the living conditions of Toronto's citizens. He was also the first president of the Board of Arts and Manufactures for Upper Canada, which awarded local scholars and artists. He died on July 26, 1864. Robert J. Burns, his biographer, summed up his life in this uninspiring obituary: "In a career only partially characterized by his official and political activities he showed a keen interest in the development of Toronto and in the welfare of its residents, and ended his life a respected patriarch of his adopted city."

SAMUEL PETERS JARVIS did not fare as well. In 1845, Samuel was removed from his appointment as the chief superintendent of Indian affairs for Upper Canada. An investigating commission alleged that Jarvis was guilty of bribery, fraud, religious discrimination, and a lack of concern for the Natives' welfare. Samuel denied any wrongdoing, but since £4,000 had been taken from the Indian Department's coffers, he was compelled to sell his land in York. This included the family's home, "Hazelburn," a fine brick house with ten acres of lawns and gardens, which was demolished in 1847. Jarvis Street came into existence as a result of the town lots formed from his divided estate.

Samuel Peters Jarvis Jr., the eldest son among his and Mary's ten children, did much to salvage his father's name. After studying law, he joined the army, serving with the 82nd Regiment during the Indian Mutiny (1857–1859). His distinguished service at the major battles of the mutiny earned him the rank of major and a medal. He went on to become the assistant adjutant-general of militia in Canada with the rank of lieutenant-colonel in the British army. During the Riel Rebellion, he was appointed to the command of the Ontario Battalion. He was later commandant of the garrison at Fort Garry, staying there until the young dominion's troops had left Manitoba. Queen Victoria later made him a Companion of the Order of St. Michael and St. George. In 1878, he was recruited for special service in South Africa's Kaffir War. Another of Samuel Peters's grandsons was Edward Aemillius Jarvis. Aemillius, as he was called, was the son of William D. P. Jarvis—a lawyer who died in 1860 at the age of thirty-nine a few months after Aemillius was born—and he followed family tradition by becoming embroiled in controversy. Aemillius was a successful financier and involved with the Steel Company of Canada, among other business ventures. An accomplished yachts-man—he was known at the Royal Canadian Yacht Club as "the Commodore"—he also was awarded the Special Service Decoration for his work in recruiting and training men for the Royal Canadian Navy during the First World War.

In 1923, Aemillius Jarvis supervised, at the Ontario government's request, the repurchasing of $18 million of provincial bonds issued in Great Britain. On the transaction, he made a commission of half a million dollars and was accused of conspiracy. The case became entangled in the scandal involving Peter Smith, the disgraced provincial treasurer in the government of E. C. Drury, who was found guilty of conspiracy to defraud the government and sentenced to three years in jail. Money from Jarvis's brokerage company was discovered in Smith's accounts. At a trial in Toronto in October 1924, Jarvis was convicted on the same charge as Smith, sentenced to six months in jail, and fined $600,000 (though it was reduced to $200,000).

———

THE NEW BRUNSWICK WING of the Jarvis clan also prospered, avoiding controversy. In the early nineteenth century, Saint John was one of the largest cities in British North America. In 1810, its population was 4,500 and by the early 1850s more than 30,000. The city faltered in the twentieth century, but in its heyday Saint John was the focus of the timber trade. In a good year, more than 300,000 tons of timber was exported from New Brunswick—a business that had a telling impact on Saint John and the entire province. It was as if New Brunswick, suggested historian Arthur Lower many years ago, was "one great lumber yard with virtually every activity in society subordinated to this undertaking." This included most notably Saint John's highly regarded shipbuilding industry that employed a small army of artisans and labourers and enabled enterprising merchants like Munson Jarvis to prosper.

The merchants of Saint John were a rare breed then and later. In 1865, a visiting journalist from Halifax summed up the typical Saint John merchant as: "The Saint Johnian is eager, ardent, and untiring. He gives all his life up to business. He opens his shop or his office at an early hour, he risks more, speculates more, loses more, makes more; he fails in business oftener, but after failure he always manages to rise again and make another fortune. . . . In [Saint John] there is no leisurely class. Everybody is hard at work. It is a city without loungers." But like many growing urban centres, there were the haves (such as the Jarvis family) and the have-nots. After the War of 1812, for instance, a continual flow of impoverished Irish immigrants and black refugees from the United States arrived in the city, taxing its resources and Christian charity.

In the early 1800s, Munson Jarvis remained one of Saint John's leading citizens. He became a vestryman at the city's Trinity Church and formed the first fire insurance company in British North America. In 1803, he established Saint John's first social club at the Exchange

Coffee House and in the following year became his city's member for the New Brunswick House of Assembly. His son William joined him in business, continuing his father's success following Munson's death in 1825, a few days after he had celebrated his eighty-third birthday. By then, the Jarvises were proud and influential members of Saint John's "Loyalist elite." As William's wife, Mary, explained to a relative in 1825, "as we are acquainted with all the people in [Nova Scotia and New Brunswick], if not personally, by name, of course we take an interest in what concerns them."

Munson Jarvis's second son, Edward James Jarvis, did not follow him into business, opting instead to study law in England. He eventually was appointed the chief justice of Prince Edward Island, and one of his sons became the private secretary of Sir Wilfrid Laurier. But Munson's eldest son, William, and his wife, Mary, maintained the family's status. Their son, William Munson Jarvis, born in 1838, became a barrister, a lieutenant-colonel in the New Brunswick Militia, and the president of the Board of Trade of the Maritime Provinces before his death in 1921. William Munson's family life was more turbulent. His first wife, Jane, died in 1866 after she had given birth to their third child and only five years after they had married. He was only twenty-seven at the time. He remarried Mary Lucretia Scovil in 1868 and had two more children.

The six children (and the thirty-six grandchildren) of Munson's widowed sister, Polly Jarvis Dibblee, also contributed to the life of the colony. William Dibblee held many public offices, including the one his Loyalist grandfather had filled in Stamford, Connecticut—that of town clerk. Walter Dibblee was at various times a crown surveyor, a teacher, and a jailer. Ebenezer Dibblee carried the mail from Fredericton to Norton, New Brunswick. Ralph Dibblee operated a store in Greenwich, New Brunswick, though he died in 1799 when he was only twenty-nine years old, leaving a wife and two young sons.

———

POLLY'S COUSIN STEPHEN JARVIS died at eighty-four years of age on April 12, 1840. Like so many other Loyalist death notices, Stephen's concealed more that it revealed about this amazing life. In two brief sentences, it reminded readers that Jarvis "took part in the many engagements during the American Rebellion. Emigrated to this Province and subsequently to Upper Canada." Stephen Jarvis and his family had watched neighbour battle neighbour, had endured separation and loss, and had ventured out in faith to start life in the northern wilds of British North America. They had been hostages to fortune, but through sweat, tears, and the odd stroke of luck, they found their feet once and again and in doing so they became—like their fellow Loyalist refugees—the vanguard of a great nation.

THE VANGUARD OF
A GREAT NATION

*The founding of the new nation grew out of the Loyalists'
perseverance against all odds. Their character and their circumstance added up to a rare moment of historical alchemy
that created Canada.*

T HE FINAL CHAPTER of the Loyalist saga played itself out in a
minor key. The exiled Loyalists' immediate past had strained
their religious ties and upset social barriers. But once the War of
1812 had confirmed their separate identities and guaranteed their
future domicile as non-Americans, their customary sea of troubles
was overtaken by the blessings of great timing and good luck. What
it added up to was the renewed sense of permanency that they had
so desperately been seeking. The melancholy burden of maintaining
their loyalties had been lifted not in any precipitous manner, but
because the ideological burdens of the past had become ever more
distant and irrelevant memories.

The doughty Loyalists had been seriously batted about by everyone. Rebel neighbours pledged their destruction and busybody
bureaucrats downgraded their plight by treating them as administrative headaches. As refugees, they had been forced into coming to

terms with all they had lost, which in most cases was nearly everything they owned. After having nothing but more troubles ahead of
them, the Loyalists who had endured the shuffling of circumstances
began to be treated with unexpected dollops of retroactive respect.
Their route to settlement was cleared by turning Canada's pristine
wilderness into their own encampments, villages, and woodsy living
quarters—primitive but cozy bungalows. Almost overnight, these
gutsy pioneers no longer joked about having to live in squalor in
what they described as "the Northern Branch of Purgatory." They
could even take time to help out with the odd barn-building bee over
at the McCurdie compound, or attend the Jarvis family's all too frequent christenings. Now, it was home.

Their victory in the War of 1812 then transformed the fleeing refugees into victorious leaders of a new homeland. It was the winning
of that strange but decisive arm-wrestling contest, fought against the
very Patriots who had once held them hostage, that had the most positive impact on the Loyalists' self-esteem. Their triumphs during this
strangest of wars resulted in not an acre of territory changing hands.
But territory was not the measure of their victory. Their onetime
persecutors were kept at bay. Their fears of another American invasion had permanently been moved off the table. Instead of merely
surviving, these early Canadians could now unabashedly thrive and
break out the maple syrup. It became permissible for them not only
to dream, but to make those whispered midnight wishes come true.

It was at this point that the Loyalists began to wave their own
flag, which was an early version of the Union Jack known as the
First Union Flag, instituted in 1606 by James I and then modified
slightly by Queen Anne in 1707. The ensign combined the Cross of
St. George, patron saint of England (a red cross on a white background), and the Cross of St. Andrew, patron saint of Scotland (a
diagonal white cross on a blue background). It remains the official
United Empire Loyalist ensign to this day, and it waves proudly in
my writing room.

WHENEVER LOYALTY DEMANDED OBEDIENCE, the Loyalists kept the faith. As New Canadians, they would be endowed with such enduring—and endearing—pledges as doing one's duty, enjoying one's sense of place, and trumping the unfair advantages of assumed privilege. These well-mannered counterrevolutionaries had convinced one another that they were eventually bound to be compensated for what they had suffered.

When the Yanks won their independence, the new Lords of the Line allocated their former fellow citizens no refunds for their illegal confiscations. They offered nothing but mayhem and individual hardships. The British government eventually paid the exiles a puny one third the value of what they were owed. And the majority did receive generous land grants, but they were chosen by lot so that you might get lucky and immediately plant abundant harvests—or end up with a crop of unmoveable boulders, offset by quicksand and tree roots with the consistency of wire cables. It was not paradise but it was enough to stop them from focusing merely on survival and to begin widening their personal and collective yearnings. That meant including and later emphasizing their desired—and by any measure, well-earned—social and political relief. They began to forge something more than a rebel republic but something less than an Anglo-Saxon pseudo-aristocracy. At last, the exiles had the time and chance to establish themselves and to relish acting out their anti-American dreams, which seemed to strengthen at each solstice.

As waves of newcomers flooded into the newly independent territory of the 1830s, the Loyalists began to entertain visions of previously denied grandeur. While supporters of Yankee independence noisily set out to create a new world order, the Loyalists felt content with nudging their status quo. They stayed true to the British Empire as an ideal, but no longer did so as a compulsion.

———————

MOST CANADIANS REMEMBER the Loyalists, if at all, as shadowy figures, left behind after a brief mention in a high school classroom on a rainy Wednesday afternoon. And yet, even if not claiming or getting much attention, these unassuming pioneers, sparse of speech and haunted by their history, deserved most of the credit as the founding mothers and fathers of our country. The Loyalists saw the world differently from their British rulers, and it was this margin of free choice that became a key factor in Canada's birth.

In fact, it is no exaggeration to contend that the birth of an independent Canada grew out of the Loyalists' dreams and visions. Initially little more than placeholders for the British Empire, they moved to occupy and own Upper Canada's available shores, untamed rivers, overflowing lakes, and—at least in theory—the whole damn country. Their ability to persevere against all odds came together in that rare moment of historical triumph that gave birth to the land, best captured by poet Al Purdy, as being "North of Summer." Those tight-lipped American refugees, who had chosen to reject the American Revolution and move to Canada, were ideally suited to realizing our pioneering ethic, with their meld of self-sufficiency and willingness to challenge authority. But if this book proves anything, it is that without them, without these ghosts of a world we scarcely knew, whose lives we would not have wanted to share—without these angels in their faded and torn coveralls, Canada would not exist.

Toronto poet Dennis Lee resolved a number of obtuse identity theories in his usual sprightly manner with four clever lines of verse from his poem "When I Went Up to Rosedale":

The Dream of Tory origins
is full of lies and blanks.
Though what remains when it is gone
proves that we're not Yanks.

That little ditty perfectly matched the central perception of the world's newest nation-state. The displaced British Americans who came north after 1776 were groping to reaffirm a classical European tradition which taught that reverence of territory was more humane than its conquest. As Lee's poem suggests, the Loyalists believed that we ought to harness sterner imperatives than the pursuit of happiness and that Canadians were bound to respond to the natural demands of favourable situations, instead of reaching out for more complicated fantasies. That any such sudden shifts should be undertaken in fear and trembling no longer fit Canada's outlook. The drumbeat imperatives of the Yanks' Manifest Destiny provided a useful rabbit hole for us, because we were never radically anti-American. (Well, not never; but that was reserved mainly for taverns—near closing time.)

Even if the Loyalists lacked the resources to reconstitute an instant culture, their dissent went just deep enough to re-emphasize that they were not pretend Yanks. The Great American Dream was not wrong—but it was their dream, not ours. Robert Calhoon, a thoughtful academic from the University of North Carolina, was on the money when he postulated that the Loyalists' ultimate ambivalence coalesced into a self-conscious realization that was "characterized by paranoia at the apparent injustices visited on them by American cruelty and British incompetence."

So be it.

Strong in spirit and dedicated to the concept and reality of duty, the Loyalists were brave in the face of long odds, clearly demonstrating that they were anything but wimps. There was much to be admired in how they responded. It was those thin shafts of light, still flickering but lit, that encouraged an early form of Canadian nationalism to take root. Remembering always that the Loyalists were Americans who were not republicans, they saw the world with a North American perspective, not a European one. That heritage would be the seedbed for what would produce, over time, true Anglophone Canadians. It was a natural evolution. Hell, they became our founding mothers and fathers, without much fuss or bother. Their call to a new form of citizenship may not have been dramatic, but it was all worthwhile. We were on the right side of history at last.

ACKNOWLEDGMENTS

T HE BRONZE TABLET bolted to the gatepost of the Williamstown cemetery, wedged into the rocky shore of the raging St. Lawrence River, commemorates the poignancy of North America's most earth-shaking epic. The tablet is inscribed with lines from Hereward Kirby Cockin's evocative poem honouring the Loyalists, who set in motion Canada's remarkable creation: "Tread softly, stranger—reverently draw near," invites its emotional inscription. "The vanguard of a nation slumbers here."

The bottom line of this great adventure was the creation of a magnificent new elephant of a country, with potential to burn. Opportunity was everywhere to be harnessed, even if its taming required the dedication of every fibre of one's being, and then some. The idea was to exchange a fixed dose of piety for a sprinkling of grace. And it worked.

This volume is the result of many minds and much study. The source of the most estimable assistance was Stephen Davidson, a retired teacher whose dedication it was to learn and to teach every detail of the Loyalists' magnificent migration. His devotion to this project went beyond the bounds of duty—and this manuscript shouts his name. Publisher Kevin Hanson, who heads Simon & Schuster of Canada, went way beyond his mandate to steer this project into safe harbour. He is a national treasure—the Jack McClelland of the New Age. His firm's editor, Brendan May, was invaluable, as was Allan Levine,

227

who has been my most dedicated researcher and editor for most of my serious writing life. In reality, Allan has become my partner—and it doesn't get any better than that.

In writing this book, I have been aware of the fact that the terminology referring to Native, Aboriginal, and Indigenous peoples has been constantly shifting. I have done my best to be sensitive to their stories while working within the boundaries of historical writing.

This is a book I never expected to write. As a fan and chronicler of Canadian history, I was drawn to the sparsely recorded saga of the Loyalists, those brave one-off souls who fathered and mothered our patches of snow into self-respecting nationhood. That was a feeling I shared as a freelancer who started to write this book about something that happened two and a half centuries ago, to unrelated settlers fighting for survival in dire circumstances. (No matter how distant the shore, I never found God's footprint.)

Still, I am trying to spend what's left of my life with a modicum of grace, and if I am convinced of anything, it is that the inner circle of Dante's Inferno is reserved not for those who fail, but for those who do not try. During my long years of living and writing—two concepts that are interchangeable—what I've learned is that if it's absurd to feel you can change things, it is much more absurd not to try.

—Peter Charles Newman
Belleville and Kingston, 2012–2016

BIBLIOGRAPHY

Acheson, T. W. *Saint John: The Making of a Colonial Community*. Toronto: University of Toronto Press, 1985.

Adams, James Truslow. *The Epic of America*. New York: Little, Brown, 1931.

Adelberg, Michael S. *The American Revolution in Monmouth County: The Theatre of Spoil and Destruction*. Charleston, SC: The History Press, 2010.

Allen, Ralph. *Ordeal by Fire*. Toronto: Doubleday Canada, 1961.

Allen, Thomas B. *Tories: Fighting for the King in America's First Civil War*. New York: HarperCollins, 2010.

Allen, Thomas B., and Todd W. Braisted. *The Loyalist Corps: Americans in the Service of the King*. Takoma Park, MD: Foxacre Press, 2011.

"An American's Experience in the British Army: The Manuscript of Colonel Stephen Jarvis." *The Journal of American History* 1:3 (1907). http://lib.jrshelby.com/jarvis.htm.

Avery, David A. *Cogs: The Ancestors and Descendants of John Gunton and Eliza Jarvis*. Belleville, ON: Mika Publishing Company, 1982.

Bailey, James Montgomery. *History of Danbury, Connecticut, 1684–1896*. New York: Burr Printing House, 1896. https://archive.org/stream/historyofdanbury-00baila#page/n9/mode/2up.

Bannister, Jerry, and Liam Riordan. *The Loyal Atlantic: Remaking the British Atlantic in the Revolutionary Era*. Toronto: University of Toronto Press, 2012.

Barkley, Murray. "The Loyalist Tradition in New Brunswick: The Growth and Evolution of an Historical Myth, 1825–1914." *Acadeinsis* 4:2 (Spring 1975): 3–45.

Barlow, Maude. *Too Close for Comfort: Canada's Future Within Fortress North America*. Toronto: McClelland & Stewart, 2005.

Bates, Walter. *Kingston and the Loyalists of the "Spring Fleet" of 1783*. Saint John: Barnes and Company, 1889.

Bell, D. G. *Early Loyalist Saint John: The Origin of New Brunswick Politics, 1783–1786*. Fredericton: New Ireland Press, 1983.

Bennett, Paul W., and Cornelius J. Jaenen. *Emerging Identities: Selected Problems and Interpretations in Canadian History*. Toronto: Prentice Hall Canada, 1986.

Berlet, Diane, and Graeme Coles. *The Loyalist Tiles of St. Albans: Encaustic Memorial Tiles of the 19th Century*. Adolphustown, ON: Adolphustown-Fredericksburgh Heritage Society, 2011.

Berman, Morris. *Why America Failed: The Roots of Imperial Decline*. New York: John Wiley & Sons, 2012.

Berton, Pierre. *The Invasion of Canada, 1812–1813*. Toronto: McClelland & Stewart, 1980.

Black, Jeremy. *George III: America's Last King*. New Haven: Yale University Press, 2006.

Blakeley, Phyllis R., and John Grant. *Eleven Exiles: Accounts of Loyalists of the American Revolution*. Toronto: Dundurn Press, 1982.

Boa Jarvis, Ann. *My Eventful Life: Stephen Jarvis, U.E., 1756–1840*. Montreal: Price-Patterson, 2002.

Borneman, Walter R. *1812: The War That Forged a Nation*. New York: HarperCollins, 2004.

Boyce, Betsy Dewar. *The Rebels of Hastings*. Toronto: University of Toronto Press, 1992.

Boyce, Gerald E. *Historic Hastings*. Belleville, ON: Ontario Intelligencer, 1967.

Brannon, Rebecca Nathan. "Reconciling the Revolution: Resolving Conflict and Rebuilding Community in the Wake of the Civil War in South Carolina, 1775–1860." PhD diss., University of Michigan, 2007. http://deepblue.lib.umich.edu/bitstream/handle/2027.42/57715/brannonr_1.pdf.

Brookhiser, Richard. *America's First Dynasty: The Adamses, 1735–1918*. New York: Free Press, 2002.

Brown, Ron. *From Queenston to Kingston: The Hidden Heritage of Lake Ontario's Shoreline*. Toronto: Dundurn Press, 2010.

Brown, Wallace. *The Good Americans: The Loyalists in the American Revolution*. New York: William Morrow, 1969.

———. "Marston, Benjamin," in *Dictionary of Canadian Biography*, vol. 4. Toronto: University of Toronto Press, 2003. http://www.biographi.ca/en/bio/marston_benjamin_4E.html.

———. *Victorious in Defeat*. Toronto: Methuen, 1984.

Browne, G. P. "Carleton, Guy, 1st Baron Dorchester," in *Dictionary of Canadian Biography*, vol. 5. Toronto: University of Toronto Press, 2003. www.biographi.ca/en/bio/carleton_guy_5E.html.

Brumwell, Stephen. *Paths of Glory: The Life and Death of General James Wolfe*. Montreal and Kingston: McGill-Queen's University Press, 2006.

Brumwell, Stephen, and William A. Speck. *Cassell's Companion to Eighteenth-Century Britain*. London: Cassell & Company, 2001.

Bumsted, J. M. "Fanning, Edward," in *Dictionary of Canadian Biography*, vol. 5. Toronto: University of Toronto Press, 2003. www.biographi.ca/en/bio/fanning_edmund_5E.html.

Burns, Robert J. "Jarvis, William," in *Dictionary of Canadian Biography*, vol. 5. Toronto: University of Toronto Press, 2003. www.biographi.ca/en/bio/jarvis_william_5E.html.

———. "Jarvis, William Botsford," in *Dictionary of Canadian Biography*, vol. 9. Toronto: University of Toronto Press, 2003. www.biographi.ca/en/bio/jarvis_william_botsford_9E.html.

Burroughs, Peter. "Parr, John," in *Dictionary of Canadian Biography*, vol. 4. Toronto: University of Toronto Press, 2003. www.biographi.ca/en/bio/parr_john_4E.html.

Burrows, Edwin G., and Mike Wallace. *Gotham: A History of New York City to 1898*. New York: Oxford University Press, 1999.

Calhoon, Robert McCluer. *The Loyalists in Revolutionary America, 1760-1781*. New York: Harcourt Brace Jovanovich, 1973.

Calloway, Colin G. *The American Revolution in Indian Country: Crisis and Diversity in Native American Communities*. New York: Cambridge University Press, 1995.

Callwood, June. *Portrait of Canada*. Garden City, NY: Doubleday, 1981.

Campbell, Steve, Janet Davis, and Ian Robertson. *Prince Edward County: An Illustrated History*. Bloomfield, ON: County Magazine, 2009.

Careless, J. M. S., W. S. MacNutt, W. J. Eccles, C. M. Johnston, L. H. Thomas, and M. A. Ormsby. *The Pioneers*. Toronto: McClelland & Stewart, 1969.

Carp, Benjamin L. *Defiance of the Patriots*. New Haven: Yale University Press, 2010.

Carroll, John. *My Boy Life, Presented in a Succession of True Stories: A Book for Old or Young*. Toronto: W. Briggs, 1882.

Carroll, Joy. *Pioneer Days, 1840–1860*. Toronto: Natural Science of Canada, 1979.

Champion, C. P. *The Strange Demise of British Canada: The Liberals and Canadian Nationalism, 1964–68*. Montreal and Kingston: McGill-Queen's University Press, 2010.

Chartrand, René. *American Loyalist Troops, 1775–1784*. New York: Osprey Publishing, 2008.

Chernow, Ron. *Washington: A Life*. New York: Penguin, 2010.

Choyce, Lesley. *Nova Scotia: Shaped by the Sea: A Living History*. Toronto: Penguin Viking, 1996.

Clark, Ellen M. *New York in the American Revolution: An Exhibition from the Library and Museum Collections of the Society of Cincinnati*. Cincinnati: Society of Cincinnati, 1998.

Clark, Alice Lavers. *Molly Brant Degonwadonti: Mohawk Heroine*. Bloomington, ID: iUniverse, 2004.

Cole, Arthur H. "The Tempo of Mercantile Life in Colonial America." *The Business History Review* 33:3 (Autumn 1959): 277–99.

Coleman, Aaron N. "Loyalists in War, Americans in Peace: The Reintegration of the Loyalists, 1775–1800. PhD diss., University of Kentucky, 2008. http://uknowledge.uky.edu/cgi/viewcontent.cgi?article=1623&context=gradschool_diss.

Collins, James P. *Autobiography of a Revolutionary Soldier* (1859), ed. John M. Roberts. New York: Arno Press, 1979.

Combs, Jerald A. *The Jay Treaty: Political Battleground of the Founding Fathers*. Berkeley: University of California Press, 1970.

Compton, Samuel Willard, ed. *Illustrated Atlas of Native American History*. Edison, NJ: Chartwell Books, 1999.

Conlin, Dan. "A Private War in the Caribbean: Nova Scotia Privateering, 1793–1805." *The Northern Mariner/Le Marin du nord* 6:4 (October 1996): 29–46.

Cooper, Barry. *It's the Regime, Stupid!* Toronto: Key Porter Books, 2009.

Craig, Gerald M. *Upper Canada: The Formative Years*. Toronto: McClelland & Stewart, 1963.

Creighton, Donald. *The Empire of the St. Lawrence*. Toronto: Macmillan Company of Canada, 1980.

Croil, James. *Dundas: A Sketch of Canadian History*. Montreal: B. Dawson & Son, 1861.

Cruikshank, E. A., ed. *The Correspondence of Lieut. Governor John Graves Simcoe*. 5 vols. Toronto: Ontario Historical Society, 1923.

Cummins, Joseph. *History's Greatest Wars: The Epic Conflicts That Shaped the Modern World*. Lion's Bay, BC: Fair Winds Press, 2011.

Cuthbertson, Brian C. *The Loyalist Governor*. Halifax: Petheric Press, 1983.

Dallison, Robert L. *The American Revolution and the Founding of New Brunswick*. The New Brunswick Military Heritage Series, vol. 2. Fredericton: Goose Lane Editions and The New Brunswick Military Heritage Project, 2003.

Davidson, Stephen. *The Burdens of Loyalty: Refugee Tales from the First American Civil War*. Saint John, New Brunswick: Trinity Enterprise, 2007.

———. "A Calamitous Situation: The Life of Polly Jarvis Dibblee." www.uelac .org/Loyalist-Info/extras/Dibblee-Fyler/Dibblee-Polly-Jarvis-biography.pdf.

———. "The Journal of a Loyalist Soldier: Stephen Jarvis." *Loyalist Trails UELAC Newsletter* (2009). www.uelac.org/Loyalist-Trails/2009/Loyalist-Trails-2009. php?issue=200947.

[Stephen Davidson is the author of more than fifty articles on Loyalists, many of which were utilized for this work. For a full listing of his articles, see the *Loyalist Trails* archives at: www.uelac.org/Loyalist-Trails/Loyalist-Trails-index.php.]

Davies, David T. *A Brief History of Fighting Ships*. New York: Carroll & Graf, 2002.

Degler, Carl N. *Out of Our Past*. New York: Harper & Row, 1962.

DeMond, Robert O. *The Loyalists in North Carolina During the Revolution*. Durham, NC: Duke University Press, 1940. Reprint by the Gemological Publishing Company, Baltimore, 1979.

Denison, Merrill. *The Barley and the Stream: The Molson Story*. Toronto: McClelland & Stewart, 1955.

Douglas, W. A. B., and Brereton Greenhous. *Out of the Shadows: Canada in the Second World War*. Toronto: Dundurn Press, 2005.

Duncan, Dorothy. *Hoping for the Best, Preparing for the Worst: Everyday Life in Upper Canada, 1812–1814*. Toronto: Dundurn Press, 2012.

Earle, Alice Morse. *Home Life in Colonial Days*. Stockbridge, MA: Berkshire Traveller Press, 1898. www.gutenberg.org.proxy2.lib.umanitoba.ca/files/22675/22675-h/22675-h.htm.

Earle, Evelyn Purvis. *Leeds the Lovely*. Toronto: Ryerson Press, 1951.

Easterbrook, W. T., and Hugh G. J. Aitkin. *Canadian Economic History*. Toronto: University of Toronto Press, 1988.

Eccles, W. J. *Canada Under Louis XIV*. Toronto: McClelland & Stewart, 1964.

Elbourne, Elizabeth. "Family Politics and Anglo-Mohawk Diplomacy: The Brant Family in Imperial Context." *Journal of Colonialism and Colonial History* 6:3 (2005). Project MUSE. https://muse.jhu.edu/.

Ellis, Joseph J. *Founding Brothers: The Revolutionary Generation*. New York: Alfred A. Knopf, 2003.

Errington, Jane. *The Lion, the Eagle, and Upper Canada: A Developing Colonial Ideology*. Montreal and Kingston: McGill-Queen's University Press, 1987.

Feinstein, Estelle F. "Stamford, Connecticut, 1641–1893: The First Two-and-a-Half Centuries." Stamford, CT: Stamford Historical Society, 1999. www.stamfordhistory.org/feinhist.htm.

Ferguson, Niall. *Empire: The Rise and Demise of the British World Order and the Lessons for Global Power*. New York: Basic Books, 2002.

Files, Angela M. "Persecution of the Loyalists," in Herman W. Witthoft, Sr. *The Descendants of Johann Conrad Kilts: Emigrant to America* (2000). http://threerivershms.com/loyalistspersecution.htm.

Fingard, Judith. "The Relief of the Unemployed Poor in Saint John, Halifax, and St. John's, 1815–1860." *Acadiensis* 5:1 (Autumn 1975): 32–53.

———. "Wentworth, Sir John," in *Dictionary of Canadian Biography*, vol. 5. Toronto: University of Toronto Press, 2003. www.biographi.ca/en/bio/wentworth_john_1737_1820_5E.html.

Finkleman, Paul. "The Monster of Monticello." *New York Times*, December 1, 2012, A25.

Finlay, J. L., and Douglas N. Sprague. *The Structure of Canadian History*. Toronto: Prentice Hall of Canada, 1979.

Firth, Edith. "Peters, Hannah," in *Dictionary of Canadian Biography*, vol. 7. Toronto: University of Toronto Press, 2003. www.biographi.ca/en/bio/peters_hannah_7E.html.

———. "Russell, Peter." in *Dictionary of Canadian Biography*, vol. 5. Toronto: University of Toronto Press, 2003. www.biographi.ca/en/bio/russell_peter_5E.html.

———. *The Town of York, 1793–1815: A Collection of Documents of Early Toronto*. Toronto: Champlain Society, 1962.

———. *The Town of York, 1815–1834: A Further Collection of Documents of Early Toronto*. Toronto: Champlain Society, 1966.

Fischer, David Hackett. *Paul Revere's Ride*. New York: Oxford University Press, 1994.

Fisher, Peter, *Sketches of New Brunswick*. Saint John: Chubb & Sears, 1825.

Fleming, Thomas. "What Life Was Like in 1776." *Wall Street Journal,* July 2, 2012.

Flick, Alexander Clarence. *Loyalism in New York During the American Revolution.* New York: Columbia University Press and Macmillan, 1901. http://archives.gnb.ca/ Exhibits/FortHavoc/html/NYLoyalism.aspx?culture=en-CA.

Fowler, William M. Jr. *An American Crisis: George Washington and the Dangerous Two Years After Yorktown, 1781–1783.* New York: Walker, 2011.

Francis, Daniel. *National Dreams: Myth, Memory, and Canadian History.* Toronto: Arsenal Pulp Press, 1997.

Fraser, Fil. *How the Blacks Created Canada.* Edmonton: Dragon Hill Publishing, 2010.

Fryer, Mary Beacock. *Buckskin Pimpernel: The Exploits of Justus Sherwood, Loyalist Spy.* Toronto: Dundurn Press, 1981.

———. *Escape: Adventures of a Loyalist Family.* Toronto: Dundurn Press, 2000.

———. *John Walden Meyers: Loyalist Spy.* Toronto: Dundurn Press, 1996.

———. *King's Men: The Soldier Founders of Ontario.* Toronto: Dundurn Press, 1980.

Fryer, Mary Beacock, and Christopher Dracott. *John Graves Simcoe, 1752–1806: A Biography.* Toronto: Dundurn Press, 1998.

Gilbert, Alan. *Black Patriots and Loyalists: Fighting for Emancipation in the War for Independence.* Chicago: University of Chicago Press, 2012.

Gilje, Paul A. *The Road to Mobocracy: Popular Disorder in New York City, 1763–1834.* Chapel Hill: University of North Carolina Press, 1987.

Glanmore National Historic Site of Canada. Belleville, ON: Essence Publishing, 2003.

Gnarowski, Michael. Foreword to *Mrs. Simcoe's Diary* by Mary Quayle Innis. Toronto: Dundurn Press, 2007.

Godfrey, W. G. "Carleton, Thomas," in *Dictionary of Canadian Biography,* vol. 5. Toronto: University of Toronto Press, 2003. www.biographi.ca/en/bio /carleton_thomas_5E.html.

Goldberg, Susan. *The Thomson Empire.* Toronto: Methuen, 1984.

Granatstein, J. L. *How Britain's Weakness Forced Canada into the Arms of the United States.* Toronto: University of Toronto Press, 1989.

Graymont, Barbara. "Koñwatsi'tsiaiéñni (Molly Brant)," in *Dictionary of Canadian Biography,* vol. 4. Toronto: University of Toronto Press, 2003. www.biographi .ca/en/bio/konwatsitsiaienni_4E.html.

———. "Thayendanegea (Joseph Brant)," in *Dictionary of Canadian Biography,* vol. 5. Toronto: University of Toronto Press, 2003. www.biographi.ca/en/bio /thayendanegea_5E.html.

Hale, R. Wallace, ed. "The Diary of Sarah Frost, 1783." http://atlanticportal.hil .unb.ca/acva/loyalistwomen/en/documents/frost/sarah_frost.pdf.

Hannon, Leslie. *Redcoats and Loyalists, 1780–1815.* Toronto: Natural Science of Canada, 1978.

Harper, Douglas. "Slavery in Connecticut." 2000. http://slavenorth.com/connecti cut.htm.

Henry, George. *The Emigrant Guide, or Canada As It Is.* Quebec: William Gray & Company, 1835.

Herrington, W. S. *Pioneer Life Among the Loyalists in Upper Canada*. Toronto: Macmillan Company of Canada, 1915.

Hitsman, J. MacKay. *The Incredible War of 1812: A Military History*. Toronto: University of Toronto Press, 1999.

Hochschild, Adam. *Bury the Chains: Prophets and Rebels in the Fight to Free an Empire's Slaves*. Boston: Houghton Mifflin, 2005.

Hogeland, William. *Declaration: The Nine Tumultuous Weeks When America Became Independent, May 1–July 4, 1776*. New York: Simon & Schuster, 2010.

———. *Inventing American History*. Cambridge: MIT Press, 2009.

Holliday, Carl. *Woman's Life in Colonial Days*. Williamstown, MA: Corner House Publishers, 1922.

Hopkins, J. Castell. *Canada: The Story of the Dominion*. Toronto: John C. Winston Company, 1901.

Horwood, Harold. *The Colonial Dream, 1497–1760*. Toronto: Natural Science of Canada, 1978.

Huey, Lois M., and Bonnie Pullis. *Molly Brant: A Legacy of Her Own*. Youngstown, NY: Old Fort Niagara Association, 1997.

Huggins, Benjamin. "Raid Across the Ice: The British Operation to Capture Washington." *Journal of the American Revolution*, December 17, 2013. http://allthingsliberty.com/2013/12/raid-across-ice-british-operation-capture-washington/.

Humphreys, Edward. *Great Canadian Battles: Heroism and Courage Through the Years*. London: Arcturus Publishing, 2008.

Hunter, Douglas. *Molson: The Birth of a Business Empire*. Toronto: Viking, 2001.

Innis, Mary Quayle. *Mrs. Simcoe's Diary*. Toronto: Dundurn Press, 2007.

Irvin, Benjamin H. "Tar and Feathers in Revolutionary America." http://revolution.h-net.msu.edu/essays/irvin.feathers.html.

Isaacson, Walter. *Benjamin Franklin: An American Life*. New York: Simon & Schuster, 2003.

Jacobs, Roberta Tansman. "The Treaty and the Tories: The Ideological Reaction to the Return of the Loyalists, 1783–1787." PhD diss., Cornell University, 1973.

Jarvis, David A. "The Jarvis Park Lot." *York Pioneer* (2013): 52–62.

Jarvis, George A., George Murray Jarvis, and William Jarvis. *The Jarvis Family*. Hartford, CT: Press of the Case, Lockwood & Brainard Company, 1879. https://archive.org/stream/jarvisfamilyorde00jarvuoft/jarvisfamilyorde00jarvuoft_djvu.txt.

Jarvis, Julia. *In Good Faith*. Toronto: n.p.1976. http://static.torontopubliclibrary.ca/da/pdfs/d37131055476832.pdf.

———. *Three Centuries of Robinsons: The Story of a Family*. Toronto: T. H. Best Printing Company, 1967.

Jasanoff, Maya. *Liberty's Exiles: American Loyalists in the Revolutionary World*. New York: Alfred A. Knopf, 2011.

Jeffery, Reginald, ed. *Dyott's Diary, 1781–1845: A Selection from the Journal of William Dyott, Sometime General in the British Army and Aide-de-Camp to His*

Majesty George III. London: Archibald Constable and Company, 1907. http://
archive.org/stream/dyottsdiaryselec01dyotuoft/dyottsdiaryselec01dyotuoft
_djvu.txt.

Johnson, J. K. "Jarvis, George Stephen Benjamin," in *Dictionary of Canadian Biography,* vol. 10. Toronto: University of Toronto Press, 2003. www.biographi.ca/
en/bio/jarvis_george_stephen_benjamin_10E.html.

Johnstone, Michael. *The Free Masons.* London: Arcturus Publishing, 2005.

Kagan, Robert. *Dangerous Nation.* New York: Random House, 2006.

———. *The World America Made.* New York: Random House, 2012.

Karg, Barb, and John K. Young. *101 Secrets of the Freemasons.* Avon, MA: F&W
Media, 2009.

Katcher, Phillip. *The American Provincial Corps, 1775–1784.* New York: Osprey
Publishing, 1973.

Kenny, Maurice. *Tekonwatonti Molly Brown, 1735–1795: Poems of War.* Buffalo, NY:
White Pines Press, 1992.

Ketchum, Richard. *Decisive Day: The Battle of Bunker Hill.* New York: Owl Books, 1999.

Kiester, Edwin Jr.. *Before They Changed the World.* Beverly, MA: Quayside Publishing Group, 2009.

Kimber, Stephen. *Loyalists and Layabouts: The Rapid Rise and Faster Fall of Shelburne,
Nova Scotia, 1783–1792.* Toronto: Random House of Canada, 2008.

Kingsford, William. *The History of Canada,* vol. VIII. Toronto: Roswell and Hutchi-
son, 1895.

Koene, William. *Loyal She Remains: A Pictorial History of Ontario.* Toronto: United
Empire Association of Canada, 1984.

Lambert, Robert Stansbury. *South Carolina Loyalists in the American Revolution.*
Clemson, SC: Clemson University Press, 2010.

Lamplugh, George R. *Politics on the Periphery: Factions and Parties in Georgia, 1783–
1806.* Cranbury, NJ: Associated University Presses, 1986.

Langguth, A. J. *Patriots: The Men Who Started the American Revolution.* New York:
Simon & Schuster, 1988.

Lapp, Eula. *To Their Heirs Forever.* Belleville, ON: Mika Publishing Company,
1977.

Latimer, Jon. *1812: War with America.* Cambridge: Harvard University Press, 2006.

Laxer, James. *The Acadians: In Search of a Homeland.* Toronto: Random House of
Canada, 2006.

———. *Tecumseh and Brock: The War of 1812.* Toronto: House of Anansi, 2012.

Lee, Dennis. *The Difficulty of Living on Other Planets: Poems.* Toronto: Macmillan of
Canada, 1987.

Leighton, Douglas, and Robert J. Burns. "Jarvis, Samuel Peters," in *Dictionary of
Canadian Biography,* vol. 8. Toronto: University of Toronto Press, 2003. www
.biographi.ca/en/bio/jarvis_samuel_peters_8E.html.

Levine, Allan. *Toronto: Biography of a City.* Vancouver: Douglas & McIntyre, 2014.

Longley, "R.S. Mob Activities in Revolutionary Massachusetts." *New England Quar-
terly* 6 (1933): 98–130.

Lord, Barry, and Gail Dexter Lord. *Artists, Patrons and the Public: Why Culture Changes*. Lanham, MD: Rowman & Littlefield, 2009.

Love, James H. "Fear of Americans and Textbooks: Cultural Survival and Social Control: The Development of a Curriculum for Upper Canada's Common Schools in 1846." *Histoire sociale-Social History* 15:30 (November 1982): 357–82.

Lower, Arthur R. M. *Canadians in the Making*. Toronto: Longmans Canada, 1969.

———. *Great Britain's Woodyard: British America and the Timber Trade, 1763–1867*. Montreal and Kingston: McGill-Queen's University Press, 1973.

Lower, J. Arthur. *Western Canada: An Outline of History*. Vancouver: Douglas & McIntyre, 1983.

MacKinnon, Neil. "The Changing Attitudes of the Nova Scotian Loyalists Towards the United States, 1783–1791." *Acadiensis* 2:2 (Spring 1973): 43–54.

———. *This Unfriendly Soil: The Loyalist Experience in Nova Scotia, 1783–1791*. Montreal and Kingston: McGill-Queen's University Press, 1986.

MacNutt, W. S. *The Atlantic Provinces: The Emergence of Colonial Society, 1712–1857*. Toronto: McClelland & Stewart, 1965.

Magee, Joan. *Loyalist Mosaic: A Multi-ethnic Heritage*. Toronto: Dundurn Press, 1984.

Malcolm, Andrew H. *The Canadians*. Toronto: Fitzhenry & Whiteside, 1985.

Marquis, Greg. "Commemorating the Loyalists in the Loyalist City: Saint John, New Brunswick, 1883–1934." *Urban History Review* 33:1 (2004): 24–33.

Marrelli, Nancy, and Simon Dardick. *The Secrets of Montreal*. Montreal: Véhicule Press, 2005.

May, Robin. *The British Army in North America, 1775–1783*. New York: Osprey Publishing, 1974.

Mayhew, Jonathan A.M., D.D., and Paul Royster, ed. "A Discourse Concerning Unlimited Submission and Non-Resistance to the Higher Powers: With Some Reflections on the Resistance Made to King Charles I. and on the Anniversary of His Death" (1750). *Electronic Texts in American Studies*. Paper 44. http://digitalcommons.unl.edu/etas/44.

McCullough, David. *John Adams*. New York: Simon & Schuster, 2001.

———. *1776*. New York: Simon & Schuster, 2005.

McEvedy, Colin. *The Penguin Atlas of North American History*. New York: Penguin, 1988.

McGahan, Elizabeth W. "Jarvis, William Munson," in *Dictionary of Canadian Biography*, vol. 15. Toronto: University of Toronto Press, 2003. www.biographi.ca/en/bio/jarvis_william_munson_15E.htm.

McMillan, Charles J. *Eminent Islanders*. Bloomington, IN: AuthorHouse, 2007.

Mealing, Stanley R. "Simcoe, John Graves," in *Dictionary of Canadian Biography*, vol. 5. Toronto: University of Toronto Press, 2003. www.biographi.ca/en/bio/simcoe_john_graves_5E.html.

Mika, Nick, and Helma Mika. *United Empire Loyalists, Pioneers of Upper Canada*. Belleville, ON: Mika Publishing Company, 1976.

Mills, David. *The Idea of Loyalty in Upper Canada 1784-1850*. Montreal and Kingston: McGill-Queen's University Press, 1988.

Minhinnick, Jeanne. *At Home in Upper Canada*. Toronto: Clarke, Irwin, 1970.

Moir, John S. *Rhymes of Rebellion*. Toronto: Ryerson Press, 1965.

Molson, Karen. *The Molsons, Their Lives and Times, 1780–2000*. Toronto: Firefly Books, 2001.

Moore, Christopher. *1867: How the Fathers Made a Deal*. Toronto: McClelland & Stewart, 1997.

———. *The Loyalists: Revolution, Exile, Settlement*. Toronto: Macmillan of Canada, 1984.

Morris, James. *Farewell the Trumpets: An Imperial Retreat*. New York: Penguin, 1979.

———. *Heaven's Command: An Imperial Progress*. New York: Penguin, 1981.

———. *Pax Britannica: The Climax of an Empire*. New York: Penguin, 1980.

Morton, Desmond. *A Military History of Canada*. Toronto: McClelland & Stewart, 1999.

Morton, W. L. *The Kingdom of Canada*. Toronto: McClelland & Stewart, 1963.

Mowat, Grace Helen. *The Diverting History of a Loyalist Town: A Portrait of St. Andrews, New Brunswick*. Fredericton: University Press of New Brunswick, 1953.

Myers, Gustavus. *History of Canadian Wealth*. Chicago: Charles H. Kerr & Company, 1914.

Nader, Ralph, Nadia Milleron, and Duff Conacher. *Canada Firsts*. Toronto: McClelland & Stewart, 1992.

Nash, Gary B. *Race and Revolution*. New York: Madison House Publishers, 1990.

———. *The Urban Crucible*. Cambridge: Harvard University Press, 1986.

Nash, Gary B., Graham Russell, and Gao Hodges. *Friends of Liberty: Thomas Jefferson, Tadeusz Kosciuszko, and Agrippa Hull*. New York: Basic Books, 2008.

Nelson, Craig. *Thomas Paine: Enlightenment, Revolution, and the Birth of Modern Nations*. New York: Penguin, 2007.

Nelson, Paul David. *General Sir Guy Carleton, Lord Dorchester: Soldier-Statesman of Early British Canada*. Madison, NJ: Fairleigh Dickinson University Press, 2000.

Nish, Cameron. *The French Canadians, 1759–1766*. Toronto: Copp Clark Publishing, 1966.

O'Callaghan, E. B. *Documents Relative to the Colonial History of the State of New York*, vol 6. Albany, NY: Weed, Parsons and Co., 1855. https://archive.org/details/documentsrelativ06brod.

Orchard, David. *The Fight for Canada: Four Centuries of Resistance to American Expansionism*. Toronto: Stoddart Publishing Company, 1993.

Parker, Phillip M. *Butterworth: Webster's Timeline History, 1647–1989*. Stamford, CT: Icon Group International, 2009.

Parmele, Mary Platt. *The Evolution of an Empire: A Brief Historical Sketch of Germany*. New York: William Beverley Harison, 1898. www.gutenberg.org/files/34072/34072-h/34072-h.htm.

Paterson, Donald G. *British Direct Investment in Canada, 1890–1914*. Toronto: University of Toronto Press, 1976.

Pen Pictures of Early Pioneer Life in Upper Canada. Toronto: William Briggs, 1905. https://archive.org/stream/penpicturesofear00scheuoft#page/n7/mode/2up.

Piecuch, Jim. *Three Peoples, One King: Loyalists, Indians, and Slaves in the Revolutionary South, 1775–1782*. Columbia: University of South Carolina Press, 2008.

Potter-MacKinnon, Janice. *While the Women Only Wept: Loyalist Refugee Women in Eastern Ontario*. Montreal and Kingston: McGill-Queen's University Press, 1995.

Purdy, Al. *The New Romans: Candid Canadian Opinions of the U.S.* Edmonton: M. G. Hurtig, 1968.

Raddall, Thomas H. *Halifax, Warden of the North*. Toronto: McClelland & Stewart, 1948.

———. *The Path of Destiny: Canada from the British Conquest to Home Rule, 1763–1850*. Toronto: Doubleday Canada, 1957.

Robinson, Helen Caister. *Mistress Molly, the Brown Lady: Portrait of Molly Brant*. Toronto: Dundurn Press, 1980.

Rokove, Jack. *Revolutionaries: A New History of the Invention of America*. Boston: Houghton Mifflin Harcourt, 2010.

Russell, David Lee. *The American Revolution in the Southern Colonies*. Jefferson, NC: McFarland, 2000.

Saul, John Ralston. *A Fair Country*. Toronto: Viking Canada, 2008.

Scadding, Henry. *Toronto of Old*. Toronto: Oxford University Press, 1966. Abridged and edited by F. H. Armstrong. First published in 1873.

Segal, Hugh. *The Right Balance: Canada's Conservative Tradition*. Vancouver: Douglas & McIntyre, 2011.

Shenstone, Susan Burgess. *So Obstinately Loyal: James Moody, 1744–1809*. Montreal and Kingston: McGill-Queen's University Press, 2000.

Silverman, Kenneth. *A Cultural History of the American Revolution*. Toronto: Fitzhenry & Whiteside, 1976.

Skeoch, Alan. *The United Empire Loyalists and the American Revolution*. Toronto: Grolier, 1982.

Smith, Gordon B. "The British Evacuate Savannah Georgia." *SAR Magazine* (Spring 2007). www.revolutionarywararchives.org/savannah.html.

Smith, Page. *A New Age Now Begins: A People's History of the American Revolution*. Toronto: McGraw-Hill, 1976.

Stephens, Henry. "De Lancey, Oliver (1749–1822)," in Leslie Stephen, ed. *Dictionary of National Biography*, vol. 14. London: Smith, Elder & Co, 1888: 303–4. www.archive.org/stream/dictionaryofnati14stepuoft#page/303/mode/1up.

Stewart, Walter. *True Blue: The Loyalist Legend*. Toronto: Collins, 1985.

Symington, Fraser. *The First Canadians*. Toronto: Natural Science of Canada, 1978.

Taylor, Alan. *The Civil War of 1812*. New York: Alfred A. Knopf, 2010.

———. *The Divided Ground: Indians, Settlers, and the Northern Borderland of the American Revolution*. New York: Random House, 2006.

Taylor, Charles. *Radical Tories*. Toronto: House of Anansi, 2006.

Thomas, Clara. *Ryerson of Upper Canada*. Toronto: Ryerson Press, 1969.

Thomas, Earl. *The Three Faces of Molly Brant: A Biography*. Kingston, ON: Quarry Press, 1996.

Thompson, Austin Seton. *Jarvis Street: A Story of Triumph and Tragedy*. Toronto: Personal Library Publishers, 1980.

Timothy, H. B. *The Galts: A Canadian Odyssey*. Toronto: McClelland & Stewart, 1977.

Tocqueville, Alexis de. *Democracy in America*. New York: Doubleday, 2006.

Troxler, Carole W. "A Loyalist Life: John Bond of South Carolina and Nova Scotia." *Acadiensis* 19:2 (Spring 1990): 72–79.

Trudel, Marcel. *The Beginnings of New France*. Toronto: McClelland & Stewart, 1973.

Trueman, Stuart. *The Ultimate History of New Brunswick*. Toronto: McClelland & Stewart, 1970.

Upton, L. F. S. *The United Empire Loyalists: Men and Myths*. Toronto: Copp Clark Publishing, 1967.

Vachon, André, Victoria Chabot, and André Desrosiers. *Dreams of Empire: Canada Before 1700*. Ottawa: Public Archives of Canada, 1982.

Van Buskirk, Judith L. *Generous Enemies: Patriots and Loyalists in Revolutionary New York*. Philadelphia: University of Pennsylvania Press, 2002.

Van Tyne, Claude Halstead. *The Loyalists in the American Revolution*. New York: Macmillan, 1902.

Vidal, Gore. *Inventing a Nation: Washington, Adams, Jefferson*. New Haven: Yale University Press, 2003.

Waldo, Samuel Putnam. *Biographical Sketches of Distinguished American Naval Heroes in the War of the Revolution, Between the American Republic and the Kingdom of Great Britain*. Hartford: Silas Andrus, 1823. https://archive.org/details/biographical sket00waldo.

Walker, George Leon. Some Aspects of the Religious Life of New England. New York: Silver, Burdett and Company, 1897. https://archive.org/details/some aspectsofrel00walk.

Walker, James W. St. G. *The Black Loyalists: The Search for a Promised Land in Nova Scotia and Sierra Leone, 1783–1870*. New York: Holmes & Meier, 1976. Reprint, University of Toronto Press, 1992.

Wallace, C. M. "Jarvis, Munson," in *Dictionary of Canadian Biography*, vol. 6. Toronto: University of Toronto Press, 2003. http://www.biographi.ca/en/bio/jarvis _munson_6E.html.

——. "Saint John Boosters and the Railroads in Mid-Nineteenth Century." *Acadiensis* 6:1 (Autumn 1976): 71–91.

Wallace, Stewart. *The United Empire Loyalists*. Glasgow: Brook & Company, 1914.

Ward, Christopher. *The War of the Revolution*. New York: Skyhorse Publishing, 2011.

Watt, Gavin K. *The Burning of the Valleys*. Toronto: Dundurn Press, 1997.

Webber, Mabel Louise, ed. *The South Carolina Historical and Genealogical Magazine* 21. Baltimore: Williams & Wilkins and Company, 1920. https://archive.org /stream/southcarolinahis2122sout/southcarolinahis2122sout_djvu.txt.

Wharton, Francis, ed. *The Revolutionary Diplomatic Correspondence of the United States*. Washington, DC: U.S. Government Printing Office, 1889. https://archive .org/details/revolutionarydi02whargoog.

Wheeler, William Bruce, and Susan D. Becker. *Discovering the American Past*. Boston: Houghton Mifflin, 2000.

Williams, Barbara. *A Gentlewoman in Upper Canada: The Journals, Letters and Art of Anne Langton*. Toronto: University of Toronto Press, 2008.

Williams, Merton Yarwood. *The Samuel Williams-Jemima Platt Family*. Ontario: M. Williams, 1967.

Wilson, William R. "Historical Narratives of Early Canada." www.uppercanada history.ca/toc.html.

Winik, Jay. *The Great Upheaval*. New York: HarperCollins, 2007.

Woodcock, George. *The Canadians*. Toronto: Fitzhenry & Whiteside, 1979.

Woods, Shirley E. Jr. *The Molson Saga, 1763–1983*. Toronto: Doubleday Canada, 1983.

Wright, Louis. *Everyday Life in Colonial America*. New York: G. P. Putnam's Sons, 1965.

Zeichner, Oscar. "The Loyalist Problem in New York After the Revolution." *New York History* 21:3 (July 1940): 284–302.

Zinn, Howard. *A People's History of the United States*. New York: HarperCollins, 2003.

INDEX

An *n* following a page number refers to text in the note section.